THE CITY & GUILDS TEXTBOOK

LEVEL 2 DIPLOMA IN

BRICKLAYING

D1612059

THE CITY & GUILDS TEXTBOOK

LEVEL 2 DIPLOMA IN
BRICKLAYING

COLIN FEARN

MIKE JONES

CLAYTON RUDMAN

SERIES TECHNICAL EDITOR
MARTIN BURDFIELD

About City & Guilds

City & Guilds is the UK's leading provider of vocational qualifications, offering over 500 awards across a wide range of industries, and progressing from entry level to the highest levels of professional achievement. With over 8500 centres in 100 countries, City & Guilds is recognised by employers worldwide for providing qualifications that offer proof of the skills they need to get the job done.

Equal opportunities

City & Guilds fully supports the principle of equal opportunities and we are committed to satisfying this principle in all our activities and published material. A copy of our equal opportunities policy statement is available on the City & Guilds website.

First edition 2014

ISBN 9780851932682

Publisher Fiona McGlade
Development Editor James Hobbs
Production Editor Lauren Cubbage

Cover design by Design Deluxe
Illustrations by Barking Dog Art and Palimpsest Book Production Ltd
Typeset by Palimpsest Book Production Ltd, Falkirk, Stirlingshire
Printed in the UK by Cambrian Printers Ltd

British Library Cataloguing in Publication Data

A catalogue record for this book is available from the British Library.

Publications

For information about or to order City & Guilds support materials, contact 0844 534 0000 or centresupport@cityandguilds.com. You can find more information about the materials we have available at www.cityandguilds.com/publications.

Every effort has been made to ensure that the information contained in this publication is true and correct at the time of going to press. However, City & Guilds' products and services are subject to continuous development and improvement and the right is reserved to change products and services from time to time. City & Guilds cannot accept liability for loss or damage arising from the use of information in this publication.

City & Guilds
1 Giltspur Street
London EC1A 9DD

0844 543 0033

www.cityandguilds.com

publishingfeedback@cityandguilds.com

CONTENTS

FOREWORD

Whether in good times or in a difficult job market, I think one of the most important things is for young people to learn a skill. There will always be a demand for talented and skilled individuals who have knowledge and experience. That's why I'm such an avid supporter of vocational training. Vocational courses provide a unique opportunity for young people to learn from people in the industry, who know their trade inside out.

Careers rarely turn out as you plan them. You never know what opportunity is going to come your way. However, my personal experience has shown that if you haven't rigorously learned skills and gained knowledge, you are unlikely to be best placed to capitalise on opportunities that do come your way.

When I left school, I went straight to work in a butcher shop, which was a fantastic experience. It may not be the industry I ended up making my career in, but being in the butchers shop, working my way up to management level and learning from the people around me was something that taught me a lot about business and about the working environment.

Later, once I trained in the construction industry and was embarking on my career as a builder, these commercial principles were vital in my success and helped me to go on to set up my own business. The skills I had learned gave me an advantage and I was therefore able to make the most of my opportunities.

Later still, I could never have imagined that my career would take another turn into television. Of course, I recognise that I have had lucky breaks in my career, but when people say you make your own luck, I think there is definitely more than a grain of truth in that. People often ask me what my most life-changing moment has been, expecting me to say winning the first series of Big Brother. However, I always answer that my most life changing moment was deciding to make the effort to learn the construction skills that I still use every day. That's why I was passionate about helping to set up a construction academy in the North West, helping other people to acquire skills and experience that will stay with them for their whole lives.

After all, an appearance on a reality TV show might have given me a degree of celebrity, but it is the skills that I learned as a builder that have kept me in demand as a presenter of DIY and building shows, and I have always continued to run my construction business. The truth is, you can never predict the way your life will turn out, but if you have learned a skill from experts in the field, you'll always be able to take advantage of the opportunities that come your way.

Craig Phillips

City & Guilds qualified bricklayer, owner of a successful construction business and television presenter of numerous construction and DIY shows

ABOUT THE AUTHORS

COLIN FEARN
CHAPTERS 1 AND 2

I was born, grew up and continue to live in Cornwall with my wife, three children, a Staffordshire bull terrier, a cat and three rabbits.

As a qualified carpenter and joiner, I have worked for many years on sites and in several joinery shops.

I won the National Wood Award for joinery work and am also a Fellow of the Institute of Carpenters, holder of the Master Craft certificate and have a BA in Education and Training.

I was until recently a full-time lecturer at Cornwall College, teaching both full-time students and apprentices.

I now work full-time as a writer for construction qualifications, practical assessments, questions and teaching materials for UK and Caribbean qualifications.

In my spare time I enjoy walks, small antiques and 'keeping my hand in' with various building projects.

CLAYTON RUDMAN
CHAPTERS 3 AND 5

The construction industry is large and varied. Personally the choice of trade to specialise in was easy. I knew from an early age that bricklaying was my future.

Working on site and studying to achieve my Level 2 and 3 qualifications was difficult, but with the right resources and tutors it was enjoyable.

I came into teaching straight from the building site as a young man, having been inspired by my tutors to pass on the experience, knowledge and skills I gained by building my own homes to others.

30 years on I still enjoy teaching.

My career progressed and over time I have taught at every level, working my way up to Head of School in one of Wales's largest further education colleges.

I am still teaching and at present combine it with a quality role within a very successful school of construction.

MIKE JONES

CHAPTERS 4 AND 6

I currently work as a Construction Lecturer and Section Leader in the Brickwork Section at Cardiff and Vale College in South Wales.

I have worked in education for the past 10 years and my previous construction industry career spanned over 30 years of work, ranging from skilled trade activities to supervisory and site management positions.

My aim in teaching practice is to impart to learners the great job satisfaction that can be gained from becoming a skilled practitioner in bricklaying. I enjoy taking the time to encourage the development of lasting talents and rewarding skills.

MARTIN BURDFIELD

SERIES TECHNICAL EDITOR

I come from a long line of builders and strongly believe that you will find a career in the construction industry a very rewarding one. Be proud of the work you produce; it will be there for others to admire for many years.

As an apprentice I enjoyed acquiring new knowledge and learning new skills. I achieved the C&G Silver Medal for the highest marks in the Advanced Craft Certificate and won the UK's first Gold Medal in Joinery at the World Skills Competition. My career took me on from foreman, to estimator and then works manager with a number of large joinery companies, where I had the privilege of working on some prestigious projects.

Concurrent with this I began working in education. I have now worked in further education for over 35 years, enjoying watching learners' skills improve during their training. For 10 years I ran the SkillBuild Joinery competitions and was the UK Training Manager and Chief Expert Elect at the World Skills Competition, training the UK's second Gold Medallist in Joinery.

Working with City & Guilds in various roles over the past 25 years has been very rewarding.

I believe that if you work and study hard that anything is possible.

HOW TO USE THIS TEXTBOOK

Welcome to your City & Guilds Level 2 Diploma in Bricklaying textbook. It is designed to guide you through your Level 2 qualification and be a useful reference for you throughout your career. Each chapter covers a unit from the 6705 Level 2 qualification, and covers everything you will need to understand in order to complete your written or online tests and prepare for your practical assessments.

Please note that not all of the chapters will cover the learning outcomes in order. They have been put into a logical sequence as used within the industry and to cover all skills and techniques required.

Throughout this textbook you will see the following features:

Screed

A mixture of cement, sand and water applied to the concrete foundation to give a smooth surface finish

Useful words – Words in bold in the text are explained in the margin to help your understanding.

INDUSTRY TIP

To reduce the dust generated by cutting or moving lightweight insulation blocks, they can be lightly sprayed with water. Be careful not to saturate them.

Industry tips – Useful hints and tips related to working in the construction industry.

ACTIVITY

What methods could be used to prevent mortar dropping onto the wall ties? Discuss this with someone else and see if you can think of two methods to prevent this.

Activities – These are suggested activities for you to complete.

FUNCTIONAL SKILLS

If one 25kg bag of adhesive lays 60 blocks, how many blocks can be laid using five bags?

Work on this activity can support FM2 (L2.1.1).

Answer: 5 x 60 = 300 blocks.

Functional Skills – These are activities that are tied to learning outcomes for the Functional Skills Maths, English and ICT qualifications.

STEP 1 Add the cement to the sand in accordance with the specified ratio.

STEP 2 Mix the sand and cement three times 'dry'.

Step by steps – These steps illustrate techniques and procedures that you will need to learn in order to carry out bricklaying tasks.

OUR HOUSE

Looking at 'Our House', can you identify any areas where decorative brick features could be included? Which ones would you choose and why?

'Our House' – These are activities that tie in directly with 'Our House' on SmartScreen to help you put the techniques in the book in context. Ask your tutor for your log-in details.

Case Study: Dave

Dave's uncle has asked him to build a new garden wall to replace a crumbling frost-damaged one. Dave goes to look at the job to work out a price for materials. He decides to reduce the labour costs since it's a job for family.

Dave explains to his uncle that the wall could be built in half-brick walling but then he would have to include attached piers to strengthen it and it wouldn't look as good from the neighbour's side. He decides it would be best to build the wall in Flemish Garden Wall bond. It's strong enough and will look good viewed from either side.

Case Studies – Each chapter ends with a case study of an operative who has faced a common problem in the industry. Some of these will reveal the solution and others provide you with the opportunity to solve the problem.

Contractors

Workers or companies working to an agreement that is legally binding.

Trade dictionary – This feature lists all of the key terms that you will pick up from reading this book.

At the end of every chapter are some 'test your knowledge' questions. These questions are designed to test your understanding of what you have learnt in that chapter. This can help with identifying further training or revision needed. You will find the answers at the end of the book.

INTRODUCTION

This book has been written to support students studying bricklaying at Level 2. By studying this book, you should receive a thorough grounding in the skills and knowledge you will need to complete your course and either progress to Level 3, or enter the workforce. You will learn about the wider construction industry and how it works, as well as the skills and techniques you will need in order to work as a bricklayer. You will be able to work safely on site using the correct tools and equipment to lay bricks and blocks in order to produce masonry structures.

In addition to the features listed on the previous pages, which are there to help you retain the information you will need to become a bricklayer, this textbook includes a large trade dictionary. Use this for reference in class and in the workshop. Become familiar with the terms and techniques, and pay attention to the skills you need to master. If you put in the effort, you will be rewarded with a satisfying and successful career in construction.

ACKNOWLEDGEMENTS

I would like to thank my dear wife Helen for her support in writing for this book. My thanks go to the other chaps (Clay, Martin and Mike) for all their help! I dedicate my work to Matt, Tasha and Daisy, and not forgetting Floyd and Mrs Dusty.

Colin Fearn

I dedicate this book to my tutor, employer, and friend Mr L E Marks from whom I developed my experience in the construction industry. Thanks also to my wife for all her support and hard work during our 28 years of building houses.

Clayton Rudman

Firstly, my thanks to John Ennis for starting my journey in education. Many thanks to my fellow authors and the staff at City & Guilds for their support and encouragement. I've also appreciated the input and suggestions of my colleagues Paul Sebburn, Craig Jones and Pete Bradwick at CAVC. Finally, thanks to my long-suffering wife Sue and the rest of my family, who supported me (and proofread my material) throughout.

Mike Jones

To my gorgeous wife Clare, without whose constant support, understanding and patience I would not have been able to continue. To Matthew and Eleanor: after not being there on too many occasions, normal service will be resumed. Finally, my parents, to whom I will always be grateful.

Martin Burdfield

City & Guilds would like to sincerely thank the following:

For invaluable bricklaying expertise

Paul Brown, Steve Everton, Glen Smith and Julian Walden.

For their help with photoshoots

Andrew Buckle (photographer), Paul Reed, Akeem Callum, Frankie Slattery, Wahidur Rahman and all of the staff at Hackney Community College, Mike Jones, Ron Lucock and Pawel Walga of Cardiff and Vale College.

For supplying pictures for the book cover

Front cover: **Construction Photography:** © Chris Henderson.
Back cover: **Construction Photography:** © Damian Gillie; © Jean-Francois Cardella; **Hackney Community College; Shutterstock:** © auremar; © Blaj Gabriel; © pryzmat.

TRADE DICTIONARY

Industry term	Definition and regional variations
Aggregates 	The coarse mineral material, such as sharp sand and graded, crushed stone (gravel), used in making mortar and concrete.
Air brick 	A perforated brick which allows ventilation through walls.
Alignment	To place something in line.
Approved Code of Practice (ACoP) 	ACoP gives practical advice for those involved in the construction industry in relation to using machinery safely. ACoP has a special legal status and employers and employees are expected to work within its guidelines.
Arch centre 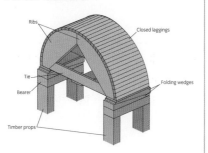	A temporary timber structure used to support the arch bricks until the mortar has set and the arch becomes self-supporting. The folding wedges allow the centre to be eased (loosened) then struck (removed).

Industry term	Definition and regional variations
Architect 	A trained professional who designs a structure and represents the client who wants the structure built. They are responsible for the production of the working drawings. They supervise the construction of buildings or other large structures.
Architectural technician 	A draftsperson who works in an architectural practice. They usually prepare the drawings for a building.
Arris 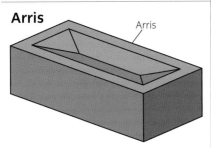	Any straight sharp edge of a brick formed by the junction of two faces.
Asbestos 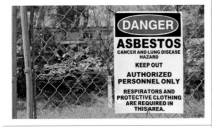	A naturally occurring mineral that was commonly used for a variety of purposes including: insulation, fire protection, roofing and guttering. It is extremely hazardous and can cause a serious lung disease known as asbestosis.
Asphalt 	A thick, sticky mixture of petroleum tars. It is used as a waterproof finish on flat roofs or to tank (line) the vertical walls of a basement.
Attached pier 	Piers that are not free-standing and are used in a structure or wall to add strength or reinforcement. The term 'attached' means that the pier is bonded into the main section of masonry following the specified bonding arrangement.

Industry term	Definition and regional variations
Ballast 	Aggregate mixture of sand and chippings up to 50mm deep, spread over a site to provide a firm surface for operatives to walk on.
Banding	Whole sections of brickwork that differ in colour and stand out from the main body of work.
Bargeboard	A board covering the ends of the rafters of a roof which would otherwise be exposed at the gable end.
Bat	Part of a brick greater than one-quarter.
Beam-filling	The brickwork between the ends of joists or beams.
Bearing	1 The portion of the lintel that sits on the wall and transmits structural weight. 2 The amount by which a piece of construction rests upon its support.
Bed	Mortar upon which the brick is laid or bedded.
Bed joint	Continuous, horizontal mortar joint supporting the bricks.
Bill of quantities BILL OF QUANTITIES (Assuming Civil Engineering Standard Method of Measu Number | Item description CLASS A: GENERAL ITEMS Specified Requirements	Produced by the quantity surveyor and describes everything that is required for the job based on the drawings, specification and schedules. It is sent out to contractors and ensures that all the contractors are pricing for the job using the same information.

Industry term	Definition and regional variations
Blade	The 'working' part of the trowel that allows manipulation of the mortar.
Blended	When bricks have gone through a process that disperses variations in colour and size of bricks to avoid unwanted patterns (banding etc) emerging.
Block splitter	A tool used to accurately cut blocks.
Bolster	A broad bladed chisel used for cutting bricks and blocks.
Bond/bonding	The arrangement or pattern of laying bricks and blocks to spread the load through the wall, also for strength and appearance.
Boundary	A line marking the end of an area.
Brick on edge coping	A masonry addition that protects the top of the wall from poor weather, where the bricks are laid on edge with the stretcher face uppermost. This type of coping can be used on walls greater than one-brick thickness by bonding the brick on edge (using Stretcher bond) across the top of the wall.

Industry term	Definition and regional variations
Brick trowel	Used for spreading and rolling mortar. *Regional variation: walling trowel*
Bridged cavity	Something that touches both skins of a cavity wall, ie lintel, tie wire, cavity liner, mortar droppings.
British Standards Institute (BSI)	The authority that develops and publishes standards in the UK.
Broken bond	The use of part bricks to make good a bonding pattern where full bricks will not fit in.
Builder's square	A tool for checking corners. A builder's square that is set at an angle of 90° will form a right-angled quoin.
Building line	The front line of the building. Note that this can be on or behind the frontage line. (*See also* Line.)
Building regulations	A series of documents that set out legal requirements for the standards of building work.
Bulking	An increase in volume of soil or earth, caused by introducing air.

Industry term	Definition and regional variations
CAD drawings	Drawings which are created using computer-aided design.
Calibrate	To adjust or correct eg to calibrate a level.
Cantilever	A beam built into a wall and held down at one end and unsupported at the other.
Capping	A brick, stone or concrete decorative feature on top of isolated piers which provides weather protection.
Castellated	Having or resembling repeated square indentations.
Cast in situ	Moulded in the position it will occupy permanently.
Cavity batten	A timber batten slightly narrower than the cavity dimension with cords or wires attached. It rests in the cavity on the wall ties to catch mortar droppings and can be withdrawn as the work progresses using the cords or wires.
Cavity tray	Membrane placed over a bridged cavity. It directs any water present in the cavity to weep holes outside the skin. (*See also* Bridged cavity.)

Industry term	Definition and regional variations
Cavity wall 	Walls built in two separate skins/leaves (usually of different materials) with a void held together by wall ties.
Chase	A narrow recess cut in the brickwork (ie to take conduit or piping).
Chimney stack 	The portion of the chimney containing the tops of the flues which passes through and projects above the roof.
Cladded 	When a surface has been covered in another material, eg plastic or timber.
Class A block 	A high quality fair-faced block.
Clipper saw 	A machine used to accurately cut bricks in quantity.
Club hammer 	A weighted hammer used to cut blocks.

Industry term	Definition and regional variations
Common bricks 	Bricks of medium quality used for ordinary walling work where no special face finish is required. Bricks are manufactured to dimensions and tolerances decided by official institutes. In the UK, this is the British Standards Institute.
Concrete	Material made up of cement, fine aggregate (sand) and course aggregate (stone) of varying sizes and in varying proportions. It is mixed with water.
Contractors	Workers or companies working to an agreement that is legally binding.
Control measures	Specific instructions to work to and control work practices.
Coping 	A masonry addition that protects the top of a wall from poor weather. (*See also* Brick on edge coping.)
Core holes	Temporary holes left in a cavity wall at ground level to enable mortar droppings to be removed from cavity.
Corner blocks 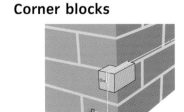	Plastic or wooden blocks used to hold the line to a stopped end.

Industry term	Definition and regional variations
Corner profiles 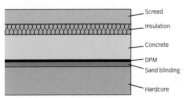	A type of profile used for marking the position of corners. Most bricklayers find corner profiles easier to use as they have level lines which can be used to form building lines in two directions. (*See also* Profiles.)
Course	A horizontal row of blocks or bricks laid on a mortar bed.
Creasing	*See* Tile creasing.
Critical path	Programme to be followed.
Cross-section	A view that shows an imaginary slice through a structure to reveal interior details.
Cure	To set hard, often using heat or pressure.
Damp proof course (DPC)	A layer or strip of watertight material placed in a joint of a wall to prevent the passage of water. Fixed at a minimum of 150mm above finished ground level. Two types of DPC are rigid and flexible.
Damp proof membrane (DPM)	A layer or sheet of watertight material, incorporated into a solid floor to prevent the rise of moisture.
Datum point 	A fixed point or height from which to take reference levels. They may be permanent Ordnance bench marks (OBMs) or temporary bench marks (TBMs). The datum point is used to transfer levels across a building site. It represents the finished floor level (FFL) on a dwelling.

Industry term	Definition and regional variations
Dead load	The self weight of all the materials used to construct the building.
Dense	Material that is hard and heavy for its volume, ie dense blocks.
Dentil course	Arrangement of bricks with an indented and protruding bricks, giving a castellated effect.
Design strength	The specific setting qualities of the adhesive used in thin joint masonry.
Detector	Used to locate the services when working on the foundations of the structure. This equipment works by sending out an electronic pulse. to tell how deep the metal of the services is.
Disc cutter	A hand held powered machine for cutting dense materials.
Dog-tooth brickwork	A type of String course, where bricks are laid diagonally in relation to the face line of the wall to give the course a serrated effect.
Double handling	Moving materials twice or even three times before use. This wastes time and energy when bricklaying.

Industry term	Definition and regional variations
Drum mixer 	Used to mix mortar on site. This can be powered by electricity, a diesel engine or a petrol engine.
Dry bond	A method of spacing bricks or blocks without mortar to sort out potential problems with the bond.
Dry silo mixer	A major piece of equipment that contains all the dry materials to produce mortar mixed on demand. It minimises waste because it only produces mortar as it is needed.
Dumpling	A mound of soil used to make good to gardens and landscapes.
Durability	How capable a product is of withstanding wear and tear or decay.
Ear defenders	A means of personal protection from the harmful effects of noise.
Efflorescence	A white deposit which may form on the surface of new bricks if the latter contain a high proportion of mineral salts.

Industry term	Definition and regional variations
Elevation	A drawing showing any face of a building or wall or object.
Engineering bricks	Hard dense bricks of regular size used for carrying heavy loads, eg in bridge buildings, heavy foundations.
English bond	A type of one-brick bond. This bond is set out with alternating courses of headers and stretchers. It is the strongest bonding arrangement possible.
English Garden Wall bond	A type of one-brick bond. The arrangement consists of three, five or seven courses of stretchers to one course of headers.
Expanded metal lathing (EML)	Metal reinforcement made out of sheet metal to form a mesh.
Face	1 The surface presented to view; the front. 2 A brick has two faces, a long side called a stretcher face and a short side called a header face.
Face plane	The alignment of all the bricks or blocks in the face of a wall to give a uniform flat appearance.

Industry term	Definition and regional variations
Fair face 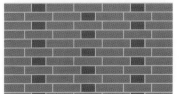	Indicating face work of neat appearance. Flemish bond is often referred to as fair-faced.
Finished floor level (FFL)	This is the height of the finished floor level in a property. Represented with a datum point, and horizontal DPC is often installed at this height.
Flashing	Flashings are commonly made from lead and are used to provide waterproofing at joints where roofing materials meet walls and around chimneys. May also be made from zinc or copper.
Flat roofs	A flat roof is defined as a roof having a pitch of 10° or less. Flat roofs are similar in design to floors, in that they are made from joists decked with timber sheet material. A waterproof layer such as bituminous felt (made from tar), plastic or fibreglass is also used.
Flaunching	The cement fillet at the junction around a chimney pot and chimney stack.
Flemish bond	A type of one-brick bond that consists of alternating headers and stretchers within a course. The headers in a course are centred above the stretchers in the course below to give a strong Quarter bond and also to produce an interesting pattern.
Flemish Garden Wall bond	A type of one-brick bond. In this bond there is a pattern of three or five stretchers followed by one header repeated along the length of each course. The header face in a course should be centred above the middle stretcher of each group of three in the course below.

Industry term	Definition and regional variations
Floors	The structured layers of a building, eg ground floor, first floor, second floor.
Flush joint	Bed and perp joint finished with a trowel flush to the material used.
Footings	The substructure below ground level. These are projecting courses at the base of a wall.
Forklift	The main piece of machinery used for moving heavy materials, such as bricks. The driver of the forklift is trained to work in a safe manner.
Foundation	Used to spread the load of a building to the subsoil.
Fracture	A crack or break in a hard object or material.
Friction	Resistance between two surfaces, for example the surface of the concrete foundation and the soil around it.

Industry term	Definition and regional variations
Frog	The indentation in a brick.
Frontage line	The front edge of the building plot, usually taken from the centre line of a road or kerb edge, from which the building line is established.
Full joint	A joint that has no gaps or voids that will allow water penetration. *Regional variation: flush joint*
Gables	The part of the wall in the triangle formed by the sloping sides of the roof.
Gauge	The dimensions of a bed joint (10mm) and a brick depth (65mm) added together (75mm). This needs to be kept uniform and accurate so that the final height of the wall is kept to specification. This is known as keeping to gauge and requires frequent checking with a tape measure or gauge rod.
Gauge rod	A timber rod with shallow gauge markings made on it with a saw. Used to measure the thickness of bed joints when keeping to gauge. *Regional variation: storey rod*
Grinder	A power tool used to grind and cut materials.

Industry term	Definition and regional variations
Half-bat Half-bat	The smallest cut allowed in half-brick walling, it measures 102.5mm. This is the same width as the header face of a full brick.
Half-bond 	This is another term for Stretcher bond which is when bricks or blocks are arranged with an overlap the width of a brick or block. This means the perp joints are exactly halfway along the face of the stretchers in the course below. (*See also* Half-brick walling.)
Half-brick walling 	Stretcher bond is often called half-bond. Since the width of the wall is almost the same as half a brick, we refer to Stretcher bond as half-brick walling.
Half-round joint 	The concave shape of the finished bed and perp joints. This is the most common form of joint. *Regional variation: bucket handle*
Hammer drill 	A power tool used to drill holes in masonry or concrete.
Hatchings Brickwork	Patterns used on a drawing to identify different materials to meet the standard BS1192.

Industry term	Definition and regional variations
Head	The horizontal top member of a door or window frame.
Header face	The end face of a brick, which is its shortest side. It is 102.5mm wide.
Hoarding	Barrier surrounding the site to protect against theft and unauthorised entry.
Honeycombed wall	A wall with bricks set so as to provide openings at regular intervals to give ventilation through the wall. Used to support ground floor joists.
Hopper	Applies wider and larger amounts of adhesive to thin joint blockwork.
Horns	The projections on a door head for building into the joints.
Hypotenuse	The longest side of a right-angled triangle. It is always opposite the right angle.
Imposed load	Additional loads that may be placed on the structure, eg people, furniture, wind and snow.
Improvement notice	Issued by an HSE or local authority inspector to formally notify a company that improvements are needed to the way it is working.

Industry term	Definition and regional variations
Indent 	A recess formed in the brickwork or blockwork to accommodate future work.
Industrial standards	Minimum standards of quality of completed work universally adopted within the industry.
Infill panels	The middle sections of a length of walling.
Inspection chamber	A masonry structure that allows inspection of services below ground level.
Insulation 	Materials used to retain heat and improve the thermal value of the building. Can also be used in managing sound transfer.
Interpret	To understand the meaning of information, eg information from working drawings and specifications.
Isolated piers 	Piers that are built separate from other masonry structures and are often used in situations such as gated entrances on a drive or pathway. If the pier is built in 1½ or 2 brick thickness (or more), it has the advantage of allowing reinforcement to be introduced within the hollow centre. The pier can then support the weight of a heavy gate.
Isometric projection 	A drawing showing detail in three dimensions. The vertical lines in the structure will be drawn at 90° to the horizontal (or bottom edge of the page) and the horizontal lines of the structure will be drawn at 30° to the horizontal on the page.
Jamb	A vertical inside face of an opening in a wall.
Joggle	Cavity into which grout is poured, often to form a joint.

Industry term	Definition and regional variations
Jointer	A tool used to provide a finish to the joints. It produces a concave finish to the mortar just before it begins to harden, to create a half-round joint.
Jointing	To make a finish to the mortar faces as work proceeds, eg half-round jointing.
Junctions	Methods of joining together walls set at angles.
Kiln	A type of large oven, used to produce moulded clay facing bricks.
Kinetic lifting	A method of lifting that ensures the risk of injury is reduced.
Lateral movement Lateral force	Movement or pressure from the side.

Industry term	Definition and regional variations
Laying trowel	A trowel only used on the first course of blockwork.
Lead-in time	The time taken between ordering an item and it being delivered.
Leaves	The two walls that make up a cavity wall to comply with current building regulations. They are tied together with wall ties. *Regional variation: skin*
Levelling	To make sure that two points are at the same height.
Lime	A fine powdered material traditionally used in mortars.
Line	The straightness of the block or brickwork.
Line and pins	A string used to guide the blocks or bricks to make them straight.

Industry term	Definition and regional variations
Lintel 	A horizontal member for spanning an opening, such as a door, to support the structure above, usually made from steel or concrete. A lintel used in a cavity wall must always be protected with the use of a cavity tray. The tray is installed above the lintel and will help catch any moisture and direct it to the outside of the wall using weep holes.
Manufacturer's instructions 	Guidelines given by the manufacturer on conditions of use.
Masonry saw 	A saw used to cut lightweight blocks.
Method statement	A description of the intended method of carrying out a task, often linked to risk assessment.
Mid girth	Often referred to as a centre line calculation, used for calculating quantities of materials.
Mortar 	A mixture of soft sand and cement mixed with water and other additives if required, eg plasticiser, colouring or lime. It is used for laying bricks.
Movement joint	A joint to allow thermal expansion in materials, enabling expansion and contraction.
Optical level 	A levelling operation using eyesight. The level is accurate up to 30m with a variation of +/–5mm. Bricklayers use optical levels when the length of construction exceeds the straight edge. The level is placed on a tripod and used with a staff or rod to transfer lines between two or more points.
Ordnance bench mark (OBM) 	They are a given height on an Ordnance Survey map. This fixed height is described as a value, eg so many metres above sea level (as calculated from the average sea height at Newlyn, Cornwall).

Industry term	Definition and regional variations
Orthographic projection 	A drawing where the front elevation of a structure has the plan view directly below it. The side or end elevations are shown directly each side of the front elevation. The most commonly used type of orthographic projection is called 'first angle projection'.
Overhand work	Facework executed from the back of the wall.
Oversailing	Projecting from the general face of the wall.
Padstone 	A masonry unit incorporated in a structure to help spread the load through a wall.
Pallets 	A storage base used to carry and store materials such as bricks or blocks.
Parapet 	A low wall along the edge of a roof or balcony.
Party wall	The dividing wall between adjoining buildings.
Perimeter 	The distance around an object or room.
Permits to work 	The permit to work is a documented procedure that gives authorisation for certain people to carry out specific work within a specified timeframe. It sets out the precautions required to complete the work safely, based on a risk assessment.

Industry term	Definition and regional variations
Perp joints	Vertical mortar joints which join two bricks or blocks together. They are at right angles (or perpendicular) to the bed.
Personal protective equipment (PPE)	This is defined in the Personal Protective Equipment at Work Regulations as 'all equipment (including clothing affording protection against the weather) which is intended to be worn or held by a person at work and which protects against one or more risks to a person's health or safety.' For example, safety helmets, gloves, eye protection, high-visibility clothing, safety footwear and safety harnesses.
Piers	Brickwork used for support in walls or as pillars, attached and detached.
Pitched roofs	Pitched roofs are constructed using rafters and come in a variety of designs, notably lean-to, gable and hipped.
Plasticiser	An additive that is used to make mortar pliable and easier to work with. This is safer and easier to use than the traditionally used hydrated lime in powder form.
Plinth	The projecting base of a wall or column.
Plumb	The verticality of brickwork. Plumbing should be started from the second course, using a spirit level.

Industry term	Definition and regional variations
Pointing	The process of applying a finish to the joints in brickwork using mortar.
Pointing hawk	Used with a pointing trowel when pointing mortar joints.
Pointing trowel	A tool used to point areas of missing adhesive in thin joint masonry, or mortar in normal masonry.
Precast	Made-up beforehand, ie a precast concrete floor.
Profiles	Boards fixed horizontally to ground pegs at the ends of a wall before construction commences in order that lines may be stretched across to mark the position of the foundations and wall. (*See also* Corner profiles.)
Programme of work	A series of events where the order of activities and the amount of time involved has been planned out. This is usually shown in the form of a bar or Gantt chart. *Regional variation: work schedule*
Prohibition notice	Issued by an HSE or local authority inspector when there is an immediate risk of personal injury. Receiving one means you are breaking health and safety regulations.
Property	A building and the land belonging to it.

Industry term	Definition and regional variations
Pulled line	A tight line fixed to bricks or blocks.
Quarter bond	Bonds in a wall that have a width equal to the length of the stretcher face of a brick (and are therefore referred to as 'one-brick' walling). The bonding arrangement shows bricks lapping each other by a quarter of a length (as in English and Flemish bond). Used where a thicker wall is needed for greater strength.
Queen Closer 46mm max.	A brick split along its length to produce a cut of 46mm. It is cut to the size of half a header face, and is used next to quoin bricks to establish the start of a bonding arrangement. Also used in indents for junction walls.
Quoins	The vertical external angles (corners) in walling. Builder's squares are used to check that the corner is square before you lay any blocks or bricks.
Racked ends	The ends of walls built without a corner to produce a vertical 'stopped' end.
Racking back Racking back	The process of building up the corners or the ends of a wall to produce a plumb reference point that guides accurate laying of the rest of the wall in between. *Regional variation: raking back*
Ranging line	A line stretched between profiles to mark the position of a wall end or foundation. The line is made from nylon and is waterproof. *Regional variation: builder's line*

Industry term	Definition and regional variations
Ranging pole	A red and white rod fixed to indicate set distance points when setting out.
Rasp	A tool used to file down a block for level.
Reclaim	To re-use resources, eg to use crushed bricks for hardcore.
Regular-shaped	To give a square, or rectangular shape to a building or masonry structure.
Reinforced	In concrete – strengthened by adding steel.
Render	When a brick, stone or block face is covered in a layer of sand and cement.
Retaining wall	A wall built to support or prevent the advance of a mass of earth or other material.
Return	The proportion of brickwork at right angles to the face of the wall.
Reveals	The masonry forming the side of a window or door opening.

Industry term	Definition and regional variations
Reverse bond 	In the same course, starting with a stretcher and ending with a header.
Risk assessment 	An assessment of the hazards and risks associated with an activity and the reduction and monitoring of them.
Rule of thumb	Industry recognised practice, eg when calculating the number of blocks required for a wall the rule of thumb is 10 blocks per 1m².
Rusticated	A blocking proud of the wall face, usually several courses of bricks followed by one or two flush, commonly used on quoins.
Saddle-back	A pointed coping, ie with sloping sides.
Scale Scale: 1:1250	The ratio of the size on a drawing to the size of the real thing that it represents. It is impossible to fit a full-sized drawing of a building onto a sheet of paper, so it is necessary to scale the size of the building to enable it to fit. Scale rules are used to draw scaled-down buildings on paper.
Scale rule 	Used with drawings to measure the dimensional line to a scale.
Scoop 	Applies wider and larger amounts of adhesive to thin joint blockwork.
Screed 	A mixture of cement, sand and water applied to the concrete foundation to give it a smooth surface.

Industry term	Definition and regional variations
Scutch hammer 	A bricklayer's hammer with interchangeable finishing heads for trimming and tidying bricks and blocks. *Regional variation: comb hammer*
Section view	Drawings that show a cut away view of a structure.
Segment	The part of a curve between two points on the circumference of a circle.
Segmental arch	If a circle was drawn, this type of arch would be formed by a segment of the circle.
Segregated waste	Separated into groups or categories, eg glass, metal and wood. Waste is often segregated to support recycling and contribute to sustainability.
Semi-circular arch	If a circle was drawn, this type of arch would be formed by half of the circle.

Industry term	Definition and regional variations
Services	Those provided by the utility companies, eg gas, electricity and water.
Set square	Used to draw square lines across materials.
Setting out	A method of locating the position of building works ready for starting work. This involves marking and positioning where a structure will be built. Accuracy is very important when setting out as mistakes here can prove costly.
Setting out chain	A tool used in measuring linear distances over a long length.
Site investigation	Looking at areas underground, such as the water table and ground conditions.
Sleeper walls	Dwarf walls erected at intervals between the main walls to provide intermediate supports to ground floor joists, usually built honey-combed.
Soffit	The underside of a part of a building, such as an arch.

Industry term	Definition and regional variations
Soldier arch 	Where bricks are laid on end with the stretcher face showing above an opening.
Soldier course 	A decorative feature where bricks are laid on end with the stretcher face showing. A contrasting brick can be used to add to the decorative appearance and the bricks can be set to project a small distance from the face line of the main wall to add more detail.
Solid walls 	Walls of a thickness of one brick and greater. Unlike cavity walls, there are usually only two materials to consider; either bricks and mortar or blocks and mortar.
Specification 	A contract document that gives information about the quality of materials and standards of workmanship required.
Spirit level 	A measuring tool to make sure the work is level and plumb. Spirit levels come in a range of sizes; the size most commonly used by bricklayers is 1.2m, but sometimes 2m spirit levels are used to help with the construction of blockwork.
Spot board 	A board made of durable material roughly 600mm x 600mm, on which mortar is placed. The boards are raised up from ground level by supporting it on blocks.
Stihl saw	A tool used to cut very hard bricks.

Industry term	Definition and regional variations
Stopped end	The vertical end of a wall.
Straight edge	An accurately proportioned implement with parallel edges made of timber or aluminium and up to 3m in length.
Straps	Plastic binding holding bricks or blocks together on a pallet. Straps are dangerous and can cut hands or legs.
Stretcher bond	Bricks or blocks arranged with an overlap the width of a brick or block. This means the perp joints are exactly halfway along the face of the stretchers in the course below.
Stretcher face	The long face of a brick when laid. It measures 215mm wide.
String course	A long narrow course projecting from the general face of the brickwork.
Struck	Refers to the mortar in pointing work being pressed inwards with the edge of the trowel.
Structural integrity	A structure's ability to safely resist the loads placed on it.
Subsoil	Earth covering the site, low compression strength.

Industry term	Definition and regional variations
Substructure	All brick and blockwork below DPC.
Superstructure	All brick and blockwork above DPC.
Sustainability	To continue to do something with minimal long-term effects on the environment. Building materials can be sustainable if they are chosen carefully.
Tape measure	A measuring tool used to set out and check dimensions. A range of tape measures in various sizes is required when setting out a structure. Tape measures vary in range from 3m to 30m.
Tarpaulin	Sheet material, usually plastic, used to protect materials.
Temporary bench mark (TBM)	Unlike an OBM, this is only temoprary and is set up on site. These can be timber pegs surrounded by concrete.
Temporary profiles	The building size and position of walls are set out onto these. A spirit level is used to transfer this on to the foundations.
Tensile forces	A measure of the ability of material to resist a force that tends to pull it apart.
Thermal movement	Changes in dimensions of masonry or concrete as a result of fluctuations in temperature over time.

Industry term	Definition and regional variations
Thermoplastic materials 	Plastics which become soft when heated and hard when cooled. Some DPCs contain thermoplastic materials.
Thin joint masonry 	A building process and method of laying lightweight insulation blocks to a dwelling in a very quick way. Unlike the sand and cement mortar used in traditional blocklaying, the blocks are laid in a very strong adhesive that is 2mm thick. The main difference between using this method and the traditional blocklaying method is that the adhesive allows for the quick fixing time and a lack of gauging.
Tile creasing 	Two courses of concrete or clay tiles, half-bonded and bedded in mortar. The creasing course oversails (projects) protecting the wall from water running down from the brick on edge course.
Timbering 	The operation of supporting earth in trench work, etc, with heavy timbers.
Tolerances	Allowable variations between the specified measurement and the actual measurement.
Tooled/ironed 	Using steel tools to create a specified type of joint.
Toothing 	Leaving the vertical end of a wall unfinished in its bond to enable the wall to be continued at a later stage.

Industry term	Definition and regional variations
Top soil	The top 150mm of soil containing vegetable matter.
Trench barrier	Barrier erected to stop traffic and personnel falling into a trench.
Trowel	Used to lay bricks. It has a 'blade', which allows you to manipulate the mortar when laying.
Truss rafters	Rafters that are already cut and fixed together before being delivered on site. The loads are calculated to ensure they are strong enough and therefore need to be fixed and braced exactly as shown on the drawings and not cut.
Turning piece	A temporary timber support used when building segmental arches to support the arch bricks until the radius is complete from one side of the opening to the other.
U-value	Rate at which heat escapes from a building.
Volatile organic compound (VOC)	The volatile organic compounds measure shows how much pollution a product will emit into the air when in use.
Wall plate	A timber bedded on the top of a wall for supporting joists or rafters.

Industry term	Definition and regional variations
Wall ties	Usually made of stainless steel, these are used to tie the two skins of a cavity wall together to strengthen it.
Weather struck joint	An angled joint, which means one side of the joint is pressed further into the joint than the other.
Weep holes	Small openings in a wall to permit the escape of water from the back of the wall.
Weighted	Use of dense cut block to weigh down the line to stop the pulled line from moving.
Well graded sand	Sand that has large, medium and small grains, such as 'pit sand' or 'sea-dredged sand'. Used in mortar.
Whisk	Used to mix adhesive in a container.
Withes	The thin division between adjoining flue liners, sometimes termed mid-feathers.

Chapter 1
Unit 201: Health, safety and welfare in construction

A career in the building industry can be a very rewarding one, both personally and financially. However, building sites and workshops are potentially very dangerous places; there are many potential hazards in the construction industry. Many construction operatives (workers) are injured each year, some fatally. Regulations have been brought in over the years to reduce accidents and improve working conditions.

By reading this chapter you will know about:

1 The health and safety regulations, roles and responsibilities.
2 Accident and emergency reporting procedures and documentation.
3 Identifying hazards in the workplace.
4 Health and welfare in the workplace.
5 Handling materials and equipment safely.
6 Access equipment and working at heights.
7 Working with electrical equipment in the workplace.
8 Using personal protective equipment (PPE).
9 The cause of fire and fire emergency procedures.

HEALTH AND SAFETY LEGISLATION

According to the Health and Safety Executive (HSE) figures, in 2011/12:

- Forty-nine construction operatives were fatally injured. Twenty-three of these operatives were self-employed. This compares with an average of 59 fatalities over the previous five years, of which an average of 19 fatally injured construction operatives were self-employed.

- The rate of fatal injury per 100,000 construction operatives was 2.3, compared with a five-year average of 2.5.

- Construction industry operatives were involved in 28% of fatal injuries across all industry sectors and it accounts for the greatest number of fatal injuries in any industry sector.

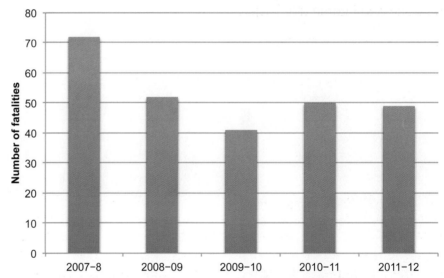

Number and rate of fatal injuries to workers in construction (RIDDOR)

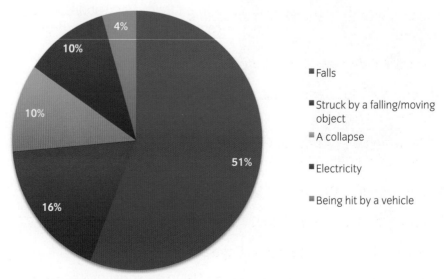

Proportion of fatalities in 2011/12 in construction

Health and safety legislation and great efforts made by the industry have made workplaces much safer in recent years. It is the responsibility of everyone involved in the building industry to continue to make it safer. Statistics are not just meaningless numbers – they represent injuries to real people. Many people believe that an accident will never happen to them, but it can. Accidents can:

■ have a devastating effect on lives and families

■ cost a lot financially in injury claims

■ result in prosecution

■ lead to job loss if an employee broke their company's safety policy.

Employers have an additional duty to ensure operatives have access to welfare facilities, eg drinking water, first aid and toilets, which will be discussed later in this chapter.

If everyone who works in the building industry pays close attention to health, safety and welfare, all operatives – including you – have every chance of enjoying a long, injury-free career.

UK HEALTH AND SAFETY REGULATIONS, ROLES AND RESPONSIBILITIES

In the UK there are many laws (legislation) that have been put into place to make sure that those working on construction sites, and members of the public, are kept healthy and safe. If these laws and regulations are not obeyed then prosecutions can take place. Worse still, there is a greater risk of injury and damage to your health and the health of those around you.

The principle legislation which relates to health, safety and welfare in construction is:

■ Health and Safety at Work Act (HASAWA) 1974

■ Control of Substances Hazardous to Health (COSHH) Regulations 2002

■ Reporting of Injuries, Diseases and Dangerous Occurrences Regulations (RIDDOR) 1995

■ Construction, Design and Management (CDM) Regulations 2007

■ Provision and Use of Work Equipment Regulations (PUWER) 1997

■ Manual Handling Operations Regulations 1992

■ Personal Protective Equipment (PPE) at Work Regulations 1992

Standard construction safety equipment

- Work at Height Regulations 2005

- Lifting Operations and Lifting Equipment Regulations (LOLER) 1998

- Control of Noise at Work Regulations 2005

- Control of Vibration at Work Regulations 2005.

HEALTH AND SAFETY AT WORK ACT (HASAWA) 1974

The Health and Safety at Work Act (HASAWA) 1974 applies to all workplaces. Everyone who works on a building site or in a workshop is covered by this legislation. This includes employed and self-employed operatives, subcontractors, the employer and those delivering goods to the site. It not only protects those working, it also ensures the safety of anyone else who might be nearby.

KEY EMPLOYER RESPONSIBILITIES

The key employer health and safety responsibilities under HASAWA are to:

- provide a safe working environment

- provide safe access (entrance) and egress (exit) to the work area

- provide adequate staff training

- have a written health and safety policy in place

- provide health and safety information and display the appropriate signs

- carry out risk assessments

- provide safe machinery and equipment and to ensure it is well-maintained and in a safe condition

- provide adequate supervision to ensure safe practices are carried out

- involve trade union safety representatives, where appointed, in matters relating to health and safety

- provide personal protective equipment (**PPE**) free of charge, ensure the appropriate PPE is used whenever needed, and that operatives are properly supervised

- ensure materials and substances are transported, used and stored safely.

PPE

This is defined in the Personal Protective Equipment at Work Regulations 1992 as 'all equipment (including clothing affording protection against the weather) which is intended to be worn or held by a person at work and which protects against one or more risks to a person's health or safety.'

Risk assessments and method statements

The HASAWA requires that employers must carry out regular **risk assessments** to make sure that there are minimal dangers to their employees in a workplace.

Risk assessment

An assessment of the hazards and risks associated with an activity and the reduction and monitoring of them

---

Risk Assessment

Activity / Workplace assessed: Return to work after accident
Persons consulted / involved in risk assessment
Date:
Reviewed on:

Location:
Risk assessment reference number:
Review date:
Review by:

Significant hazard	People at risk and what is the risk Describe the harm that is likely to result from the hazard (e.g. cut, broken leg, chemical burn etc.) and who could be harmed (e.g. employees, contractors, visitors etc.)	Existing control measure What is currently in place to control the risk?	Risk rating Use matrix identified in guidance note Likelihood (L) Severity (S) Multiply (L) * (S) to produce risk rating (RR)				Further action required What is required to bring the risk down to an acceptable level? Use hierarchy of control described in guidence note when considering the controls needed	Actioned to: Who will complete the action?	Due date: When will the action be complete by?	Completion date: Initial and date once the action has been completed
			L	S	RR	L/M/H				
Uneven floors	Operatives	Verbal warning and supervision	2	1	2	m	None applicable	Site supervisor	Active now	Ongoing
Steps	Operatives	Verbal warning	2	1	2	m	None applicable	Site supervisor	Active now	Ongoing
Staircases	Operatives	Verbal warning	2	2	4	m	None applicable	Site supervisor	Active now	Ongoing

		Likelihood		
		1 **Unlikely**	**2** **Possible**	**3** **Very likely**
Severity	**1** Slight/minor injuries/minor damage	1	2	3
	2 Medium injuries/significant damage	2	4	6
	3 Major injury/extensive damage	3	6	9

Likelihood
3 – Very likely
2 – possible
1 – Unlikely

Severity
3 – major injury/extensive damage
2 – medium injury/significant damage
1 – Slight/minor damage

1 – Low risk, action should be taken to reduce the risk if reasonably practicable
2, 3, 4 – Medium risk, is a significant risk and would require an appropriate level of resource
6 & 9 – High risk , may require considerable resource to mitigate. Control should focus on elimination of risk, if not possible control should be obtained by following the hierarchy of control

123 type risk assessment

A risk assessment is a legally-required tool used by employers to:

- identify work hazards

- assess the risk of harm arising from these hazards

- adequately control the risk.

Risk assessments are carried out as follows:

1 Identify the hazards. Consider the environment in which the job will be done. Which tools and materials will be used?

2 Identify who might be at risk. Think about operatives, visitors and members of the public.

3 Evaluate the risk. How severe is the potential injury? How likely is it to happen? A severe injury may be possible but may also be very improbable. On the other hand a minor injury might be very likely.

4 If there is an unacceptable risk, can the job be changed? Could different tools or materials be used instead?

5 If the risk is acceptable, what measures can be taken to reduce the risk? This could be training, special equipment and using PPE.

6 Keep good records. Explain the findings of the risk assessment to the operatives involved. Update the risk assessment as required – there may be new machinery, materials or staff. Even adverse weather can bring additional risks.

A **method statement** is required by law and is a useful way of recording the hazards involved in a specific task. It is used to communicate the risk and precautions required to all those involved in the work. It should be clear, uncomplicated and easy to understand as it is for the benefit of those carrying out the work (and their immediate supervisors).

Inductions and tool box talks

Any new visitors to and operatives on a site will be given an induction. This will explain:

- the layout of the site

- any hazards of which they need to be aware

- the location of welfare facilities

- the assembly areas in case of emergency

- site rules.

Tool box talks are short talks given at regular intervals. They give timely safety reminders and outline any new hazards that may have arisen because construction sites change as they develop. Weather conditions such as extreme heat, wind or rain may create new hazards.

KEY EMPLOYEE RESPONSIBILITIES

The HASAWA covers the responsibilities of employees and subcontractors:

- You must work in a safe manner and take care at all times.

- You must make sure you do not put yourself or others at risk by your actions or inactions.

Method statement

A description of the intended method of carrying out a task, often linked to a risk assessment

INDUSTRY TIP

The Construction Skills Certification Scheme (CSCS) was set up in the mid-90s with the aim of improving site operatives' competence to reduce accidents and drive up on-site efficiency. Card holders must take a health and safety test. The colour of card depends on level of qualification held and job role. For more information see www.cscs.uk.com

ACTIVITY

Think back to your induction. Write down what was discussed. Did you understand everything? Do you need any further information? If you have not had an induction, write a list of the things you think you need to know.

INDUSTRY TIP

Remember, if you are unsure about any health and safety issue always seek help and advice.

- You must co-operate with your employer in regard to health and safety. If you do not you risk injury (to yourself or others), prosecution, a fine and loss of employment. Do not take part in practical jokes and horseplay.

- You must use any equipment and safeguards provided by your employer. For example, you must wear, look after and report any damage to the PPE that your employer provides.

- You must not interfere or tamper with any safety equipment.

- You must not misuse or interfere with anything that is provided for employees' safety.

FIRST AID AND FIRST-AID KITS

First aid should only be applied by someone trained in first aid. Even a minor injury could become infected and therefore should be cleaned and a dressing applied. If any cut or injury shows signs of infection, becomes inflamed or painful seek medical attention. An employer's first-aid needs should be assessed to indicate if a first-aider (someone trained in first aid) is necessary. The minimum requirement is to appoint a person to take charge of first-aid arrangements. The role of this appointed person includes looking after the first-aid equipment and facilities and calling the emergency services when required.

First-aid kits vary according to the size of the workforce. First-aid boxes should not contain tablets or medicines.

First-aid kit

Labels on image: Eye wash, Foil blanket, Bandages, Cleaning wipes, Microporous tape, Safety pins, Scissors, Burn dressing, Resuscitation face shield, Nitrate gloves, Plasters

INDUSTRY TIP

The key employee health and safety responsibilities are to:
- work safely
- work in partnership with your employer
- report hazards and accidents as per company policy.

INDUSTRY TIP

Employees must not be charged for anything given to them or done for them by the employer in relation to safety.

INDUSTRY TIP

In the event of an accident, first aid will be carried out by a qualified first aider. First aid is designed to stabilise a patient for later treatment if required. The casualty may be taken to hospital or an ambulance may be called. In the event of an emergency you should raise the alarm.

ACTIVITY

Your place of work or training will have an appointed first-aider who deals with first aid. Find out who they are and how to make contact with them.

ACTIVITY

Find the first-aid kit in your workplace or place of training. What is inside it? Is there anything missing?

SOURCES OF HEALTH AND SAFETY INFORMATION

Source	How they can help
Health and Safety Executive (HSE)	A government body which oversees health and safety in the workplace. It produces health and safety literature such as the **Approved Code of Practice** (ACoP).
Construction Skills	The construction industry training body produces literature and is directly involved with construction training.
The Royal Society for the Prevention of Accidents (ROSPA)	It produces literature and gives advice.
The Royal Society for Public Health	An independent, multi-disciplinary charity which is dedicated to the promotion and protection of collective human health and wellbeing.
Institution of Occupational Safety and Health (IOSH)	A chartered body for health and safety practitioners. The world's largest health and safety professional membership organisation.
The British Safety Council	It helps businesses with their health, safety and environmental management.

HEALTH AND SAFETY EXECUTIVE (HSE)

The HSE is a body set up by the government. The HSE ensures that the law is carried out correctly and has extensive powers to ensure that it can do its job. It can make spot checks in the workplace, bring the police, examine anything on the premises and take things away to be examined.

If the HSE finds a health and safety problem that breaks health and safety law it might issue an **improvement notice** giving the employer a set amount of time to correct the problem. For serious health and safety risks where there is a risk of immediate major injury, it can issue a **prohibition notice** which will stop all work on site until the health and safety issues are rectified. It may take an employer, employee, self-employed person (subcontractor) or anyone else

Approved Code of Practice

ACoP gives practical advice for those in the construction industry in relation to using machinery

INDUSTRY TIP

There are many other trade organisations, eg the Timber Research and Development Association (TRADA) which also offer advice on safe practices.

ACTIVITY

You have been asked to give a tool box talk because of several minor injuries involving tripping on site. What topics would you include in this talk?

INDUSTRY TIP

To find out more information on the sources in the table, enter their names into a search engine on the internet.

Improvement notice

Issued by an HSE or local authority inspector to formally notify a company that improvements are needed to the way it is working

Prohibition notice

Issued by an HSE or local authority inspector when there is an immediate risk of personal injury. They are not issued lightly and if you are on the receiving end of one, you are clearly breaking a health and safety regulation

involved with the building process to court for breaking health and safety legislation.

The HSE provides a lot of advice on safety and publishes numerous booklets and information sheets. One example of this is the Approved Code of Practice (ACoP) which applies to wood working machinery. The ACoP has a special legal status and employers and employees are expected to work within its guidelines.

The duties of the HSE are to:

- give advice

- issue improvement and prohibition notices

- caution

- prosecute

- investigate.

The Approved Code of Practice booklet is available free online

CONTROL OF SUBSTANCES HAZARDOUS TO HEALTH (COSHH) REGULATIONS 2002

The Control of Substances Hazardous to Health (COSHH) Regulations 2002 controls the use of dangerous substances, eg preservatives, fuel, solvents, adhesives, cement and oil-based paint. These have to be moved, stored and used safely without polluting the environment. It also covers hazardous substances produced while working, eg wood dust produced when sanding or drilling.

Hazardous substances may be discovered during the building process, eg lead-based paint or asbestos. These are covered by separate regulations.

When considering substances and materials that may be hazardous to health an employer should do the following to comply with COSHH:

- Read and check the COSHH safety data sheet that comes with the product. It will outline any hazards associated with the product and the safety measures to be taken.

- Check with the supplier if there are any known risks to health.

- Use the trade press to find out if there is any information about this substance or material.

- Use the HSE website, or other websites, to check any known issues with the substance or material.

Example of COSHH data sheet

When assessing the risk of a potentially dangerous substance or material it is important to consider how operatives could be exposed to it. For example:

- by breathing in gas or mist

- by swallowing it

- by getting into their eyes

- through their skin, either by contact or through cuts.

Safety data sheets

Products you use may be 'dangerous for supply'. If so, they will have a label that has one or more hazard symbols. Some examples are given here.

These products include common substances in everyday use such as paint, bleach, solvent or fillers. When a product is 'dangerous for supply', by law, the supplier must provide you with a safety data sheet. Note: medicines, pesticides and cosmetic products have different legislation and don't have a safety data sheet. Ask the supplier how the product can be used safely.

Safety data sheets can be hard to understand, with little information on measures for control. However, to find out about health risks and emergency situations, concentrate on:

- Sections 2 and 16 of the sheet, which tell you what the dangers are;
- Sections 4-8, which tell you about emergencies, storage and handling.

Since 2009, new international symbols have been gradually replacing the European symbols. Some of them are similar to the European symbols, but there is no single word describing the hazard. Read the hazard statement on the packaging and the safety data sheet from the supplier.

European symbols

Toxic · Very toxic · Harmful · Irritant

Highly flammable · Extremely flammable · Explosive · Dangerous to the environment

Oxidising · Corrosive

New International symbols

Hazard checklist

- ☐ Does any product you use have a danger label?
- ☐ Does your process produce gas, fume, dust, mist or vapour?
- ☐ Is the substance harmful to breathe in?
- ☐ Can the substance harm your skin?
- ☐ Is it likely that harm could arise because of the way you use or produce it?
- ☐ What are you going to do about it?
  - Use something else?
  - Use it in another, safer way?
  - Control it to stop harm being caused?

CONTROL MEASURES

The control measures below are in order of importance.

1 Eliminate the use of the harmful substance and use a safer one. For instance, swap high **VOC** oil-based paint for a lower VOC water-based paint.

2 Use a safer form of the product. Is the product available ready-mixed? Is there a lower strength option that will still do the job?

VOC

The volatile organic compounds measure shows how much pollution a product will emit into the air when in use

INDUSTRY TIP

Product data sheets are free and have to be produced by the supplier of the product.

3 Change the work method to emit less of the substance. For instance, applying paint with a brush releases fewer VOCs into the air than spraying paint. Wet grinding produces less dust than dry grinding.

4 Enclose the work area so that the substance does not escape. This can mean setting up a tented area or closing doors.

5 Use extraction or filtration (eg a dust bag) in the work area.

6 Keep operatives in the area to a minimum.

7 Employers must provide appropriate PPE.

Paint with high VOC content

European symbols

Toxic

Very toxic

Harmful

Irritant

Highly flammable

Extremely flammable

Explosive

Dangerous to the environment

Oxidising

Corrosive

New International symbols

Toxic

May explode when heated

Irritant

Causes fire

Explosive

Dangerous to the environment

Intensifies fire

Long term health hazard

Corrosive

COSHH symbols. The international symbols will replace the European symbols in 2015.

INDUSTRY TIP

For more detailed information on RIDDOR visit the HSE webpage at www.hse.gov.uk/riddor.

REPORTING OF INJURIES, DISEASES AND DANGEROUS OCCURRENCES REGULATIONS (RIDDOR) 1995

Despite all the efforts put into health and safety, incidents still happen. The Reporting of Injuries, Diseases and Dangerous Occurrences Regulations (RIDDOR) 1995 state that employers must report to the HSE all accidents that result in an employee needing more than seven days off work. Diseases and dangerous occurrences must also be reported. A serious occurrence which has not caused an injury (a near miss) should still be reported because next time it happens things might not work out as well.

Below are some examples of injuries, diseases and dangerous occurrences which would need to be reported:

- A joiner cuts off a finger while using a circular saw.

- A plumber takes a week off after a splinter in her hand becomes infected.

- A ground operative contracts **leptospirosis**.

- A labourer contracts dermatitis (a serious skin problem) after contact with an irritant substance.

- A scaffold suffers a collapse following severe weather, unauthorised alteration or overloading but no-one is injured.

Leptospirosis

Also known as Weil's disease, this is a serious disease spread by rats and cattle

The purpose of RIDDOR is to enable the HSE to investigate serious incidents and collate statistical data. This information is used to help reduce the number of similar accidents happening in future and to make the workplace safer.

INDUSTRY TIP

Accidents do not just affect the person who has the accident. Work colleagues or members of the public might be affected and so will the employer. The consequences may include:

- a poor company image (this may put potential customers off)
- loss of production
- insurance costs increasing
- closure of the site
- having to pay sick pay
- other additional costs.

New HSE guidelines require employers to pay an hourly rate for time taken by the HSE to investigate an accident. This is potentially very costly.

An F2508 injury report form

Although minor accidents and injuries are not reported to HSE, records must be kept. Accidents must be recorded in the accident book. This provides a record of what happened and is useful for future reference. Trends may become apparent and the employer may take action to try and prevent that particular type of accident occurring again.

CONSTRUCTION, DESIGN AND MANAGEMENT (CDM) REGULATIONS 2007

The Construction, Design and Management (CDM) Regulations 2007 focus attention on the effective planning and management of construction projects, from the design concept through to maintenance and repair. The aim is for health and safety considerations to be integrated into a project's development, rather than be an inconvenient afterthought. The CDM Regulations reduce the risk of harm to those that have to work on or use the structure throughout its life, from construction through to **demolition**.

ACTIVITY

You have identified a potential risk. What action should you take? Make notes.

The CDM regulations play a role in safety during demolition

Demolition

When something, often a building, is completely torn down and destroyed

CDM Regulations protect workers from the construction to demolition of large and complex structures

The CDM Regulations apply to all projects except for those arranged by private clients, ie work that isn't in furtherance of a business interest. Property developers need to follow the CDM Regulations.

Under the CDM Regulations, the HSE must be notified where the construction work will take:

- more than 30 working days or

- 500 working days in total, ie if 100 people work for 5 days (500 working days) the HSE will have to be notified.

DUTY HOLDERS

Under the CDM Regulations there are several duty holders, each with a specific role.

Duty holder	Role
Client	This is the person or organisation who wishes to have the work done. The client will check that: - all the team members are competent - the management is suitable - sufficient time is allowed for all stages of the project - welfare facilities are in place before construction starts. HSE notifiable projects require that the client appoints a CDM co-ordinator and principal contractor, and provides access to a health and safety file.
CDM co-ordinator	Appointed by the client, the co-ordinator advises and assists the client with CDM duties. The co-ordinator notifies the HSE before work starts. This role involves the co-ordination of the health and safety aspects of the design of the building and ensures good communication between the client, designers and contractors.
Designer	At the design stages the designer removes hazards and reduces risks. The designer provides information about the risks that cannot be eliminated. Notifiable projects require that the designer checks that the client is aware of their CDM duties and that a CDM co-ordinator has been appointed. The designer will also supply information for the health and safety file.
Principal contractor	The principal contractor will plan, manage and monitor the construction in liaison with any other involved contractors. This involves developing a written plan and site rules before the construction begins. The principle contractor ensures that the site is made secure and suitable welfare facilities are provided from the start and maintained throughout construction. The principal contractor will also make sure that all operatives have site inductions and any further training that might be required to make sure the workforce is competent.
Contractor	Subcontractors and self-employed operatives will plan, manage and monitor their own work and employees, co-operating with any main contractor in relation to site rules. Contractors will make sure that all operatives have any further training that might be required to make sure they are competent. A contractor also reports any incidents under RIDDOR to the principal contractor.
Operatives	Operatives need to check their own competence: Can you carry out the task you have been asked to do safely? Have you been trained to do this type of activity? Do you have the correct equipment to carry out this activity? You must follow all the site health and safety rules and procedures and fully co-operate with the rest of the team to ensure the health and safety of other operatives and others who may be affected by the work. Any health and safety issues must be reported.

A client, a contractor and an operative looking over building plans ahead of construction

WELFARE FACILITIES REQUIRED ON SITE UNDER THE CDM REGULATIONS

The table below shows the welfare facilities that must be available on site.

Facility	Site requirement
Sanitary conveniences (toilets) 	■ Suitable and sufficient toilets should be provided or made available. ■ Toilets should be adequately ventilated and lit and should be clean. ■ Separate toilet facilities should be provided for men and women.
Washing facilities 	■ Sufficient facilities must be available, and include showers if required by the nature of the work. ■ They should be in the same place as the toilets and near any changing rooms. ■ There must be a supply of clean hot (or warm) and cold running water, soap and towels. ■ There must be separate washing facilities provided for men and women unless the area is for washing hands and the face only.

Facility	Site requirement
Clean drinking water 	■ This must be provided or made available. ■ It should be clearly marked by an appropriate sign. ■ Cups should be provided unless the supply of drinking water is from a water fountain.
Changing rooms and lockers 	■ Changing rooms must be provided or made available if operatives have to wear special clothing and if they cannot be expected to change elsewhere. ■ There must be separate rooms for, or separate use of rooms by, men and women where necessary. ■ The rooms must be have seating and include, where necessary, facilities to enable operatives to dry their special clothing and their own clothing and personal effects. ■ Lockers should also be provided.
Rest rooms or rest areas 	■ They should have enough tables and seating with backs for the number of operatives likely to use them at any one time. ■ Where necessary, rest rooms should include suitable facilities for pregnant women or nursing mothers to rest lying down. ■ Arrangements must be made to ensure that meals can be prepared, heated and eaten. It must also be possible to boil water.

ACTIVITY

What facilities are provided at your workplace or place of training?

PROVISION AND USE OF WORK EQUIPMENT REGULATIONS (PUWER) 1997

The Provision and Use of Work Equipment Regulations (PUWER) 1997 place duties on:

■ people and companies who own, operate or have control over work equipment

■ employers whose employees use work equipment.

Work equipment can be defined as any machinery, appliance, apparatus, tool or installation for use at work (whether exclusively or not). This includes equipment which employees provide for their own use at work. The scope of work equipment is therefore extremely wide. The use of work equipment is also very widely interpreted and, according to the HSE, means 'any activity involving work equipment and includes starting, stopping, programming, setting, transporting, repairing, modifying, maintaining, servicing and cleaning.' It includes equipment such as diggers, electric planers, stepladders, hammers or wheelbarrows.

Under PUWER, work equipment must be:

- suitable for the intended use

- safe to use

- well maintained

- inspected regularly.

Regular inspection is important as a tool that was safe when it was new may no longer be safe after considerable use.

Additionally, work equipment must only be used by people who have received adequate instruction and training. Information regarding the use of the equipment must be given to the operator and must only be used for what it was designed to do.

Protective devices, eg emergency stops, must be used. Brakes must be fitted where appropriate to slow down moving parts to bring the equipment to a safe condition when turned off or stopped. Equipment must have adequate means of isolation. Warnings, either by signs or other means such as sounds or lights, must be used as appropriate. Access to dangerous parts of the machinery must be controlled. Some work equipment is subject to additional health and safety legislation which must also be followed.

Employers who use work equipment must manage the risks. ACoPs (see page 9) have been developed in line with PUWER. The ACoPs have a special legal status, as outlined in the introduction to the PUWER ACoP:

Following the guidance is not compulsory and you are free to take other action. But if you do follow the guidance you will normally be doing enough to comply with the law. Health and safety inspectors seek to secure compliance with the law and may refer to this guidance as illustrating good practice.

MANUAL HANDLING OPERATIONS REGULATIONS 1992

Employers must try and avoid manual handling within reason if there is a possibility of injury. If manual handling cannot be avoided then they must reduce the risk of injury by means of a risk assessment.

An operative lifting heavy bricks

LIFTING AND HANDLING

Incorrect lifting and handling is a serious risk to your health. It is very easy to injure your back – just ask any experienced builder. An injured back can be very unpleasant, so it's best to look after it.

Here are a few things to consider when lifting:

■ Assess the load. Is it too heavy? Do you need assistance or additional training? Is it an awkward shape?

■ Can a lifting aid be used, such as any of the below?

Wheelbarrow

Gin lift

Scissor lift

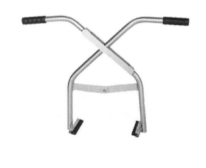

Kerb lifter

■ Does the lift involve twisting or reaching?

■ Where is the load going to end up? Is there a clear path? Is the place it's going to be taken to cleared and ready?

How to lift and place an item correctly

If you cannot use a machine, it is important that you keep the correct posture when lifting any load. The correct technique to do this is known as **kinetic lifting**. Always lift with your back straight, elbows in, knees bent and your feet slightly apart.

Kinetic lifting

A method of lifting that ensures that the risk of injury is reduced

Safe kinetic lifting technique

ACTIVITY

Try it out. Place a box on the floor and lift it using the technique shown.

ACTIVITY

Consider this list of materials: plywood, cement, aggregates, sawn timber joists, glass, drainage pipes, and kerbs. Make a table to show how you would transport and stack them around your place of work.

INDUSTRY TIP

Most workplace injuries are a result of manual handling. Remember pushing or pulling an object still comes under the Manual Handling Operations Regulations.

When placing the item, again be sure to use your knees and beware of trapping your fingers. If stacking materials, be sure that they are on a sound level base and on bearers if required.

Heavy objects that cannot easily be lifted by mechanical methods can be lifted by several people. It is important that one person in the team is in charge, and that lifting is done in a co-operative way. It has been known for one person to fall down and the others then drop the item!

CONTROL OF NOISE AT WORK REGULATIONS 2005

Under the Control of Noise at Work Regulations 2005, duties are placed on employers and employees to reduce the risk of hearing damage to the lowest reasonable level practicable. Hearing loss caused by work is preventable. Hearing damage is permanent and cannot be restored once lost.

ACTIVITY

Watch this link to find out more about hearing loss and damage: www.hse.gov.uk/noise/video/hearingvideo.htm

EMPLOYER'S DUTIES UNDER THE REGULATIONS

An employer's duties are:

- To carry out a risk assessment and identify who is at risk.

- To eliminate or control its employees exposure to noise at the workplace and to reduce the noise as far as practicable.

- To provide suitable hearing protection.

- To provide health surveillance to those identified as at risk by the risk assessment.

■ To provide information and training about the risks to their employees as identified by the risk assessment.

EMPLOYEES' DUTIES UNDER THE REGULATIONS

Employees must:

■ Make full and proper use of personal hearing protectors provided to them by their employer.

■ If they discover any defect in any personal hearing protectors or other control measures they must report it to their employer as soon as is practicable.

Ear defenders

Ear plugs

NOISE LEVELS

Under the Regulations, specific actions are triggered at specific noise levels. Noise is measured in decibels and shown as dB(A). The two main action levels are 80 dB(A) and 85 dB(A).

Requirements at 80 dB(A) to 85 dB(A):

■ Assess the risk to operatives' health and provide them with information and training.

■ Provide suitable ear protection free of charge to those who request ear protection.

Requirements above 85 dB(A):

■ Reduce noise exposure as far as practicable by means other than ear protection.

■ Set up an ear protection zone using suitable signage and segregation.

■ Provide suitable ear protection free of charge to those affected and ensure they are worn.

PERSONAL PROTECTIVE EQUIPMENT (PPE) AT WORK REGULATIONS 1992

Employees and subcontractors must work in a safe manner. Not only must they wear the PPE that their employers provide they must also look after it and report any damage to it. Importantly, employees must not be charged for anything given to them or done for them by the employer in relation to safety.

ACTIVITY

Think about your place of work or training. What PPE do you think you should use when working with cement or using a powered planer?

The hearing and respiratory PPE provided for most work situations is not covered by these Regulations because other regulations apply to it. However, these items need to be compatible with any other PPE provided.

The main requirement of the Regulations is that PPE must be supplied and used at work wherever there are risks to health and safety that cannot be adequately controlled in other ways.

The Regulations also require that PPE is:

- included in the method statement

- properly assessed before use to ensure it is suitable

- maintained and stored properly

- provided to employees with instructions on how they can use it safely

- used correctly by employees.

An employer cannot ask for money from an employee for PPE, whether it is returnable or not. This includes agency workers if they are legally regarded as employees. If employment has been terminated and the employee keeps the PPE without the employer's permission, then, as long as it has been made clear in the contract of employment, the employer may be able to deduct the cost of the replacement from any wages owed.

Using PPE is a very important part of staying safe. For it to do its job properly it must be kept in good condition and used correctly. If any damage does occur to an article of PPE it is important that this is reported and it is replaced. It must also be remembered that PPE is a last line of defence and should not be used in place of a good safety policy!

FUNCTIONAL SKILLS

Using an internet search engine, research what to consider when selecting and using PPE. Write down four considerations.

Work on this activity can support FICT2.A and FE 2.2.1.

ACTIVITY

Check the date on your safety helmet. Always update your safety helmet if it is out of date.

INDUSTRY TIP

Remember, you also have a duty of care for your own health.

A site safety sign showing the PPE required to work there

The following table shows the type of PPE used in the workplace and explains why it is important to store, maintain and use PPE correctly. It also shows why it is important to check and report damage to PPE.

PPE	Correct use
Hard hat/safety helmet 	Hard hats must be worn when there is danger of hitting your head or danger of falling objects. They often prevent a wide variety of head injuries. Most sites insist on hard hats being worn. They must be adjusted to fit your head correctly and must not be worn back to front! Check the date of manufacture as plastic can become brittle over time. Solvents, pens and paints can damage the plastic too.
Toe-cap boots or shoes  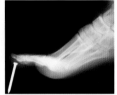 Safety boots A nail in a construction worker's foot.	Toe-cap boots or shoes are worn on most sites as a matter of course and protect the feet from heavy falling objects. Some safety footwear has additional insole protection to help prevent nails going up through the foot. Toe caps can be made of steel or lighter plastic.
Ear defenders and plugs  Ear defenders Ear plugs	Your ears can be very easily damaged by loud noise. Ear protection will help prevent hearing loss while using loud tools or if there is a lot of noise going on around you. When using earplugs always ensure your hands are clean before handling the plugs as this reduces the risk of infection. If your ear defenders are damaged or fail to make a good seal around your ears have them replaced.
High visibility (hi-viz) jacket 	This makes it much easier for other people to see you. This is especially important when there is plant or vehicles moving in the vicinity.
Goggles and safety glasses   Safety goggles Safety glasses	These protect the eyes from dust and flying debris while you are working. It has been known for casualties to be taken to hospital after dust has blown up from a dry mud road. You only get one pair of eyes, look after them!

PPE	Correct use
Dust masks and respirators 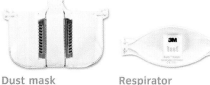 Dust mask Respirator	Dust is produced during most construction work and it can be hazardous to your lungs. It can cause all sorts of ailments from asthma through to cancer. Wear a dust mask to filter this dust out. You must ensure it is well fitted. Another hazard is dangerous gases such as solvents. A respirator will filter out hazardous gases but a dust mask will not! Respirators are rated P1, P2 and P3, with P3 giving the highest protection.
Gloves  Latex glove Nitrile glove  Gauntlet gloves Leather gloves	Gloves protect your hands. Hazards include cuts, abrasions, dermatitis, chemical burns or splinters. Latex and nitrile gloves are good for fine work, although some people are allergic to latex. Gauntlets provide protection from strong chemicals. Other types of gloves provide good grip and protect the fingers. 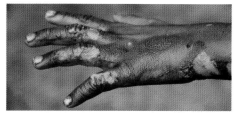 A chemical burn as a result of not wearing safety gloves
Sunscreen 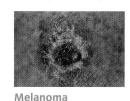 Suncream Melanoma	Another risk, especially in the summer months, is sunburn. Although a good tan is sometimes considered desirable, over-exposure to the sun can cause skin cancer such as melanoma. When out in the sun, cover up and use sunscreen (ie suncream) on exposed areas of your body to prevent burning.
Preventing HAVS 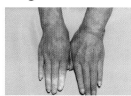	Vibration white finger (VWS) is a symptom of an industrial injury known as HAVS and is caused by using vibrating power tools (such as a hammer drill, vibrating poker and vibrating plate) for a long time. This injury is controlled by limiting the time such power tools are used. For more information see page 31.

ACTIVITY

You are working on a site and a brick falls on your head. Luckily, you are doing as you have been instructed and you are wearing a helmet. You notice that the helmet has a small crack in it. What do you do?

1 Carry on using it as your employer will charge you for a new one, after all it is only a small crack.
2 Take it to your supervisor as it will no longer offer you full protection and it will need replacing.
3 Buy a new helmet because the old one no longer looks very nice.

INDUSTRY TIP

The most important pieces of PPE when using a disc cutter are dust masks, glasses and ear protection.

WORK AT HEIGHT REGULATIONS 2005

The Work at Height Regulations 2005 put several duties upon employers:

■ Working at height should be avoided if possible.

■ If working at height cannot be avoided, the work must be properly organised with risk assessments carried out.

■ Risk assessments should be regularly updated.

■ Those working at height must be trained and competent.

■ A method statement must be provided.

Operatives working at height as a roof is lifted into place

Several points should be considered when working at height:

■ How long is the job expected to take?

■ What type of work will it be? It could be anything from fitting a single light bulb, through to removing a chimney or installing a roof.
  • How is the access platform going to be reached? By how many people?
  • Will people be able to get on and off the structure safely? Could there be overcrowding?

■ What are the risks to passers-by? Could debris or dust blow off and injure anyone on the road below?

■ What are the conditions like? Extreme weather, unstable buildings and poor ground conditions need to be taken into account.

A cherry picker can assist you when working at height

ACCESS EQUIPMENT AND SAFE METHODS OF USE

The means of access should only be chosen after a risk assessment has been carried out. There are various types of access.

Ladders

Ladders are normally used for access onto an access platform. They are not designed for working from except for light, short-duration work. A ladder should lean at an angle of 75°, ie one unit out for every four units up.

Roof ladder

Resting ladders on plastic guttering can cause it to bend and break

Strong upper resting point

Adequate lap on extension ladders

Ground back slope not exceeding 6°

Ground side slope not exceeding 16°, clean and free of slippery algae and moss

Using a ladder correctly

The following images show how to use a ladder or stepladder safely.

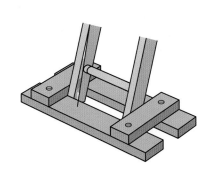

A ladder secured at the base.

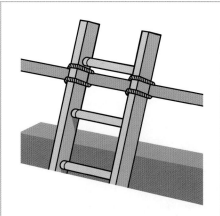

A ladder secured at the top of a platform for working from.

Access ladders should extend 1m above the landing point to provide a strong handhold.

Certain stepladders are unsafe to work from the top three rungs.

Don't overreach, and stay on the same rung.

Grip the ladder when climbing and remember to keep three points of contact.

INDUSTRY TIP

Always complete ladder pre-checks. Check the stiles (the two uprights) and rungs for damage such as splits or cracks. Do not use painted ladders because the paint could be hiding damage! Check all of the equipment including any stays and feet.

Stepladders

Stepladders are designed for light, short-term work.

Working from the side can make stepladders unstable. Do not overreach

Don't stand on the top three steps

Stepladder is fully open

Locked open firm and level on the ground

Using a stepladder correctly

FUNCTIONAL SKILLS

Using information on stepladders on the HSE website, write down two examples of what sort of job stepladders could be used for and two jobs they should not be used for.

Work on this activity can support FICT 2.A and FE 2.2.2.

Trestles

This is a working platform used for work of a slightly longer duration.

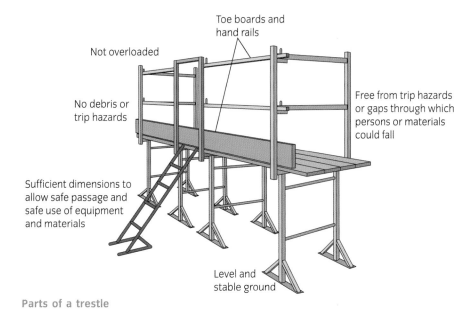

Toe boards and hand rails

Not overloaded

No debris or trip hazards

Free from trip hazards or gaps through which persons or materials could fall

Sufficient dimensions to allow safe passage and safe use of equipment and materials

Level and stable ground

Parts of a trestle

Tower scaffold

These are usually proprietary (manufactured) and are made from galvanised steel or lightweight aluminium alloy. They must be erected by someone competent in the erection and dismantling of mobile scaffolds.

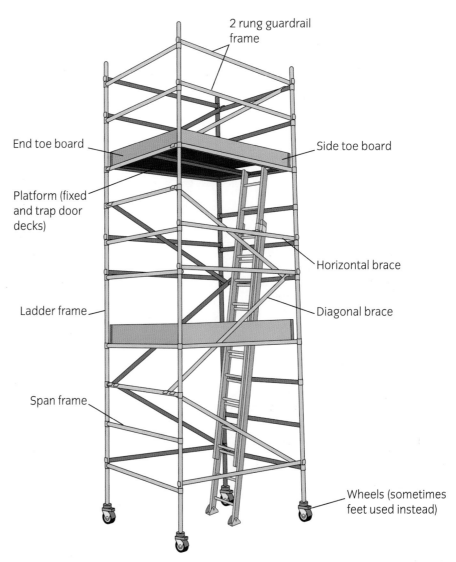

2 rung guardrail frame

End toe board

Side toe board

Platform (fixed and trap door decks)

Horizontal brace

Ladder frame

Diagonal brace

Span frame

Wheels (sometimes feet used instead)

Parts of a tower scaffold

To use a tower scaffold safely:

- Always read and follow the manufacturer's instruction manual.

- Only use the equipment for what it is designed for.

- The wheels or feet of the tower must be in contact with a firm surface.

- Outriggers should be used to increase stability. The maximum height given in the manufacturer's instructions must not be exceeded.

- The platform must not be overloaded.

- The platform should be unloaded (and reduced in height if required) before it is moved.

- Never move a platform, even a small distance, if it is occupied.

INDUSTRY TIP

Remember, even a mobile access tower should have toe boards and guard rails fitted at all times when in use.

Tubular scaffold

This comes in two types:

- independent scaffold has two sets of standards or uprights

- putlog scaffold is built into the brickwork.

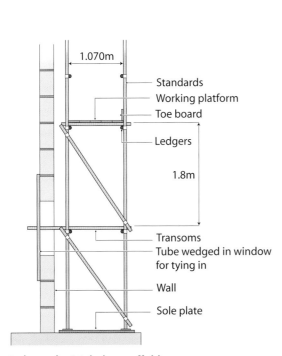

Independent tubular scaffold

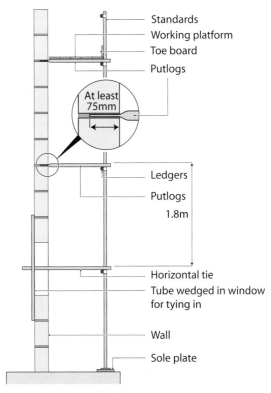

Putlog tubular scaffold

Tubular scaffold is erected by specialist scaffolding companies and often requires structural calculations. Only trained and competent scaffold erectors should alter scaffolding. Access to a scaffold is usually via a tied ladder with three rungs projecting above the step off at platform level.

OUR HOUSE

You have been asked to complete a job that requires gaining access to the roof level of a two-storey building. What equipment would you choose to get access to the work area? What things would you take into consideration when choosing the equipment? Take a look at 'Our House' as a guide for working on a two-storey building.

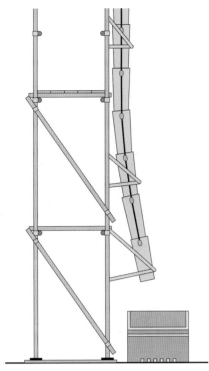

A debris chute for scaffolding

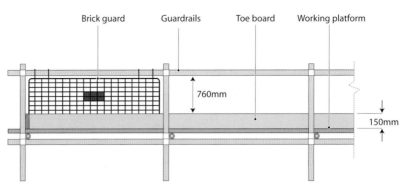

Brick guard   Guardrails   Toe board   Working platform

760mm

150mm

A safe working platform on a tubular scaffold

All scaffolding must:

- not have any gaps in the handrail or toe boards

- have a safe system for lifting any materials up to the working height

- have a safe system of debris removal.

Fall protection devices include:

- harnesses and lanyards

- safety netting

- air bags.

A harness and lanyard or safety netting will stop a person falling too far, leaving them suspended in the air. Air bags (commonly known as 'bouncy castles') are set up on the ground and inflated. If a person falls, they will have a soft landing. Air bags have fallen out of favour somewhat as some operatives use them as an easy way to get off the working platform – not the purpose they were intended for!

A safe scaffolding set up

LIFTING OPERATIONS AND LIFTING EQUIPMENT REGULATIONS (LOLER) 1998

The Lifting Operations and Lifting Equipment Regulations (LOLER) 1998 put responsibility upon employers to ensure that the lifting equipment provided for use at work is:

- strong and stable enough for the particular use and marked to indicate safe working loads

- positioned and installed to minimise any risks

- used safely, ie the work is planned, organised and performed by competent people

- subject to on-going thorough examination and, where appropriate, inspection by competent people.

THE CONTROL OF VIBRATION AT WORK REGULATIONS 2005

Vibration white finger or hand–arm vibration syndrome (HAVS), see page 23, is caused by using vibrating tools such as hammer drills, vibrating pokers or hand held breakers over a long period of time. The most efficient and effective way of controlling exposure to hand-arm vibration is to look for new or alternative work methods which remove or reduce exposure to vibration.

An operative taking a rest from using a power tool

Follow these steps to reduce the effects of HAVS:

■ Always use the right tool for each job.

■ Check tools before using them to make sure they have been properly maintained and repaired to avoid increased vibration caused by faults or general wear.

■ Make sure cutting tools are kept sharp so that they remain efficient.

■ Reduce the amount of time you use a tool in one go, by doing other jobs in between.

■ Avoid gripping or forcing a tool or work piece more than you have to.

■ Encourage good blood circulation by:
  • keeping warm and dry (when necessary, wear gloves, a hat, waterproofs and use heating pads if available)
  • giving up or cutting down on smoking because smoking reduces blood flow
  • massaging and exercising your fingers during work breaks.

Damage from HAVS can include the inability to do fine work and cold can trigger painful finger blanching attacks (when the ends of your fingers go white).

Don't use power tools for longer than you need to

CONSTRUCTION SITE HAZARDS

DANGERS ON CONSTRUCTION SITES

Study the drawing of a building site. There is some demolition taking place, as well as construction. How many hazards can you find? Discuss your answers.

Dangers	Discussion points
Head protection	The operatives are not wearing safety helmets, which would prevent them from hitting their head or from falling objects.
Poor housekeeping	The site is very untidy. This can result in slips trips and falls and can pollute the environment. An untidy site gives a poor company image. Offcuts and debris should be regularly removed and disposed of according to site policy and recycled if possible.
Fire	There is a fire near a building; this is hazardous. Fires can easily become uncontrollable and spread. There is a risk to the structure and, more importantly, a risk of operatives being burned. Fires can also pollute the environment.

Dangers	Discussion points
Trip hazards	Notice the tools and debris on the floor. The scaffold has been poorly constructed. There is a trip hazard where the scaffold boards overlap.
Chemical spills	There is a drum leaking onto the ground. This should be stored properly – upright and in a lockable metal shed or cupboard. The leak poses a risk of pollution and of chemical burns to operatives.
Falls from height	The scaffold has handrails missing. The trestle working platform has not been fitted with guard rails. None of the operatives are wearing hard hats for protection either.
Noise	An operative is using noisy machinery with other people nearby. The operative should be wearing ear PPE, as should those working nearby. Better still, they should be working elsewhere if at all possible, isolating themselves from the noise.
Electrical	Some of the wiring is 240V as there is no transformer, it's in poor repair and it's also dragging through liquid. This not only increases the risk of electrocution but is also a trip hazard.
Asbestos or other hazardous substances	Some old buildings contain **asbestos** roofing which can become a hazard when being demolished or removed. Other potential hazards include lead paint or mould spores. If a potentially hazardous material is discovered a supervisor must be notified immediately and work must stop until the hazard is dealt with appropriately.

Asbestos

A naturally occurring mineral that was commonly used for a variety of purposes including: **insulation**, fire protection, roofing and guttering. It is extremely hazardous and can cause a serious lung disease known as asbestosis

Insulation

A material that reduces or prevents the transmission of heat

FUNCTIONAL SKILLS

Using the data you collected in the Functional Skills task on page 3, produce a pie chart to show the proportion of occupational cancer that is caused by asbestosis.

Work on this activity can support FM L2.3.1 and C2.4.

Cables can be a trip hazard on site

Boiler suit

Hand cleaner

PERSONAL HYGIENE

Working in the construction industry can be very physical, and it's likely to be quite dirty at times. Therefore you should take good care with your personal hygiene. This involves washing well after work. If contaminants are present, then wearing a protective suit, such as a boiler suit, that you can take off before you go home will prevent contaminants being taken home with you.

You should also wash your hands after going to the toilet and before eating. This makes it safer to eat and more pleasant for others around you. The following step by steps show a safe and hygienic way to wash your hands.

STEP 1 Apply soap to hands from the dispenser.

STEP 2 Rub the soap into the lather and cover your hands with it, including between your fingers.

STEP 3 Rinse hands under a running tap removing all of the soap from your hands.

STEP 4 Dry your hands using disposable towels. Put the towel in the bin once your hands are dry.

WORKING WITH ELECTRICITY

Electricity is a very useful energy resource but it can be very dangerous. Electricity must be handled with care! Only trained, competent people can work with electrical equipment.

THE DANGERS OF USING ELECTRICAL EQUIPMENT

The main dangers of electricity are:

- shock and burns (a 230V shock can kill)

- electrical faults which could cause a fire

- an explosion where an electrical spark has ignited a flammable gas.

VOLTAGES

Generally speaking, the lower the voltage the safer it is. However, a low voltage is not necessarily suitable for some machines, so higher voltages can be found. On site, 110V (volts) is recommended and this is the voltage rating most commonly used in the building industry. This is converted from 230V by use of a transformer.

110V 1 phase – yellow

230V (commonly called 240V) domestic voltage is used on site as battery chargers usually require this voltage. Although 230V is often used in workshops, 110V is recommended.

410V (otherwise known as 3 phase) is used for large machinery, such as joinery shop equipment.

230V 1 phase – blue

Voltages are nominal, ie they can vary slightly.

BATTERY POWER

Battery power is much safer than mains power. Many power tools are now available in battery-powered versions. They are available in a wide variety of voltages from 3.6V for a small screwdriver all the way up to 36V for large masonry drills.

410V 3 phase – red

The following images are all examples of battery powered tools you may come across in your workplace or place of training.

Battery drill   Battery-powered planer   Battery-powered jigsaw

WIRING

The wires inside a cable are made from copper, which conducts electricity. The copper is surrounded by a plastic coating that is colour coded. The three wires in a cable are the live (brown), which works with the neutral (blue) to conduct electricity, making the appliance work. The earth (green and yellow stripes) prevents electrocution if the appliance is faulty or damaged.

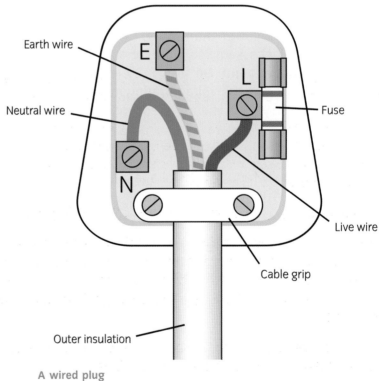

A wired plug

POWER TOOLS AND CHECKS

Power tools should always be checked before use. Always inform your supervisor if you find a fault. The tool will need to be repaired, and the tool needs to be kept out of use until then. The tool might be taken away, put in the site office and clearly labelled 'Do not use'.

Power tool checks include:

- *Look for the powered appliance testing (PAT) label*: PAT is a regular test carried out by a competent person (eg a qualified electrician) to ensure the tool is in a safe electrical condition. A sticker is placed on the tool after it has been tested. Tools that do not pass the PAT are taken out of use.

PAT testing labels

- *Cable*: Is it damaged? Is there a repair? Insulation tape may be hiding a damaged cable. Damaged cables must be replaced.

- *Casing*: Is the casing cracked? Plastic casings ensure the tool is double-insulated. This means the live parts inside are safely shielded from the user. A cracked casing will reduce the protection to the user and will require repair.

- *Guards and tooling*: Are guards in place? Is the tooling sharp?

- *Electricity supply leads*: Are they damaged? Are they creating a trip hazard? You need to place them in such a way that they do not make a trip hazard. Are they protected from damage? If they are lying on the floor with heavy traffic crossing them, they must be covered.

- *Use appropriate equipment for the size of the job*: For example, too many splitters can result in a web of cables.

- *Storage*: After use, power tools and equipment should be stored correctly. Tools must be returned to the boxes, including all the guards and parts. Cables need to be wound onto reels or neatly coiled as they can become tangled very easily.

Cable protection

Cable reel

INDUSTRY TIP

Remember, always fully unroll an extension lead before use because it could overheat and cause a fire.

FIRE

Fire needs three things to start; if just one of them is missing there will be no fire. If all are present then a fire is unavoidable:

1 *Oxygen*: A naturally occurring gas in the air that combines with flammable substances under certain circumstances.

2 *Heat*: A source of fire, such as a hot spark from a grinder or naked flame.

3 *Fuel*: Things that will burn such as acetone, timber, cardboard or paper.

The fire triangle

If you have heat, fuel and oxygen you will have a fire. Remove any of these and the fire will go out.

PREVENTING THE SPREAD OF FIRE

Being tidy will help prevent fires starting and spreading. For instance:

- Wood offcuts should not be left in big piles or standing up against a wall. Instead, useable offcuts should be stored in racks.

- Put waste into the allocated disposal bins or skips.

- Always replace the cap on unused fuel containers when you put them away. Otherwise they are a potential source of danger.

- Flammable liquids (not limited to fuel-flammable liquids) such as oil-based paint, thinners and oil must be stored in a locked metal cupboard or shed.

- Smoking around flammable substances should be avoided.

- Dust can be explosive, so when doing work that produces wood dust it is important to use some form of extraction and have good ventilation.

FIRE EXTINGUISHERS AND THEIR USES

You need to know where the fire extinguishers and blankets are located and which fire extinguishers can be used on different fires. The table below shows the different classes of fire and which extinguisher to use in each case.

Class of fire	Materials	Type of extinguisher
A	Wood, paper, hair, textiles	Water, foam, dry powder, wet chemical
B	Flammable liquids	Foam, dry powder, CO_2
C	Flammable gases	Dry powder, CO_2
D	Flammable metals	Specially formulated dry powder
E	Electrical fires	CO_2, dry powder
F	Cooking oils	Wet chemical, fire blanket

Fire blanket

CO_2 extinguisher

Dry powder extinguisher

Water extinguisher

Foam extinguisher

It is important to use the correct extinguisher for the type of fire as using the wrong one could make the danger much worse, eg using water on an electrical fire could lead to the user being electrocuted!

EMERGENCY PROCEDURES

In an emergency, people tend to panic. If an emergency were to occur, such as fire, discovering a bomb or some other security problem, would you know what to do? It is vital to be prepared in case of an emergency.

It is your responsibility to know the emergency procedures on your work site:

■ If you discover a fire or other emergency you will need to raise the alarm:
  • You will need to tell a nominated person. Who is this?
  • If you are first on the scene you will have to ring the emergency services on 999.

■ Be aware of the alarm signal. Is it a bell, a voice or a siren?

■ Where is the assembly point? You will have to proceed to this point in an orderly way. Leave all your belongings behind, they may slow you or others down.

■ At the assembly point, there will be someone who will ensure everyone is out safely and will do so by taking a count. Do you know who this person is? If during a fire you are not accounted for, a firefighter may risk their life to go into the building to look for you.

■ How do you know it's safe to re-enter the building? You will be told by the appointed person. It's very important that you do not re-enter the building until you are told to do so.

Emergency procedure sign

ACTIVITY

What is the fire evacuation procedure at your workplace or place of training?

SIGNS AND SAFETY NOTICES

The law sets out the types of safety signs needed on a construction site. Some signs warn us about danger and others tell us what to do to stay safe.

The following table describes five basic types of sign.

Type of sign	Description
Prohibition 	These signs are red and white. They are round. They signify something that must *not* be done.
Mandatory	These signs are blue. They are round. They signify something that *must* be done.

Type of sign	Description
Caution 	These signs are yellow and black. They are triangular. These give warning of hazards.
Safe condition 	These signs are green. They are usually square or rectangular. They tell you the safe way to go, or what to do in an emergency.
Supplementary 	These white signs are square or rectangular and give additional important information. They usually accompany the signs above.

Case Study: Miranda

A site has a small hut where tools are stored securely, and inside the hut there is a short bench that has some sharpening equipment including a grinding wheel.

Miranda wished to grind her plane blade, but before using it found that the grinding wheel was defective as the side of the wheel had been used, causing a deep groove.

She found another old grinding wheel beneath the bench which looked fine. She fitted it to the grinder and used it.

Afterwards, she wondered if she should have asked someone else to change the wheel for her.

- What health and safety issues are there with this scenario?

- What training could Miranda undertake?

TEST YOUR KNOWLEDGE

Work through the following questions to check your learning.

1 Which of the following must be filled out prior to carrying out a site task?

   a Invoice

   b Bill of quantities

   c Risk assessment

   d Schedule

2 Which of the following signs shows you something you *must* do?

   a Green circle

   b Yellow triangle

   c White square

   d Blue circle

3 Two parts of the fire triangle are heat and fuel. What is the third?

   a Nitrogen

   b Oxygen

   c Carbon dioxide

   d Hydrogen sulphite

4 Which of the following types of fire extinguisher would best put out an electrical fire?

   a CO_2

   b Powder

   c Water

   d Foam

5 Which piece of health and safety legislation is designed to protect an operative from ill health and injury when using solvents and adhesives?

   a Manual Handling Operations Regulations 1992

   b Control of Substances Hazardous to Health (COSHH) Regulations 2002

   c Health and Safety (First Aid) Regulations 1981

   d Lifting Operations and Lifting Equipment Regulations (LOLER) 1998

6 What is the correct angle at which to lean a ladder against a wall?

   a 70°

   b 80°

   c 75°

   d 85°

7 Which are the most important pieces of PPE to use when using a disc cutter?

   a Overalls, gloves and boots

   b Boots, head protection and overalls

   c Glasses, hearing protection and dust mask

   d Gloves, head protection and boots

8 Which of these is not a lifting aid?

   a Wheelbarrow

   b Kerb lifter

   c Gin lift

   d Respirator

9 Which of these is a 3 phase voltage?

   a 410V

   b 230V

   c 240V

   d 110V

10 Above what noise level must you wear ear protection?

   a 75 dB(A)

   b 80 dB(A)

   c 85 dB(A)

   d 90 dB(A)

Chapter 2
Unit 202: Principles of building construction, information and communication

Working in the building industry involves more than just the physical construction of buildings such as laying blocks, screwing timber together or soldering pipes. Building is an expensive business and for the work to progress smoothly (and on budget) the work needs to be well organised.

This involves interpreting information such as drawings, specifications and schedules. It also involves calculating quantities and dimensions and knowing how to communicate well with others.

By reading this chapter you will know about:

1 How to select types of building information.
2 Environmental considerations in relation to construction.
3 The construction of foundations.
4 Construction of internal and external walls.
5 Construction of floors.
6 Construction of roofs.
7 How to communicate in the workplace.

TECHNICAL INFORMATION

This section will discuss the three main sources of technical information that are used when constructing buildings:

- working drawings and **specifications**
- schedules
- **bill of quantities**.

These are all essential information and form the contract documents (those that govern the construction of a building). All documentation needs to be correctly interpreted and correctly used. The contract documents need to be looked after and stored (filed) correctly and safely. If documents are left lying around they will become difficult to read and pages may be lost, leading to errors. The contract documents will need to be **archived** at the end of the contract, so they can be referred back to in case of any query or dispute over the work carried out or the materials used.

DRAWING SCALES

It is impossible to fit a full-sized drawing of a building onto a sheet of paper, so it is necessary to **scale** (shrink) the size of the building to enable it to fit. The building has to be shrunk in proportion; this makes it possible to convert measurements on the drawing into real measurements that can be used. Scale rules are made specifically for this purpose.

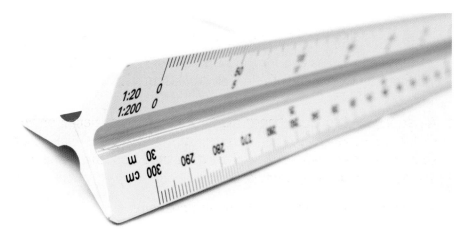

Triangular scale rule

How do scale rules work? Let's say we are using a scale of 1:5. That means that what we draw – using the sizes on the scale rule – will be five times smaller on the drawing than the object's actual size. So, a line 30mm long will represent an object 150mm long (30 × 5 = 150).

Specification

A contract document that gives information about the quality of materials and standards of workmanship required

Bill of quantities

A document containing quantities, descriptions and cost of works and resources

Archived

Kept in storage

Scale

The ratio of the size on a drawing to the size of the real thing that it represents

INDUSTRY TIP

Do not scale from photocopies because these can easily become distorted in the process of photocopying.

INDUSTRY TIP

If a drawing has **dimensions**, use these instead of using a scale rule to take a measurement.

Dimension

A measurement

The British Standards Institute's BS 1192 (Drawing office practice) gives a range of standard scales that are used for various drawing types and scale rules are manufactured to meet this purpose.

British Standards Institute

The British Standards Institute (BSI) is the UK authority which develops and publishes standards in the UK

SCALES IN COMMON USE

Scale	Use
1:1	Full size (used for rods)
1:2 1:5 1:10	Building details
1:20 1:50 1:100 1:200	Plans, elevations and sections
1:200 1:500 1:1250	Site plans
1:1250 1:2500	Location plans

The documents these scales are used for are described on pages 49–51.

FUNCTIONAL SKILLS

Work out the following:

Scale size	Scale	Actual size
10mm	1:10	100mm
25mm	1:20	a)
b)	1:50	300mm
50mm	1:200	c)

Work on this activity can support FM L2.3.2 and C2.3.

Answers: a) 500mm, b) 6mm, c) 10m

DATUM POINTS

Heights of buildings and the relative heights of components within the building are calculated from a common **datum point**. Datum points are determined by transferring a known fixed height from a bench mark. There are two types of datum point:

- A permanent Ordnance bench mark (OBM) is a given height on an Ordnance Survey map. This fixed height is described as a value, eg so many metres above sea level (as calculated from the average sea height at Newlyn, Cornwall).

- A temporary bench mark (TBM) is set up on site.

Datum point

A fixed point or height from which reference levels can be taken. The datum point is used to transfer levels across a building site. It represents the finished floor level (FFL) on a dwelling

Ordnance and temporary bench marks

ACTIVITY

Find your local OBM or your site TBM. What is the height of your OBM or TBM?

BASIC DRAWING SYMBOLS (HATCHINGS)

Standard symbols, also known as hatching symbols, are used on drawings as a means of passing on information simply. If all the parts of a building were labelled in writing, the drawing would soon become very crowded. Additionally, it is important to use standard symbols so that everyone can read them and it means the same to everyone. The following images are just some of the standard symbols used.

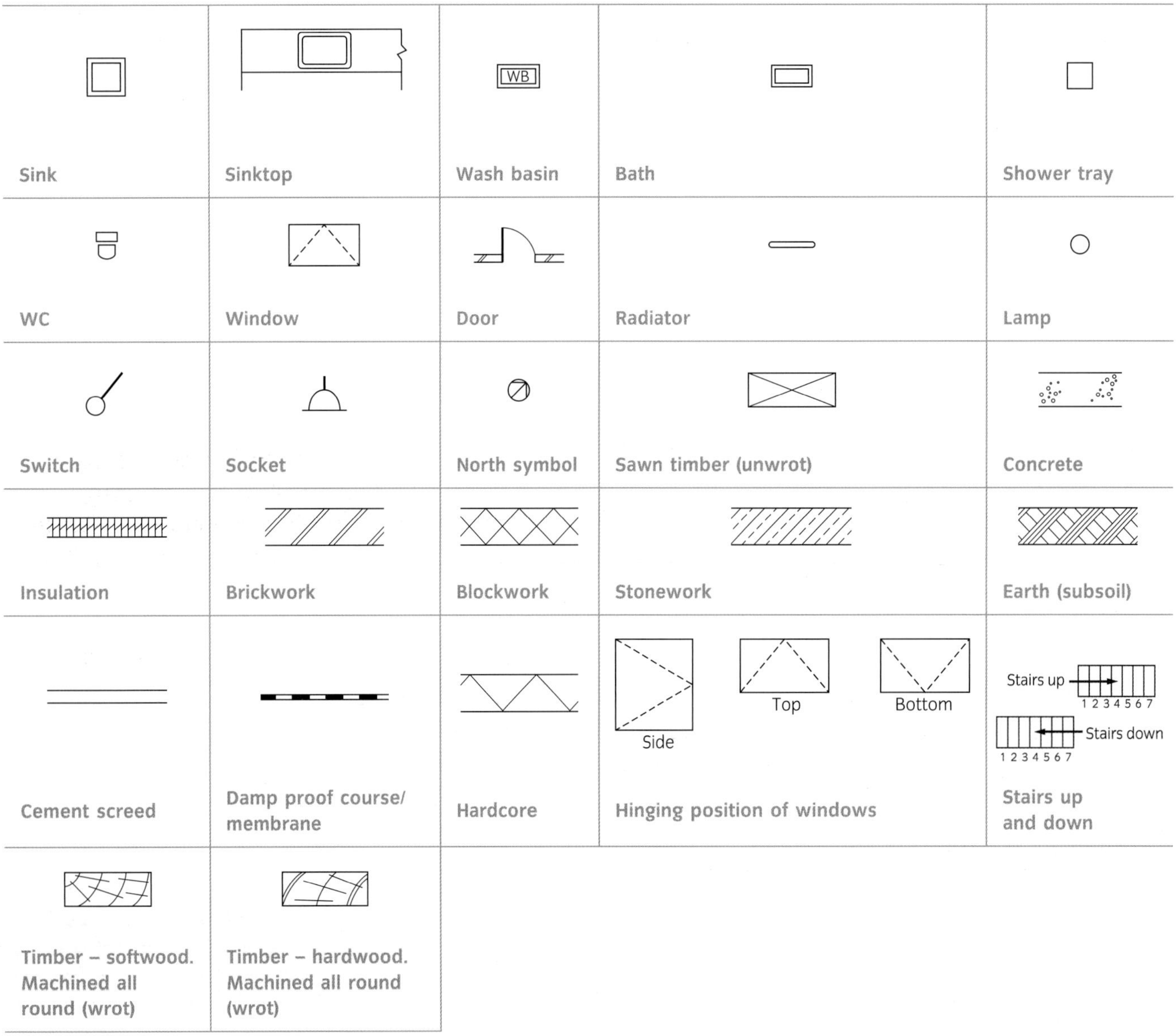
WB
Sink
Sinktop
Wash basin
Bath
Shower tray
WC
Window
Door
Radiator
Lamp
Switch
Socket
North symbol
Sawn timber (unwrot)
Concrete
Insulation
Brickwork
Blockwork
Stonework
Earth (subsoil)
Side
Top
Bottom
Stairs up
1 2 3 4 5 6 7
Stairs down
1 2 3 4 5 6 7
Cement screed
Damp proof course/ membrane
Hardcore
Hinging position of windows
Stairs up and down
Timber – softwood. Machined all round (wrot)
Timber – hardwood. Machined all round (wrot)

INFORMATION SOURCES

Type of drawing	Description
Location drawings	Usually prepared by an **architect** or **architectural technician**. Show the location of the building plot, position of the building and areas within the building. Location drawings covers all of the drawings in this table.
Block plans 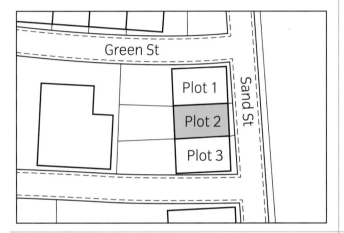	Show the proposed development in relation to its surrounding properties. The scales used are 1:1250 or 1:2500. Very little detail is available from this type of plan. The direction North is usually shown.
Site plans 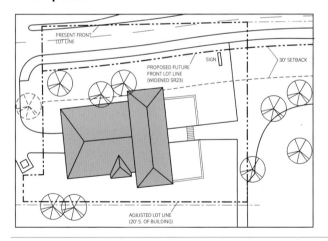	Show the plot in more detail, with drain runs, road layouts and the size and position of the existing building (and any extensions proposed) in relation to the property boundary. A scale of 1:200 or 1:500 is used. The Planning Portal sometimes refers to site plans as block plans, but the two types of plan have been distinguished in this book.

Architect

A trained professional who designs a structure and represents the client who wants the structure built. They are responsible for the production of the working drawings. They supervise the construction of buildings or other large structures

Architectural technician

A draftsperson who works in an architectural practice

Type of drawing	Description
Floor plans 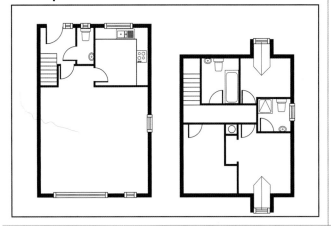	Show the positioning of walls, size of rooms along with the positioning of elements within the building such as units.
Elevations 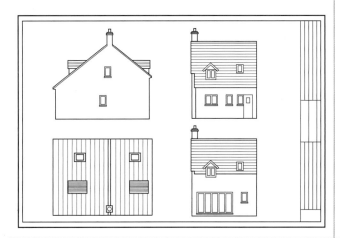	Show a building from a particular side and show the positioning of features such as doors and windows.
Sections 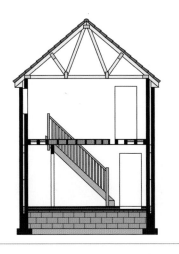	Show in greater detail what the section of a component looks like and how it might fit in relation to another component. A typical example would be a cross-section of a window showing the size of the features and how it fits together. Using these drawings it is possible to determine the positions of rooms, windows, doors, kitchen units and so on. Elevations are shown. These drawings are more detailed, and are often scaled to provide construction measurements. Some of the scales used are 1:200, 1:100, 1:50, 1:10, 1:5 and 1:1. A scale of 1:1 is full size.

Type of drawing	Description
Construction drawings (detail drawings) 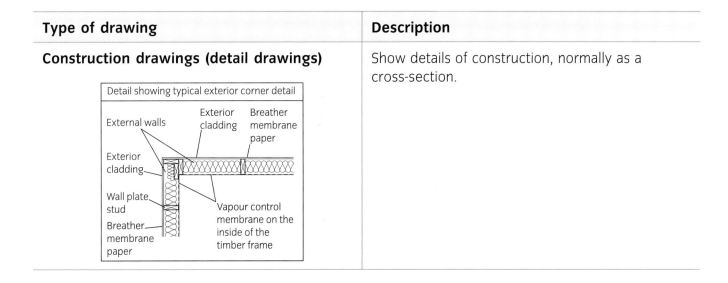	Show details of construction, normally as a cross-section.

PERMITS TO WORK

The permit to work is a documented procedure that gives authorisation for certain people to carry out specific work within a specified time frame. It sets out the precautions required to complete the work safely, based on a risk assessment. The following is an example of permit-to-work documentation that must be filled out.

PERMIT TO WORK

1. Area	2. Date
3. Work to be Done	4. Valid From
	5. Valid To
6. Company	
7. Man in Charge	8. No of Men
9. Safety Precautions	

10. Safety Planning Certificate (cancelled if alarm sounds)

I have inspected the above job which has been safely prepared according to requirements of a safety planning certificate

Signed ....

11. Approval of Permit to Work

I am satisfied that this permit is properly authorised, that safe access is provided, and that all persons affected by this job have been informed

Signed ....

12. Electrical Equipment

All power has been isolated/locked/tagged/tried*
Circuits are live for troubleshooting only

Signed ....

13. Acceptance of Permit to Work

I/we* have read and understood the above precautions and will observe them. All equipment complies with relevant standards. I understand the site emergency plan.

Signed ....

14. Completion of Permit to Work

I/we* certify that this job is complete/incomplete*, all guards have been replaced and secured and all equipment has been removed. The job site has been left clean and tidy.

Permit to work

SIGNS AND NOTICES

As mentioned in Chapter 1, signs are used to keep operatives safe, and the law sets out the types of safety signs needed on a construction site. Some signs warn us about danger and others tell us what to do to stay safe. There are five basic types of sign on a site: prohibition, mandatory, caution, safe condition and supplementary. For more information on the colour, shape and use of these signs, see Chapter 1, pages 41–42.

Examples of safe condition and caution signs

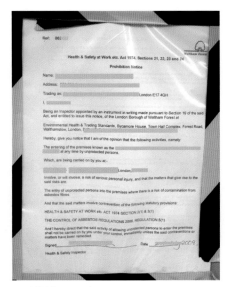

Prohibition notice

Notices are also used on construction sites, and again these are covered in Chapter 1, page 8. Two that you need to know are improvement notices and prohibition notices, both of which are issued by the HSE. An improvement notice is issued by an HSE or local authority inspector to formally notify a company that improvements are needed to the way it is working. A prohibition notice is issued by an HSE or local authority inspector when there is an immediate risk of personal injury. They are not issued lightly and if you receive one, you are clearly breaking a health and safety regulation. The HASAWA workplace notice is also important.

SPECIFICATIONS

A specification accompanies the working drawings. It gives further information that cannot be shown on the drawings because the drawings need to be clear and not covered in notes. A specification would include information such as:

- the colour of paint required

- a specific timber species

- the brick type required

- the plaster finish required.

It is prepared by construction professionals such as architects and building services engineers. They can be produced from previous project specifications, in-house documents or master specifications such as the National Building Specification (NBS). The NBS is owned by the Royal Institute of British Architects (RIBA).

System Outline

102 External cavity walling

✗ • Drawing references:
✗ • Parameters:
   • Walling below ground:
      - Type: Cavity walling, concrete filled.
      - Masonry units: Common bricks.
      - Mortar: Class M6 mortar.
   • Dpc at ground floor: Flexible cavity trays.
   • Walling above ground:
      - External leaf above ground:
         Masonry units: Facing bricks.
         Bond or coursing: Flemish bond.
      - Internal leaf above ground:
         Masonry units: Aerated concrete blocks.
      - Mortar:
         Type: Class M4 mortar.
         Joint profile to external   Bucket handle.
         faces:
      - Wall ties: Insulation retaining wall ties.
      - Cavity insulation: Full fill cavity insulation.
      - Ventilation components: Air bricks and sub-floor ventilation ducts.
✗   - Items supplied by others:
   • Openings:
      - Lintels:
         Type: Manufactured stone lintels.
         Cavity tray over: Flexible cavity trays.
      - Cavity closers: Flexible insulated dpcs.
      - Sills:
         Type:
         Dpc below: Manufactured stone sills.
   • Abutments: Natural stone sills.
      - Cavity trays and dpcs: Precast concrete sills.
      - Flashings built into masonry: As drawings.

Example of a specification

COMPONENT RANGE DRAWINGS

A component range drawing shows the range of components available from a manufacturer. It includes:

- sizes available

- coding for ordering purposes

- availability (whether it can be bought off-the-shelf or if pre-ordering is required).

Availability is particularly important when planning delivery dates. Schedules reference this type of drawing.

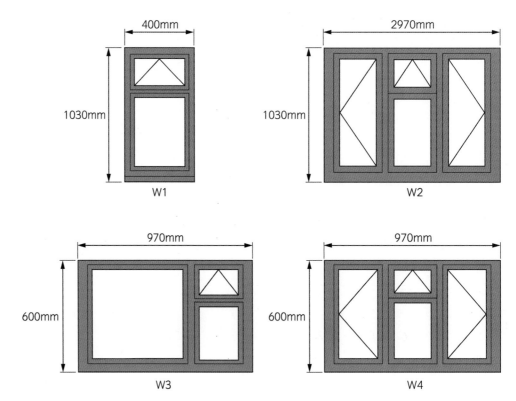

Component range drawing of windows

SCHEDULES

A schedule is used to record repeated design information that applies to a range of components or fittings, such as:

- windows

- doors

- kitchen units

- joinery fittings.

A schedule is mainly used on bigger sites where there are multiples of several designs of houses, with each type having different components and fittings. It avoids the wrong component or fitting being put in the wrong house.

A schedule is usually used in conjunction with a component range drawing, a detail drawing and a floor plan.

A detail drawing shows just that – a detail of a particular part of a building and how it is constructed.

In a typical plan, the doors and windows are labelled D1, D2, W1, W2 etc. These components would be included in the schedule, which would provide additional information on them. For example, see the following schedule.

Master Internal Door Schedule							
Ref:	Door size	S.O. width	S.O. height	Lintel type	FD30	Self closing	Floor level
D1	838×1981	900	2040	BOX	Yes	Yes	GROUND FLOOR
D2	838×1981	900	2040	BOX	Yes	Yes	GROUND FLOOR
D3	762×1981	824	2040	BOX	No	No	GROUND FLOOR
D4	838×1981	900	2040	N/A	Yes	No	GROUND FLOOR
D5	838×1981	900	2040	BOX	Yes	Yes	GROUND FLOOR
D6	762×1981	824	2040	BOX	Yes	Yes	FIRST FLOOR
D7	762×1981	824	2040	BOX	Yes	Yes	FIRST FLOOR
D8	762×1981	824	2040	N/A	Yes	No	FIRST FLOOR
D9	762×1981	824	2040	BOX	Yes	Yes	FIRST FLOOR
D10	762×1981	824	2040	N/A	No	No	FIRST FLOOR
D11	686×1981	748	2040	N/A	Yes	No	SECOND FLOOR
D12	762×1981	824	2040	BOX	Yes	Yes	SECOND FLOOR
D13	762×1981	824	2040	100 HD BOX	Yes	Yes	SECOND FLOOR
D14	686×1981	748	2040	N/A	No	No	SECOND FLOOR

Example of a schedule

BILL OF QUANTITIES

A bill of quantities is produced by the quantity surveyor and describes everything that is required for the job based on the drawings, specification and schedules. A bill of quantities contains the following information:

- *Preliminaries*: General information including the client and architect, details of the work and descriptions of the site.

- *Preambles*: Like the specification, this outlines the quality and description of materials and workmanship, etc.

- *Measured quantities*: A description of how each task and material is to be measured, with measurements in metres (linear and square), hours, litres, kilogrammes and the number of components required.

The completed document is sent out to contractors who will then price the work and enter the costs into the blank spaces. The bill of quantities ensures that all the contractors are pricing for the job using the same information.

BILL OF QUANTITIES

Number	Item Description	Unit	Quantity	Rate	Amount	
					£	p
	CLASS A: GENERAL ITEMS					
	Specified Requirements					
	Testing of Materials					
A250	Testing of recycled and secondary aggregates	sum				
	Information to be provided by the Contractor					
A290	Production of Materials Management Plan	sum				
	Method Related Charges					
	Recycling Plant/Equipment					
A339.01	Mobilise; Fixed	sum				
A339.02	Operate; Time-Related	sum				
A339.03	De-mobilise; Fixed	sum				
	CLASS D: DEMOLITION AND SITE CLEARANCE					
	Other Structures					
D522.01	Other structures; Concrete	sum				
D522.02	Grading/processing of demolition material to produce recycled and secondary aggregates	m³	70			
D522.03	Disposal of demolition material offsite	m³	30			
	CLASS E: EARTHWORKS					
	Excavation Ancillaries					
E542	Double handling of recycled and secondary aggregates produced from demolition material	m³	70			
	Filling					
E615	Importing primary aggregates for filling to structures	m³	15			
E619.1	Importing recycled and secondary aggregates for filling to structures	m³	15			

WORK SCHEDULES

It is very important indeed that the progress of work is planned out. A work schedule or programme of work is an easy way of showing what work is to be carried out and when. This is usually shown in the form of a bar chart called a Gantt chart. The chart lists the tasks that need to be done on the left-hand side and shows a timeline across the top. The site manager or trade supervisors can quickly tell from looking at this chart:

- if work is keeping to schedule

- what materials, equipment and labour are required

- when they are required.

Materials very often have a **lead-in time** and so cannot be delivered immediately. These need to be ordered and delivered at the correct time. Labour planning is also required otherwise the trades may be working elsewhere when needed.

INDUSTRY TIP

Use of a planning document such as a gantt chart will reduce waste and ensure effective use of labour.

Lead-in time

The time taken between ordering an item and it being delivered

Task	Time (days)						
	1	2	3	4	5	6	7
Prepare the ground	░	░					
Spread foundations			░	░			
Lay cables for services				░	░		
Build walls up to DPC						░	░
	Proposed time in orange						

Gantt chart

CALCULATING QUANTITIES FOR MATERIALS

Calculations are required throughout the building process. It is important that these calculations are accurate, as mistakes can be very expensive. A company can lose a lot of money if it underestimates:

- the amount of materials required

- how much they cost

- how long it will take to complete a job.

It could also lead to the company gaining a bad reputation for not being able to complete a job on time and in budget.

Materials are usually better priced if bought in bulk, whereas a buy-as-you go approach can cost more.

FUNCTIONAL SKILLS

You have been asked to provide a quote for building a garage. Find the prices online for all the costs, and record them using a spreadsheet. Remember to include labour, plant costs and VAT. Don't forget to make a profit!

Work on this activity can support FICT 2.C and FM C2.9.

Consider these points when buying materials:

- Is there sufficient storage room for delivered materials?

- Is there a risk of the materials being damaged if there is nowhere suitable to store them or if they are delivered too early?

- Will it be a problem to obtain the same style, colour or quality of product if they are not all ordered at the same time?

- Will over-ordering cause lots of wastage?

These and many other considerations will help determine when and in what quantity materials are ordered.

Some wastage is unavoidable. Allowances must be made for wastage, eg cut bricks that cannot be re-used, short ends of timber, partly full paint cans. Up to 5% waste is allowed for bricks and blocks and 10% for timber and paint.

It may be that all the materials are ordered by the office or supervisory staff, but you still need to know how to recognise and calculate material requirements. Deliveries have to be checked before the delivery note is signed and the driver leaves. Any discrepancies in the type or quantity of materials, or any materials that have arrived damaged, must be recorded on the delivery note and reported to the supervisor. Any discrepancies will need to be followed up and new delivery times arranged.

You must be able to identify basic materials and carry out basic calculations. You will often have to collect sufficient materials to carry out a particular operation. Being able to measure accurately will mean you can make the most economic use of materials and therefore reduce waste.

INDUSTRY TIP

Wastage is impossible to avoid, so make sure enough materials are ordered as it might be difficult to order additional materials that match exactly, such as tiles or wallpaper.

Deliveries must be checked before signing the delivery note

UNITS OF MEASUREMENT

The construction industry uses metric units as standard; however, you may come across some older measures called imperial units.

Units for measuring	Metric units	Imperial units
Length	millimetre (mm) metre (m) kilometre (km)	inch (in) or " eg 6" (6 inches) foot (ft) or ' eg 8' (8 foot)
Liquid	millilitre (ml) litre (l)	pint (pt)
Weight	gramme (g) kilogramme (kg) tonne (t)	pound (lb)

Units for measuring	Quantities	Example
Length	There are 1,000mm in 1m There are 1,000m in 1km	1mm × 1,000 = 1m 1m × 1,000 = 1km 6,250mm can be shown as 6.250m 6,250m can be shown as 6.250km
Liquid	There are 1,000ml in 1l	1ml × 1,000 = 1l
Weight	There are 1,000g in 1kg There are 1,000kg in 1t	1g × 1,000 = 1kg 1kg × 1,000 = 1t

ACTIVITY

Look online to find out:
- What other imperial units are still commonly used?
- How many millimetres are there in an inch?
- How many litres are there in a gallon?

INDUSTRY TIP

Although everything supplied in the construction industry is measured in metric units, many materials still use the imperial equivalent. For example, a plywood sheet will be 1.22m × 2.44m. This is actually the equivalent of an 8 foot by 4 foot board. It is worth noting these differences as it can cause problems.

CALCULATIONS

Four basic mathematical operations are used in construction calculations.

ADDITION

The addition of two or more numbers is shown with a plus sign (**+**).

Example

A stack of bricks 3 bricks long and 2 bricks high contains 6 bricks.

$$3 + 3 = 6$$

More examples:

$$5 + 2 = 7$$

$$19 + 12 = 31$$

$$234 + 105 = 339$$

Pallet of bricks

SUBTRACTION

The reduction of one number by another number is shown with a minus sign (**–**).

Example

A pallet containing 100 bricks is delivered on site, but you only need 88 bricks. How many are left over?

$$100 - 88 = 12$$

More examples:

$$5 - 2 = 3$$

$$19 - 12 = 7$$

$$234 - 105 = 129$$

MULTIPLICATION

The scaling of one number by another number is shown with a multiplication sign (×).

> **Example**
>
> A stack of bricks is 3 bricks long and 2 bricks high. It contains 6 bricks.
>
> $$3 \times 2 = 6$$
>
> More examples:
>
> $$19 \times 12 = 228$$
>
> $$234 \times 10 = 2,340$$
>
> $$234 \times 105 = 24,570$$

In the last two examples, the comma (,) is used to show we are in the thousands. In words we would say, twenty four thousand, five hundred and seventy.

DIVISION

Sharing one number by another number in equal parts (how many times it goes into the number) is shown with a division sign (÷).

> **Example**
>
> $$4 \div 2 = 2$$
>
> $$36 \div 12 = 3$$
>
> $$600 \div 4 = 150$$

LINEAR MEASUREMENTS

Linear means how long a number of items would measure from end to end if laid in a straight line. Examples of things that are calculated in linear measurements are:

- skirting board
- lengths of timber
- rope
- building line
- wallpaper.

We use this form of measurement when working out how much of one of the materials listed above we need, eg to find out how much

The quantity of skirting required is calculated using linear measurements

CALCULATING QUANTITIES FOR MATERIALS

A joiner measuring a room

Perimeter

The distance around an object or room

skirting board is required for a room. First, we need to measure the **perimeter** (sides) of a room. To find the linear length we add the length of all four sides together. This can be done in two ways: adding or multiplying.

Example 1

A site carpenter has been asked how many metres of skirting are required for the rooms below.

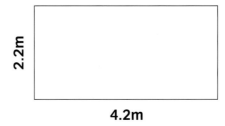

They can add all the sides together:
2.2 + 4.2 + 2.2 + 4.2 = 12.8m

Or, they can multiply each side by 2, and add them together:
(2.2 × 2) + (4.2 × 2) = 12.8m

Either way, **12.8m** is the correct answer.

Example 2

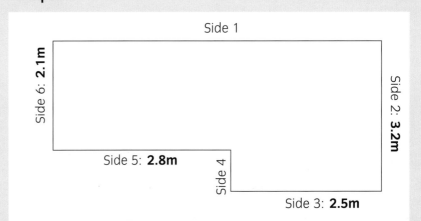

To work out the perimeter of this room we need to add all the sides together. In this example each side has been given a reference number, so all we need to do is add all the sides together, like this:

side 1 (side 3 + side 5) + side 2 + side 3 + side 4 (side 2 − side 6) + side 5 + side 6

Now, let's show the working out: 2.8 + 2.5 + 3.2 + 2.5 + 3.2 − 2.1 + 2.8 + 2.1 = 17m

The amount of skirting board required is **17m**.

Now let's put some door openings in. This symbol ⟷ represents an opening.

Example 3

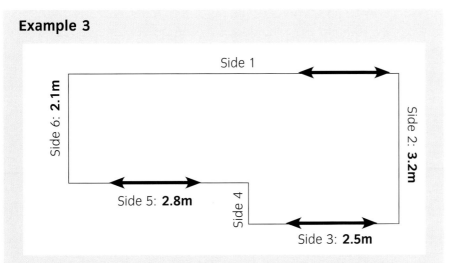

On side 1 there is an opening 0.9m wide, on side 3 there is an opening 1.5m wide and on side 5 there is an opening 2.1m wide.

We know from Example 2 that the perimeter of the room is 17m. We now need to remove the openings. Skirting board will not be needed for the openings.

Step 1

Add together the lengths of the three combined openings:

0.9 + 1.5 + 2.1 = 4.5m

Step 2

Deduct this from 17m:

17 − 4.5 = 12.5m

The linear length of skirting board required is 12.5m.

Step 3

However, this calculation does not take into account any waste. We would normally add 10% extra to allow for waste:

12.5 + 10% = 12.5 + 1.25 = 13.75m

The total amount of skirting board required is **13.75m**.

PERCENTAGES

An easy way to find a percentage (%) of a number is to divide the number by 100 and then multiply it by the percentage you require.

ACTIVITY

5   Increase 49m by 10%
6   Increase 27m by 20%
7   Increase 34m by 17.5%
8   Decrease 22m by 5%

4) 20.9m
Answers: 1) 53.9m, 2) 32.4m, 3) 39.95m,

Example

Increase 19m by 12%

19 ÷ 100 = 0.19

0.19 × 12 = 2.28

19 + 2.28 = 21.28m

Total required **21.28m**.

AREA

To find out how much material is required to cover a surface such as a **floor** or wall you need to calculate its area. Area is the measurements of a two dimensional surface, eg the surface of floors, walls, glass or a roof.

Floors

The structured layers of a building, eg ground floor, first floor, second floor

To find the area of a surface you need to multiply its length by its width (L × W) or one side by the other. This will give you an answer which is expressed in square units (²). For example, mm², m² or km².

Example 1

A bricklayer has been asked to work out the area of the floors below.

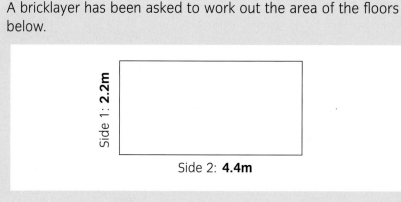

Side 1: **2.2m**

Side 2: **4.4m**

side 1 × side 2 = floor area

2.2 × 4.4 = 9.68m²

The total floor area is **9.68m²**.

Irregularly shaped areas can be calculated by breaking up the area into sections that can be worked out easily, and then adding them together.

Example 2

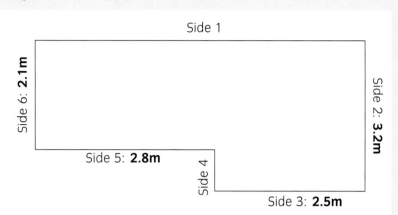

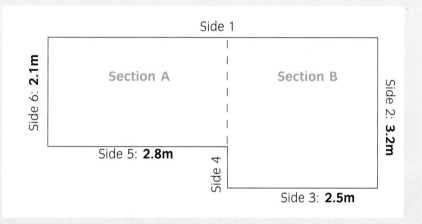

Irregularly shaped rooms can be split into sections to calculate the area

Step 1

Divide the area into two parts, and then calculate the area of each part. The easiest way to do this is to divide it into two smaller sections:

Step 2

Work out the area of section A and section B:

section A = 2.1 × 2.8 = 5.88m²

section B = 2.5 × 3.2 = 8m²

Step 3

Add the areas of section A and section B together:

section A + section B = total floor area

5.88 + 8 = 13.88m²

The total floor area is 13.88m².

A tiler tiling a floor

INDUSTRY TIP

Remember, there are 1,000mm in a metre so we show the sum as 0.305m in Example 3.

ACTIVITY

Find the area of the following measurements:

1 2.1m × 2.4m
2 0.9m × 2.7m
3 250mm × 3.4m

Answers: 1) 5.04m, 2) 2.43m, 3) 0.85m

Now let's say the floor requires tiling. The tiler needs to calculate the number of floor tiles required.

Example 3

The size of each floor tile is 305mm × 305mm. We can also show this as 0.305m × 0.305m.

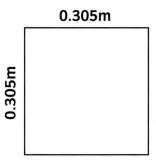

0.305m

0.305m

How many floor tiles are required for the floor area in Example 2? The total floor area is 13.88m².

Step 1

Calculate the area of one tile. As the floor area is given in m², we need to calculate the size of the tile in the same unit, ie m².

$0.305 \times 0.305 = 0.093m^2$

Step 2

Now you need to divide the total floor area by the area of one tile to find out the total number tiles required.

total floor area ÷ area of one tile = total number of tiles

$13.88 \div 0.093 = 149.247$ tiles

This number is rounded up to the next full tile, so a total of 150 floor tiles are required.

Step 3

However, this total does not allow for any waste.

Add 5% to allow for waste:

150 + 5% = 158 tiles (to the next full tile)

Let's look at the working out:

$150 \div 100 = 1.5$ tiles (this is 1%)

$1.5 \times 5 = 7.5$ tiles (this is 5%)

5% of 150 tiles, rounded up to the next full tile, is 8 tiles.

Therefore **158 tiles** are required.

AREA OF A TRIANGLE

Sometimes you will be required to work out an area that includes a triangle.

Example 1

A painter has been asked to work out how much paint will be needed to paint the front of this house.

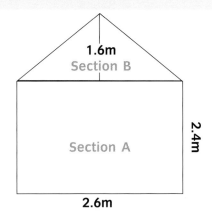

A decorator measuring the height of a room

Step 1

Divide the area up into a rectangular section (section A) and a triangular section (section B).

Step 2

Find the area of section A:

2.4 × 2.6 = 6.24m²

The area of section A is 6.24m².

Step 3

Find the area of section B.

The area of a triangle can be found by multiplying the base by the height, then dividing by 2.

(base × height) ÷ 2 = area

2.6 × 1.6 = 4.16

4.16 ÷ 2 = 2.08m²

The area of section B is 2.08m².

Step 4

area of section A + area of section B = total wall area

6.24 + 2.08 = 8.32m²

The total wall area is **8.32m²**.

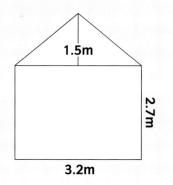

Hypotenuse

The longest side of a right-angled triangle. It is always opposite the right angle

Now let's look at the simple triangle below. It has three sides, A, B and C. Pythagorean theorem tells us that in a right-angled triangle the **hypotenuse** is equal to the sum of the square of the lengths of the two other sides, in other words $a^2 + b^2 = c^2$. In this example the hypotenuse is side C.

Using the Pythagorean theorem we can work out the length of any side.

Example 1

If side A is 3m long and side B is 4m long, what is the length of side C?

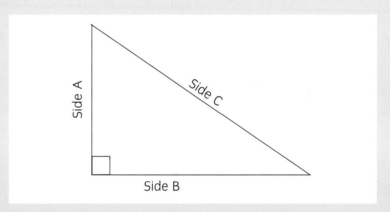

$3 \times 3 = 9$

$4 \times 4 = 16$

$9 + 16 = 25$

$\sqrt{25} = 5$

($\sqrt{}$ means square root, or a number that is multiplied by itself, in this case $5 \times 5 = 25$)

Side C is **5m** long.

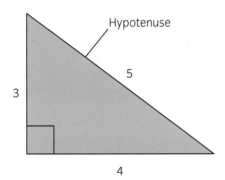

The hypotenuse

INDUSTRY TIP

If a triangle has a small square in the corner, this shows you the corner is a right angle.

Example 2

A joiner has been asked to work out the length of a roof (side C).

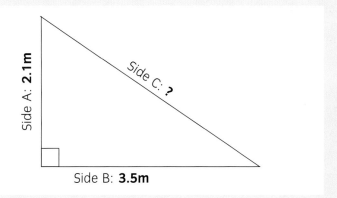

2.1 × 2.1 (side A) = 4.41

3.5 × 3.5 (side B) = 12.25

4.41 + 12.25 = 16.66

$\sqrt{16.66}$ = 4.08m

The length of side C is 4.08m.

Example 3

A bricklayer needs to find the rise of a roof (side A).

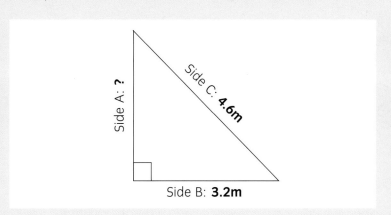

3.2 × 3.2 (side B) = 10.24

4.6 × 4.6 (side C) = 21.16

21.16 − 10.24 = 10.92

$\sqrt{10.92}$ = 3.30m

The length of side A is 3.3m.

Use Pythagorean theorem to answer following questions:

1   What is the length of side B?

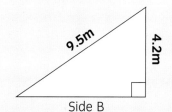

2   What is the length of side C?

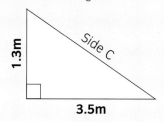

Answers: 1) 8.5m², 2) 3.73m

PERIMETERS AND AREAS OF CIRCLES

Circumference

The distance around the edge of a circle

Diameter

The length of a straight line going through the centre of a circle connecting two points on its circumference

Sometimes you are required to find the perimeter or **circumference** of a circle.

circumference of a circle = π × **diameter**

$$C = πd$$

π (or 'pi') is the number of times that the diameter of a circle will divide into the circumference.

π = 3.142

This is equal to the number of diameters in one revolution of a circle. It is the same for any sized circle.

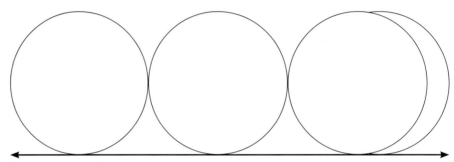

There are 3.142 diameters in one complete revolution

Example 1

A joiner is making a circular window that has a diameter of 600mm. Its circumference is:

0.600 × 3.142 = **1.885m**

The diameter of a circle from a given circumference is:

diameter = circumference ÷ π

Example 2

A window has a circumference of 2.250m. Its diameter is:

2.250 ÷ 3.142 = **0.716m** (or 716mm)

Radius

The length of a line from the centre to a point on the circumference of a circle. It is exactly half the length of the diameter

The area of a circle is found by:

area of a circle = π × **radius²** (radius is equal to half the diameter)

Example 3

A painter needs to paint a circle that is 1.2m in diameter and is required to find the area of the circle to enable them to order the correct quantity of paint.

1.2 ÷ 2 = **0.6m** (the radius)

3.142 × 0.6m² = **1.13m²**

VOLUME

The volume of an object is the total space it takes up, eg a tin of paint, a foundation for a wall or the capacity of a concrete mixer, and is shown as m³ (cubic metres). To find the volume of an object you must multiply length by width by height.

$$\text{volume} = \text{length} \times \text{width} \times \text{height}$$

Example 1

Each side of this cube is 1m. The total space it takes up is 1m³

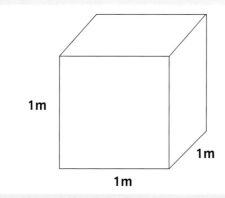

1m × 1m × 1m = **1m³**

Example 2

A bricklayer has been asked to work out how many m³ of **concrete** is required for a strip foundation. The size of the foundation is 3.2m long, 0.600m wide and 0.900m deep.

length × width × height = volume

3.2 × 0.600 × 0.900 = 1.728m³

The volume of concrete needed for the strip foundation is **1.728m³**.

INDUSTRY TIP

Remember r² is the same as r × r (r= radius).

A bricklayer taking levels

Concrete

Composed of cement, fine aggregate (sand) and course aggregate (stone) of varying sizes and in varying proportions

To work out the volume of a cylinder:

$$\text{volume} = \pi r^2 h \; (\pi \times r^2 \times h)$$

Example 3

A joiner has a tin of presevative and needs to know its volume. The tin has a diameter of 250mm and a height of 700mm.

$\pi r^2 h \; (\pi \times r^2 \times h) = \text{volume}$

The radius (r) is half the diameter:

$250 \div 2 = 125\text{mm}$

$3.142 \times 0.125^2 \times 0.700 = 0.034\text{m}^3$

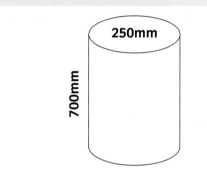

The volume of the tin of paint is **0.034m³**.

COMMUNICATION

Good communication is vital to the smooth running of any building project.

Communication involves sharing thoughts, information and ideas between people. For communication to be effective, information must be:

- given in a clear way
- received without misunderstanding.

It has been said that to be a good communicator it is just as important to be a good listener as it is to be a good speaker! Good communication leads to a safer and more efficient workplace, not to mention helping to maintain a pleasant working environment.

Most sites will have policies and procedures in place that govern the chain of command and communication between supervisory staff and workers.

WRITTEN COMMUNICATION

There are many methods of communication within the building industry. In this chapter we have discussed drawings, schedules and specifications etc. The architect uses these methods to communicate details about the building to the team who will **tender** for and erect the building.

Communication is usually electronic via email (with or without attachments) or through intranet sites. Drawings are very commonly distributed in electronic formats which are printed on to paper when required. Messages are often given via text.

Sometimes communication will be via a memorandum (memo), a written form of communication.

Site rules, risk assessments and method statements (see Chapter 1) communicate safety information.

Tender

The process of supplying the client with a fixed quotation for the work

INDUSTRY TIP

Messages that are passed on by word of mouth are open to interpretation, so written messages often can be more clear.

FUNCTIONAL SKILLS

Thinking about the garage that you worked out the costs for on page 57 and using a computer, write a letter to the client outlining the cost and other details such as when the work would start and any basic terms regarding payment.

Work on this activity can support FE 2.3.1.

SITE PAPERWORK

Communication on site is aided by the use of paperwork and without it no building site could operate. It is an important method of communication between operatives and supervisory staff, builders, architects and clients.

Type of paperwork	Description
Timesheet **Timesheet** Employer: CPF Building Co. — Employee Name: Louise Miranda — Week starting: 17/6/13 Date: 21/6/13 	Day	Job/Job Number	Start Time	Finish Time	Total Hours	Overtime
Monday	Penburthy, Falmouth 0897	9am	6pm	8	
Tuesday	Penburthy, Falmouth 0897	9am	6pm	8	
Wednesday	Penburthy, Falmouth 0897	8.30am	5.30pm	8	
Thursday	Trelawney, Truro 0901	11am	8pm	8	2
Friday	Trelawney, Truro 0901	11am	7pm	7	1
Saturday	Trelawney, Truro 0901	9am	1pm	4	
Totals				43	3 | Employee's signature: _____ Supervisor's signature: _____	Used to record the hours completed each day, and is usually the basis on which pay is calculated. Timesheets also help to work out how much the job has cost in working hours, and can give information for future estimating work when working up a tender.

Type of paperwork	Description
Job sheet **CPF Building Co** Job sheet **Customer name:** Henry Collins **Date:** 9/12/13 **Address:** 57 Green St Kirkham London **Work to be carried out** Finishing joint work to outer walls **Instructions** Use weather struck and half round	Gives details of a job to be carried out, sometimes with material requirements and hours given to complete the task.
Variation order **Confirmation notice** **Architect's instruction** **CPF Building Co** Variation order **Project Name:** Penburthy House, Falmouth, Cornwall **Reference Number:** 80475 **Date:** 14/11/13 **From: :** _____ **To:** _____ | Reason for change:	Tick
Customer requirements	☑
Engineer requirements	☐
Revised design	☐ | **Instruction:** Entrance door to be made from Utile hardwood with brushed chrome finished ironmongery (changed from previous detail, softwood with brass ironmongery). Signature _____	Sometimes alterations are made to the contract which changes the work to be completed, eg a client may wish to move a door position or request a different brick finish. This usually involves a variation to the cost. This work should not be carried out until a variation order and a confirmation notice have been issued. Architect's instructions are instructions given by an architect, first verbally and then in writing to a site agent as work progresses and questions inevitably arise over details and specifications.

Type of paperwork	Description
Requisition order	Filled out to order materials from a supplier or central store. These usually have to be authorised by a supervisor before they can be used.

CPF Building Co
Requisition order

Supplier Information: Construction Supplies Ltd   Date: 9/12/13

Contract Address/Delivery Address: Penburthy House, Falmouth, Cornwall

Tel number: 0207294333

Order Number: 26213263CPF

Item number	Description	Quantity	Unit/Unit Price	Total
X22433	75mm 4mm gauge countersunk brass screws slotted	100	30p	£30
YK7334	Brass cups to suit	100	£5	£500
V23879	Sadikkens water based clear varnish	1 litre	£20.00	£20.00
Total:				£550.00

Authorised by: Denzil Penburthy

Delivery note	Accompanies a delivery. Goods have to be checked for quantity and quality before the note is signed. Any discrepancies are recorded on the delivery note. Goods that are not suitable (because they are not as ordered or because they are of poor quality) can be refused and returned to the supplier.

Construction Supplies Ltd
Delivery note

Customer name and address:
CPF Building Co
Penburthy House
Falmouth
Cornwall

Delivery Date: 16/12/13
Delivery time: 9am

Order number: 26213263CPF

Item number	Quantity	Description	Unit Price	Total
X22433	100	75mm 4mm gauge countersunk brass screws slotted	30p	£30
YK7334	100	Brass cups to suit	£5	£500
V23879	1 litre	Sadikkens water based clear varnish	£20	£20

Subtotal	£550.00
VAT	20%
Total	£660.00

Discrepancies: ....

Customer Signature: ....

Print name: ....

Date: ....

Type of paperwork	Description
Delivery record 	Every month a supplier will issue a delivery record that lists all the materials or hire used for that month.
Invoices 	Sent by the supplier. They list the services or materials supplied along with the price the contractor is requested to pay. There will be a time limit within which to pay. Sometimes there will be a discount for quick payment or penalties for late payment.
Site diary	This will be filled out daily. It records anything of note that happens on site such as deliveries, absences or occurrences, eg delay due to the weather.

Content of delivery record image:

Davids & Co
Monthly delivery record

Customer name and address: CPF Building Co Penburthy House Falmouth Cornwall			Customer order date: 28th May 2013	
Item number	**Quantity**	**Description**	**Unit Price**	**Date Delivered**
BS3647	2	1 ton bag of building sand	£60	3/6/13
CM4324	12	25kg bags of cement	£224	17/6/13

Customer Signature: ....

Print name: ....

Date: ....

Content of invoice image:

Davids & Co
Invoice

Invoice number: 75856   Date: 2nd January 2014
PO number: 4700095685

Company name and address: Davids & Co 228 West Retail Park Ivybridge Plymouth	Customer name and address: CPF Building Co Penburthy House Falmouth Cornwall

VAT registration number: 663694542

For:

Item number	Quantity	Description	Unit Price
BS3647	2	1 ton bag of building sand	£30
CM4324	12	25kg bags of cement	£224

Subtotal	£2748.00
VAT	20%
Total	£3297.60

Please make cheques payable to Davids & Co

Payment due in 30 days

VERBAL COMMUNICATION

Often, managers, supervisors, work colleagues and trades communicate verbally. This can be face to face or over a telephone. Although this is the most common form of communication, it is also the most unreliable.

Mistakes are often made while communicating verbally. The person giving the information might make an error. The person receiving the information might misunderstand something because the information is unclear or it is noisy in the background, or because they later forget the details of the conversation.

Confusion can be minimised by recording conversations or by using a form of written communication. If there is a record it can be used for future reference and help to clear up any misunderstandings.

TAKING A TELEPHONE MESSAGE

It is a good idea to take down details of telephone calls and many companies provide documentation for this purpose. When taking a message it is important to record the following details:

- *Content*: This is the most important part of the message – the actual information being relayed. Take and write down as many details as possible.

- *Date and time*: Messages are often **time sensitive**, and may require an urgent response.

- *Who the message is for*: Ensure the person gets the message by giving it to them or leaving it in a place where they will find it.

- *Contact name and details*: Write down the name of the person leaving the message, and how to get back to them with a response.

UNACCEPTABLE COMMUNICATION

When communicating, it is very important to stay calm. Think about what you are going to say. An angry word will often encourage an angry response. However, keeping calm and composed will often diffuse a stressful situation. A shouting match rarely ends with a good or productive result.

There are several types of communication that are unacceptable and could result in unemployment. Unacceptable communication includes:

- aggressive communication such as swearing or using inappropriate hand gestures

ACTIVITY

Find a partner. Choose a particular health and safety issue – this may be something you have seen at your training centre or on site. Prepare some basic notes. Assume the roles of operative and supervisor and discuss the issue. Swap roles and discuss the problem again. Afterwards, write down the solutions on which you agreed.

What type of approach works best? Does preparation help? Why should you write down the results of your discussion?

An operative taking notes during a phone call

Time sensitive

When something must be dealt with quickly

INDUSTRY TIP

It is often a good idea to prepare what you are going to say before making a call, and having all the information you require to hand.

- racist or sexist comments or gestures

- showing prejudice against people with disabilities.

This type of behaviour shows a lack of respect for others and does not create a safe or pleasant working environment. It will also give your company a poor image if customers see or hear this behaviour. Acting in this way is likely to result in trouble for you and your employer and could even result in a **tribunal** and loss of employment.

Tribunal

A judgement made in court

KNOWLEDGE OF THE CONSTRUCTION INDUSTRY AND BUILT ENVIRONMENT

Buildings come in a wide variety of types in relation to appearance and methods of construction. Despite the variety of buildings, they all have design features in common. In this section we will discuss various parts of buildings and their purpose.

We will also discuss sustainable construction – how buildings can be designed to sit better within the environment, with lower pollution levels and energy requirements both during the building process and when in use.

A house with solar panels

FOUNDATIONS

Foundation

Used to spread the load of a building to the subsoil

Foundations serve as a good base on which to put the building. They need to be capable of carrying the weight of the building and any further load that may be put upon it. These are known as **dead loads** and **imposed loads**.

Foundations must be designed to resist any potential movement in the ground on which the building will sit. Ground conditions can vary widely. Soil samples are taken to help decide on the type of foundation to use. This usually takes the form of bore holes dug or drilled around the site. These samples are sent away for testing in a laboratory. The results will identify:

- the soil condition (clay or sandy)

- the depth of the soil

- the depth of the water table

- if any contaminations are present.

The soil condition is important: clay soil drains poorly and can move if it gets waterlogged or dries out completely. Sandy soils drain very well, but can become unstable. A foundation that is suitable for the ground type and load of the building will be designed.

CONCRETE

Foundations are made from concrete. Concrete is made from fine and coarse aggregate (crushed stone), sand and cement mixed with water. Water reacts with the cement causing it to harden. This process is called hydration and it locks the aggregates together. Concrete is very strong under compression (when weight is put upon it) but is weak when it is pulled (put under tension). Tension can be caused in a foundation when it has to bridge softer sections of ground or when ground conditions are unstable. To prevent failure of the foundation, the concrete may need to be reinforced with steel which is cast into the concrete before it hardens.

Dead load

The weight of all the materials used to construct the building

Imposed load

Additional loads that may be placed on the structure, eg people, furniture, wind and snow

INDUSTRY TIP

The type of foundation to be used will usually be decided by the architect and a structural engineer and will be the result of tests.

INDUSTRY TIP

Remember, cement will give chemical burns so use the correct PPE while using and mixing it.

Concrete with steel reinforcement

Sulphate-resisting cement

Sulphate-resisting cement, such as Sulphate Resisting Portland Cement, is more resistant than ordinary cement to the action of mineralised water containing sulphates. It also hardens more slowly and has a higher frost resistance. The ratio of cement to aggregate in concrete will also affect its strength. Concrete can be mixed in a number of ratios to suit the type of foundation design and the strength of foundation needed to cope with different ground conditions. The ratios are outlined below.

Concrete name	Ratio	Usage
C7.5 (low strength)	1:3:6 or 7 (cement:sand: coarse aggregate)	For general non-structural use.
C10 to C15 (medium strength)	1:4:6 to 1:4:5 (cement:sand: medium aggregate)	Used in typical house foundations.
C20 (strong)	1:2:4 (cement:sand: medium aggregate)	Used as a foundation mix in house construction in softer ground and for slabs.
C25 (stronger)	1:1.5:3 (cement:sand: medium aggregate)	Can be used for foundations to larger houses and for creating floors.
C30 (very strong)	1:2:3 (cement:sand: fine aggregate)	A general-purpose, strong concrete.
C35 (industrial strength)	1:1.5:2.5 (cement: sand:fine aggregate)	Structural concrete.

Additives are used to slow down or speed up the curing process if required (known as a retardant or accelerant respectively) and for frost resistance as frost can damage concrete that has not had a chance to harden sufficiently.

TYPES OF FOUNDATION

Different types of structures, such as detached houses, high-rise and low-rise buildings, will all require different types of foundation.

Low-rise building

High-rise building

Detached house

OUR HOUSE

What type of foundation does the building you are sitting in have? How can you tell? Why was that foundation type chosen? Look at the foundations used in 'Our House' as a further guide.

Strip foundations

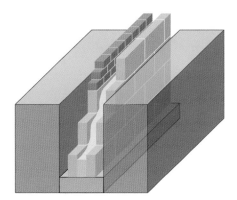

Traditional strip foundation

A strip foundation is the traditional type of foundation used for residential developments (ordinary houses). It is formed by digging a trench to the required width and depth as determined by the soil conditions and the weight of the structure. It is either filled with concrete or a layer of concrete is poured into the bottom. This layer must be a minimum of 150mm thick and is commonly 225mm thick.

Footings

The substructure below ground level. These are projecting courses at the base of a wall

Damp proof course (DPC)

A layer of plastic that prevents damp rising up through a wall needs to be positioned at least 150mm above ground level

Footings are brought up to the level of the **damp proof course** (DPC) using concrete blocks or bricks. These are set out from the centre of the strip of concrete in order to spread the weight evenly. A variety of specialist bricks and blocks are used for this purpose. They need to be able to resist water penetration and therefore frost damage.

Engineering brick

Trench block

It can be economical to fill the trench up to the top with concrete rather than build a substructure – this is known as trench fill. Sometimes it is necessary to build on the edge of the concrete – this is known as an eccentric foundation.

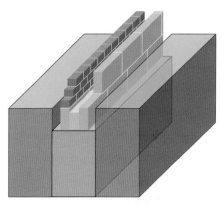
Trench fill foundation

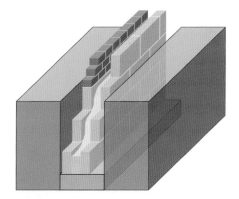
Eccentric foundation

Wide strip foundations

A wide strip foundation is very similar to strip foundation in most of its aspects. The main difference between the two is that a wide strip foundation has steel reinforcements placed within the concrete. The steel gives considerably more strength to the foundation and enables greater loads to be placed on it. Without the steel reinforcements the foundation would need to be much deeper and would need vast amounts of concrete.

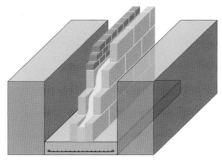

Wide strip foundation

Pad foundations

A pad foundation is used to support a point load such as a column in a steel-framed building. This type of foundation often has bolts set into the top ready for fixing the steel.

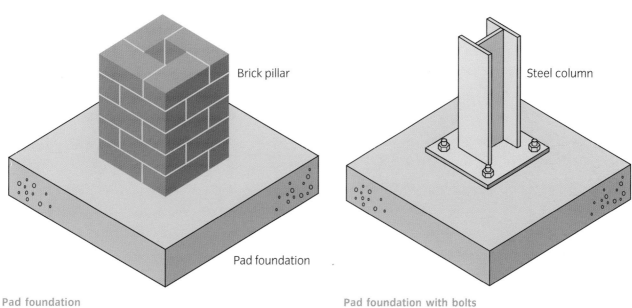

Brick pillar

Steel column

Pad foundation

Pad foundation

Pad foundation with bolts

Pile foundations

Deep **piles** are used to transfer the load through unsuitable soil layers into the harder layers of ground below, even down to rock if required (known as end bearing). Some piles use **friction** to provide support. This is known as skin friction. Tall buildings (and especially narrow buildings such as chimneys or towers) have large lateral forces due to side winds and pile foundations resist these forces well.

Pile

A cylindrical foundation used on large, heavy buildings, or where the ground has poor loadbearing capabilities

Friction

Resistance between the surface of the concrete foundation and the soil around it

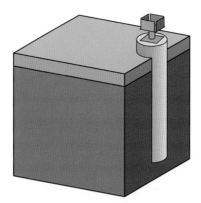

A cylindrical pile foundation

Raft foundations

A raft foundation is often laid over an area of softer soil that would be unsuitable for a strip foundation. A raft foundation is a slab of concrete covering the entire base of the building; it spreads the weight of the building over a wider area but still maintains a deeper base around the load bearing walls.

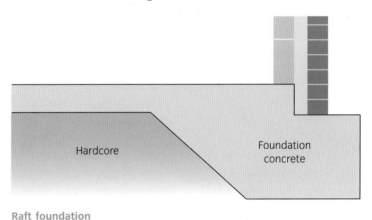

Hardcore

Foundation concrete

Raft foundation

FLOORS

Floors can be divided into two main categories:

■ ground floors

■ upper floors.

Floors are required to be load bearing, and there is a wide variety of construction methods depending on the type of building and potential load that will be imposed upon the floor. Floors also may need to prevent:

■ heat loss

■ transfer of sound

■ moisture penetration.

GROUND FLOORS

These may be either solid ground floors or suspended floors.

Solid floors

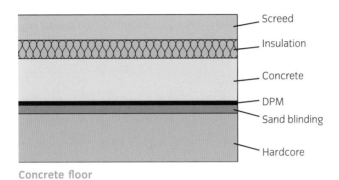

Concrete floor

Solid concrete floors are laid upon **hardcore** and have a **damp proof membrane** (DPM) built into them to prevent damp coming up through the floor. **Insulation** is also laid into the floor to reduce heat loss. It is important that the insulation is not affected by the high water content of the wet concrete when being poured.

A finish to a concrete floor is called a screed. It can be laid 'lean' which consists of a mix of sand and cement that only has a little water added to it. Another type is known as 'self-levelling' which is mixed up very wet and finds its own level. It can be bought in bags as a powder that needs to be mixed, or delivered in a lorry and poured in.

As mentioned earlier, steel reinforcement can also be used within the concrete to increase strength and reduce cracks.

Hollow and suspended floors

Upper floors and some ground floors are suspended or hollow, meaning that instead of resting on the ground beneath the load is transferred via beams to the walls.

Two types of beam used are Posi-Joist and I-beam. Posi-Joists are strong yet lightweight as they are made from two smaller beams connected with metal struts. It is easier to accommodate large services such as soil pipes when using this type of floor. Timber I-beams are similar to Posi-Joists, but the middle of the beam is made from a timber sheet material. Timber joists are usually covered with either chipboard or solid timber floorboards. A sleeper wall is built beneath the floor to carry the joists, making the floor stronger and reducing movement.

Hardcore

A mixture of crushed stone and sand laid and compacted to give a good base for the concrete

Damp proof membrane (DPM)

An impermeable layer that prevents damp coming up through the floor. A layer of sand known as blinding is placed below the DPM to prevent any sharp stones below piercing the membrane when the concrete is poured

Insulation

Materials used to retain heat and improve the thermal value of a building, may also be used for managing sound transfer

Modern timber frame

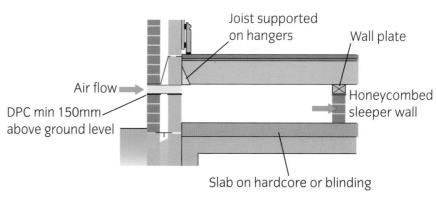

Suspended wood floor

Joist supported on hangers

Wall plate

Air flow

DPC min 150mm above ground level

Honeycombed sleeper wall

Slab on hardcore or blinding

Posi-Joist

I-beam

Suspended concrete floors can be made using two methods. They can either be cast 'in situ', which means that formwork (a mould) is set up and concrete is poured into it. Alternately, precast floors involve using concrete beams or rafts that have been made off site in a factory and are set onto walls. Concrete is then poured on top to finish the floor.

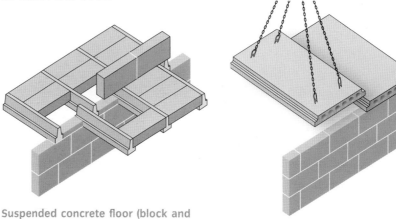

Suspended concrete floor (block and beam)

Precast floor

UPPER FLOORS

In most domestic dwellings timber floor joists are used and laid in the same way as hollow timber ground floors, while in large commercial and industrial buildings solid concrete floors are used.

WALLS

Walling for a building can usually be divided in two categories:

- external

- internal.

Walling can be load or non-load bearing. Load bearing walls carry the weight of the floors and roof and transfer this weight down to the foundations. A non-load bearing wall carries no weight.

Walls often have openings in them, eg doors and windows, which will weaken them if they are not constructed correctly. Openings require support (via a **lintel** or arch) across the top to give the wall support and **bond** it together.

Lintel

A horizontal member for spanning an opening to support the structure above

Bond

The arrangement or pattern of laying bricks and blocks to spread the load through the wall, also for strength and appearance

Solid wall

Walls of a thickness of one brick and greater

Cavity wall

Walling built in two separate skins (usually of different materials) with a void held together by wall ties

EXTERNAL WALLING

External walls need to:

- keep the elements (wind and rain) out of the building

- look good

- fit into the surrounding landscape.

Several methods of construction are used for external walling. Common construction methods are:

- **solid wall**

- **cavity wall**

- timber framing.

Solid walls

Many older traditional buildings have solid walls made from brick, block or stone – see the table on the next page. Solid walls have the disadvantage of being more easily penetrated by damp. Older solid walls are often upgraded by having insulating and waterproofing layers applied to the outside of the wall.

ACTIVITY

What are the walls in the building you are sitting in made from? Why do you think these materials were chosen? What are the advantages or disadvantages of these materials?

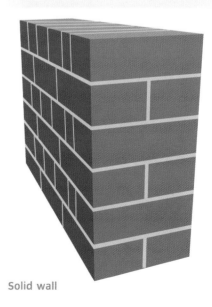

Solid wall

Material used	Description
Bricks 	A very traditional building material made from fired clay, calcium-silicate or concrete. A standard sized brick is 215mm × 102.5mm × 65mm.
Blocks 	These are made of either concrete (crushed stone and cement) or a lightweight cement mixture. They are much bigger than a brick, and are available in various sizes. The most commonly used size is 440mm × 215mm × 100mm. Wider blocks are used for walls where more strength or improved sound insulation is required. Lightweight blocks made from aerated concrete are easier to lay and cut and have greater thermal resistance. However, they are more costly and do not have the same structural properties as standard dense concrete blocks.
Stone 	A natural building material which varies widely in use and appearance from area to area. Stone may be cut to a uniform size before use or used in its quarried state.
Mortar 	This is used between bricks, blocks and stones to bind them together and increase the strength of the wall. It is a mixture of soft sand and cement mixed with water and other additives if required, eg **plasticiser**, colouring or **lime**. It is important that the strength of the mortar is correct for the type of material that is being used to construct the wall. If the mortar has too much cement in the mix it will be so strong it will not allow movement in the walling due to settlement, and the bricks could crack resulting in the wall needing to be rebuilt. Other additives (retardant and accelerant) can slow down or accelerate this curing process and help protect from frost. Mortars are mixed to a ratio of materials, eg 1:6. The first number is always the proportion of cement with the second being the proportion of sand. A typical mix ratio for masonry walling is 1:5.

Plasticiser

An additive that is used to make the mortar more pliable and easier to work with

Lime

A fine powdered material traditionally used in mortar

Bonding is the interlocking pattern that the brick and block **leaves** are laid in, which increases the strength of the wall. There are many bond types. Here are three common examples.

Leaves

The two walls or skins that make up a cavity wall to comply with current building regulations

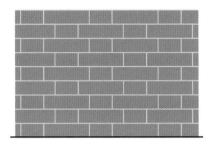

Flemish bond

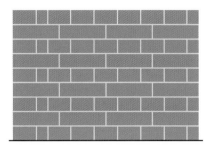

English bond

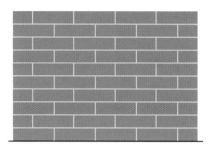

Stretcher bond

Cavity walls

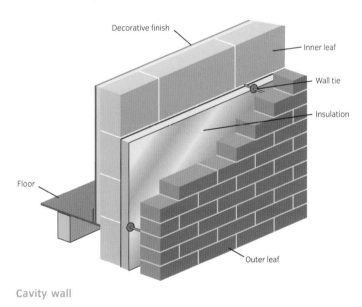

Cavity wall

The most common type of external walling used today is cavity wall construction.

Cavity walls are two masonry walls built side by side to form an inner and outer leaf (sometimes called skins). The leaves are held together with wall ties. These ties are made from rust and rot proof material and are built in as the walls are being constructed. The cavity is partially filled with insulation (typically fibreglass batts or polystyrene boards) as required by the **building regulations**. This reduces heat loss and saves energy.

The inner leaf usually carries any loads from the roof and floors down to the foundations and has a decorative finish on the inside, typically plaster which is either painted or papered. The outer leaf resists the elements and protects the inside of the building.

Building regulations

A series of documents that set out legal requirements for the standards of building work

ACTIVITY

State the minimum performance standards required for a cavity wall to meet current building regulations.

ACTIVITY

Find out the current minimum width of cavity allowed.

Timber framing

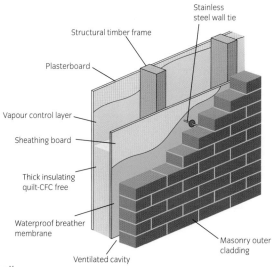

Stainless
steel wall tie

Structural timber frame

Plasterboard

Vapour control layer

Sheathing board

Thick insulating
quilt-CFC free

Waterproof breather
membrane

Ventilated cavity

Masonry outer
cladding

Timber frame wall

Elizabethan oak frame

Timber framing is both a traditional and modern method of building. Traditional buildings using timber framing were made mostly from oak with various in-fills such as brick or plaster to form the walls. Modern timber frame homes are generally built from softwood and have an outer skin of masonry or are clad with timber or plaster to waterproof the structure. Oak framing, as a traditional building method, is becoming increasingly popular again.

Prefabricated walls

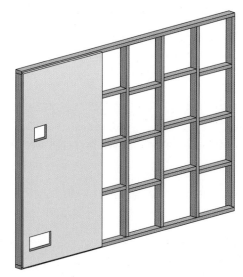

Prefabricated wall panel

Services

Those provided by the utility companies, eg gas, electric and water

There are a variety of prefabricated products available, generally made in a factory and then transported to site to be erected. These products enable quick and easy building. Often the **services** are pre-installed.

INTERNAL WALLING

Internal walling can be load or non-load bearing. Internal partitions divide large internal spaces into smaller rooms.

Internal partitions can be made from studwork or masonry. Studwork partitions consist of studs (which can be made from timber or metal) covered with a sheet material (usually plasterboard).

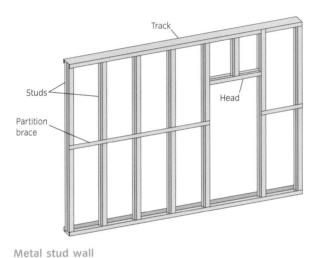

Metal stud wall

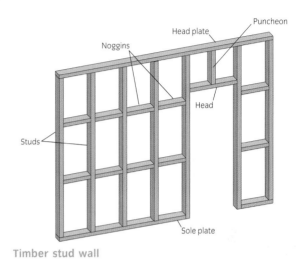

Timber stud wall

WALL FINISHES

External walls made from brick usually have no further finishes added while ones made from blocks are rendered. This is a covering of sand and cement mortar which is then finished with masonry paint.

Internal walls are most often plastered with a thin layer of gypsum plaster over plasterboard; this gives a very smooth hardwearing finish which is then usually finished with emulsion paint or papered coverings.

It is important to **size** new plaster to give a good base before applying further coverings of paint or paper coverings. This first coat of paint or paste is usually thinned down by 10% with clean water.

INDUSTRY TIP

At least two coats of emulsion are usually required for new plaster.

Size

To apply a watered down or mist-coat of paint or paste to new plaster

ROOFS

Roofs are designed to protect the structure below by keeping the weather out. As heat rises, the roof must be well insulated to prevent heat loss and improve the energy efficiency of the building.

TYPES OF ROOFS

Roofs come in a wide variety of designs, but they come under two main categories of 'flat' and 'pitched'.

Flat roofs

Flat roofs are similar in design to floors, in that they are made from joists decked with timber sheet material. A waterproof layer such as bituminous felt (made from tar), plastic or fibreglass is also used. Although flat roofs tend to be cheaper to install than pitched roofs, they do not last as long and they can suffer from leaks.

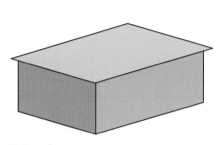

Flat roof

House with a flat roof

Pitched roofs

Pitched roofs are constructed using rafters, and come in a variety of designs. The simplest design of pitched roof is the 'lean-to', where a roof leans up against a wall. 'Gable-ended roofs' are a very common design, with walls covering the ends of the roof. These walls are known as gables or gable ends, which gives the roof its name. The weather can drive into these gables, and very often lengths of timber known as bargeboards are used to keep the elements out. 'Hipped roofs' are more complex (and rather more expensive). The roof ends are covered, making the roof more resistant to the elements. It is common to find a combination of the above roofs in the same building.

House with a pitched roof

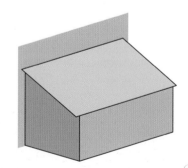

Lean-to roof

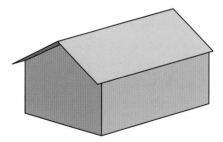

Gable-ended roof

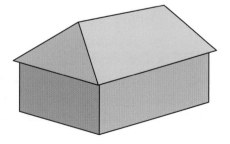

Hipped roof

ROOF COMPONENTS

You will need to know the different components of roofs. Study the illustrations below to learn what these are and how they are used to assemble a roof.

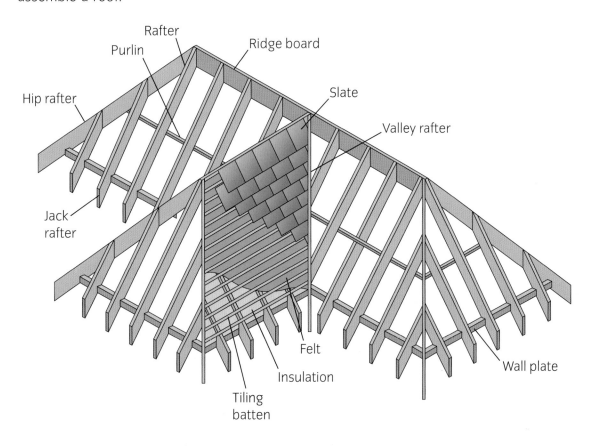

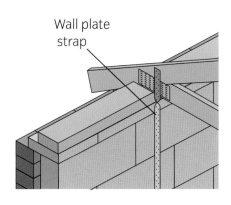

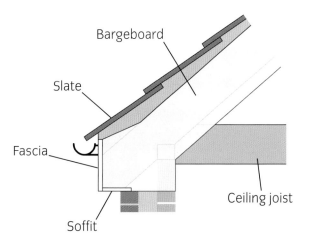

Roofs are usually constructed using **truss rafters**. This method of building a roof is quicker to install than a cut roof (where all of the components are cut and assembled on site). Roofs can be constructed using a combination of trusses and cut rafters. One type of commonly used truss is called a Fink truss (see next page).

Truss rafters

Rafters that are already cut and fixed together before being delivered on site

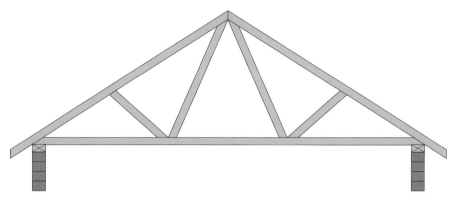

Commonly used standard Fink truss

Roofs are commonly covered with slates or tiles. Slates are a natural product. Slate is a type of mineral that can be split into thin sheets. Artificial cement fibre slates are also available; these are thin and uniform. Tiles can be made from clay or concrete.

Slate

Cement fibre slate

Roof tiles

A felt is laid below the roofing material to provide additional protection in case some water gets through the tiles.

Flashings are commonly made from lead and are used to provide waterproofing at joints where roofing materials meet walls and around chimneys.

Flashing providing waterproofring

Flashing around a chimney

Timber requires protection from the elements (rain, wind and sun) and this is done using timber coatings. Knotting is applied to prevent heat from the sun drawing resin out of knots in the timber. Primer is applied to give a good key to the paint or stain that is used to provide a finish. Paint also requires undercoat to be applied to give a good finish. Paint and stain can be water or solvent borne (water- or oil-based).

SERVICES

Buildings contain services such as:

- water
- electricity
- gas supplies.

Additionally, waste such as sewage and water run-off have to be considered.

WATER

Water is brought into a building using pipes. Supply pipes used are usually made of plastic, with internal domestic plumbing being made from plastic or copper. Plumbing is installed using a variety of fittings including tees, elbows, and reducers. Bathrooms, kitchens and most heating systems require plumbing.

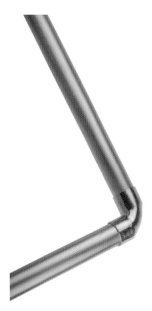

Copper pipe

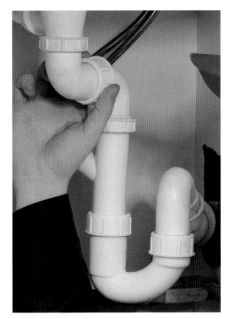

Plastic waste water pipe

Pipe fittings: Tee   Elbow   Reducer

ACTIVITY

What services are being used in the building you are sitting in? How are they brought into the building?

Not only is water carried into a building, it is also taken away. Rainwater run-off is collected into gutters and taken away via downpipes and drains and returned to the ground. It may also be stored for later use in raintanks; this is known as rainwater harvesting.

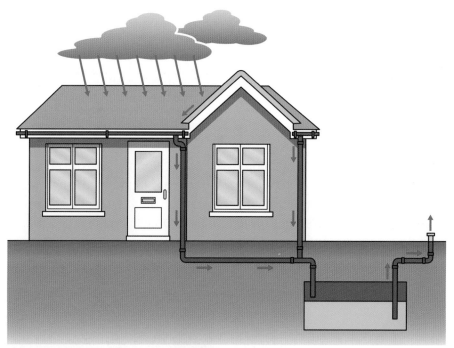

Rainwater flowing down pipes and into an underground raintank

SEWAGE

Sewage is taken away from the building via drains and is disposed of either into a sewer or into a septic tank/sewage treatment plant.

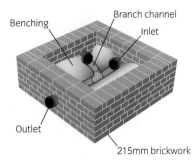

Benched drain

Septic tank

Sewage treatment plant

ELECTRICITY

Electricity is an important service provided to buildings. It powers lighting and heating. It is brought into a building through cables.

GAS

Gas is brought into a building using pipes. Gas powers heating systems and provides fuel for cooking.

OTHER SERVICES

Other services that are installed include telephone systems and other data cables for broadband and entertainment systems.

Electricity cables, switches and socket

SUSTAINABILITY

Our planet is a fixed size. Fossil fuels, eg oil and coal, which we take from the ground are not infinite, ie they will run out one day. However, the wind, the sun and the tides will always be there. These are sustainable sources of energy.

Pipework to boiler

Building materials can be sustainable if they are chosen carefully. For example, the process of manufacturing concrete uses a lot of fuel and produces a lot of carbon dioxide (a gas that some say is damaging the climate).

On the other hand, trees absorb carbon dioxide as they grow, look nice and the timber they produce is an excellent building material. However, some timber is harvested from rainforests without thought for the surrounding environment, or are harvested to such an extent that certain species are close to extinction. Managed forests where trees are replanted after harvesting provide a sustainable source of timber.

Here are some questions to consider regarding sustainability in construction.

MATERIALS

- How far have the materials been brought? Locally sourced materials do not have to be transported far, thus reducing fuel use.

- Are the materials sustainably sourced? Has the timber come from a managed forest or has it come from a rainforest with no regard to the environment?

- Have the materials been manufactured with the minimum of energy and waste?

DESIGN

Is there an alternative design that can be used that uses more sustainable materials? For example, a timber frame could be used instead of concrete block or brick.

The table below shows some sustainable materials:

Material	Image
Straw bales	
Cob (soil)	
Timber	 Redwood Spruce Oak
Bamboo	

Material	Image
Lime	
Sheep wool	

ENERGY EFFICIENCY

Energy is expensive and is only going to get more expensive. As the population increases, more and more energy will be required. This needs to come from somewhere and its production can be damaging to the environment. The less power a building uses the better and if it can produce its own that is a bonus. Energy-saving measures can save a lot of power consumption.

Insulation

Light, air-filled materials tend to have better thermal insulation properties than heavy, dense materials. This means that heat cannot easily pass from one side to another, and so if these materials are used in a building it will require less heating during the winter and will remain cooler during the summer.

The following drawing shows how much heat a typical home loses through different parts of the property. Better insulation will reduce the amount of heat lost.

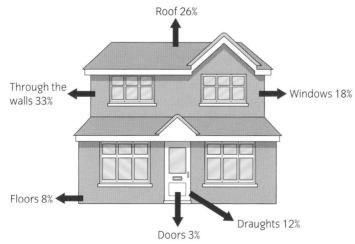

Sources of heat loss from a house

INDUSTRY TIP

There are many ways of reducing the energy consumption of buildings, such as the use of low-energy light bulbs or lights that only come on when a sensor detects movement and turn off when there is no one about.

What insulation has been used in the building you are sitting in? Is the building energy efficient? Is it cold? Does it take a lot of heating? Take a look at 'Our House' and identify the insulation measures used there.

The table below shows some examples of insulation:

Type of insulation	Description
Blue jean and lambswool 	Lambswool is a natural insulator. Blue jean insulation comes from recycled denim.
Fibreglass/mineral wool 	This is made from glass, often from old recycled bottles or mineral wool. It holds a lot of air within it and therefore is an excellent insulator. It is also cheap to produce. It does however use up a fair bit of room as it takes a good thickness to comply with building regulations. Similar products include plastic fibre insulation made from plastic bottles and lambswool.
PIR (polyisocyanurate)	This is a solid insulation with foil layers on the faces. It is lightweight, rigid and easy to cut and fit. It has excellent insulation properties. Polystyrene is similar to PIR. Although it is cheaper, its thermal properties are not as good.
Multifoil	A modern type of insulation made up of many layers of foil and thin insulation layers. These work by reflecting heat back into the building. Usually used in conjunction with other types of insulation.

Type of insulation	Description
Double glazing and draught proofing measures 	The elimination of draughts and air flows reduces heat loss and improves efficiency.

MAKING BETTER USE OF EXISTING AND FREE ENERGY

Solar power

The sun always shines and during the day its light reaches the ground (even on cloudy days). This energy can be used. A simple use of this is to allow sunlight to enter a building. With a little thought in design, light can reach deep into a building via roof lights and light tunnels. This means that internal artificial lighting requirements are reduced, therefore saving energy.

Solar panels can generate hot water or electricity, and once the cost of installation has been covered the energy they produce is totally free.

Solar panel

A panel that absorbs sun rays to generate electricity or hot water

Solar panels

Air conditioning unit

Turbines

A machine designed to allow continuous movement to create electrical energy

Heat source and recovery

Humans give off a fair bit of energy as they go through a normal day (eg body heat, heat given off by hairdryers, cookers, refrigerators and other activities) and this can be conserved. Modern air-conditioning systems take the heat from stale air and put it into the fresh air coming in.

Heat can be taken from the ground and even the air outside.

Wind power

Wind power is becoming more widespread. However, some people feel that wind **turbines** are damaging the visual environment as they spoil the appearance of the countryside. Individuals will have their own opinion on whether wind power is a good thing or not as there are many considerations to be taken into account.

Wind turbines

Water power

Water is another source of power, whether that be hydro-electric (water from dams turning turbines) or wave power (which is currently under development).

Another method is through extracting heat energy contained in the air and ground. This can be extracted by the use of a heat exchanger. Water in pipes buried in the ground circulates, picking up heat, which is then taken out and used in the building. This can also be achieved with air from outside.

Biomass heating

Biomass heating (using wood and other non-fossil fuels) is also becoming more popular as these systems can heat water efficiently as well as heat rooms, and of course a well-insulated building does not require a lot of heating.

Energy efficient goods and appliances

Energy efficient electrical goods (eg low-energy light bulbs) and appliances (eg dishwashers, fridges and washing machines) which use a reduced amount of power and less water are available.

PROTECTING THE ENVIRONMENT

Building work can create a lot of waste, and can pollute the environment. To avoid this, careful consideration needs to be given to how waste is disposed of. There are many regulations that control the management of waste (ie COSHH, see Chapter 1 page 9) that also need to be followed.

Proper stock control and efficient use of materials reduces waste. Dust and fumes can be reduced by using water or LEV (local exhaust ventilation), which sucks dust from the air. Materials such as glass or plastics can be recycled, very often into other building materials. Timber can be reused instead of being thrown away or taken to a salvage yard. The waste that is left (the waste that cannot be recycled or reused) then needs to be disposed of carefully in a skip. Hazardous waste such as asbestos is usually removed by specialists.

A hydroelectric dam

Biomass fuel

An energy efficient light bulb

Case Study: Tristan

Tristan has been asked to help design and produce specifications for a house. He has been asked to research how to make the house energy efficient. The house will have four bedrooms and has a gable roof that faces south.

Tristan consulted manufacturers' catalogues and websites to determine the most efficient system for generating energy. As the roof faces south, Tristan decides that panels on the roof are a good option. Tristan decides that five solar thermal collectors will be enough to provide hot water for the occupants of the house. Ground source will provide additional heating for the house.

The walls, roof, windows and floor are to be insulated. The building regulations provide minimum requirements that Tristan refers to. Again, using manufacturers' information he decides which is the best insulation systems to use, balancing effectiveness with cost.

- Do you agree with Tristan's design?

- Could it be improved?

- Are there any drawbacks to his design?

Work through the following questions to check your learning.

1 Which **one** of the following identifies the details of materials needed for a project?

a Specification

b Programme of work

c Delivery note

d Site diary

2 Which scale should be used for a detail drawing?

a 1:5

b 1:75

c 1:500

d 1:7500

3 What is the hatching symbol shown below?

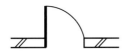

a Door

b Roof light

c Window

d Hallway

4 What is the hatching symbol shown below?

a Plastic

b Insulation

c Timber

d Blockwork

5 What is the point shown below?

a A point of a known height used for setting out

b A point of unknown height used for setting out

c A point of known position used to determine the building line

d A point of unknown position used to determine the building line

6 What type of brick is shown below?

a Flemish

b Concrete

c Trench

d Air

7 What foundation type covers the footprint of the building?

a Strip

b Raft

c Pile

d Pad

8   In a concrete mix ratio of 1:2:3, the 3 represents

   a   Retardant

   b   Fine aggregate

   c   Coarse aggregate

   d   Cement

9   What part of a roof retains heat within the building?

   a   Insulation

   b   Restraint strap

   c   DPC

   d   Concrete tiles

10 What brick bond is shown below?

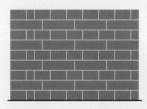

   a   German

   b   English

   c   French

   d   Flemish

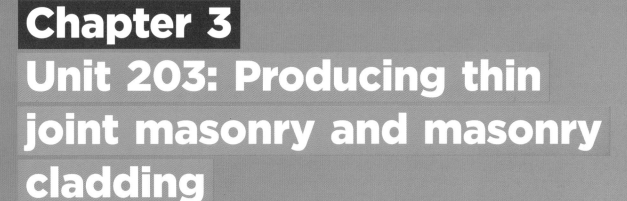

Chapter 3
Unit 203: Producing thin joint masonry and masonry cladding

Producing thin joint masonry and masonry cladding for buildings are essential skills to possess as an operative in the bricklaying industry. Expanding on the knowledge that you will have obtained at Level 1, this chapter goes into further detail on the knowledge required when assembling cavity walls. It also provides further insight into DPC and bonding and summarises the techniques and materials used in cladding internal walls.

By reading this chapter you will know how to:

1 Construct thin joint masonry for use with concrete and steel-framed buildings.

WHAT IS THIN JOINT MASONRY AND CLADDING?

Thin joint blockwork is a building process and method of laying lightweight insulation blocks to a dwelling in a very quick way. Unlike the sand and cement mortar used in traditional blocklaying, the blocks are laid in a very strong adhesive that is 2mm thick and sets in 20 minutes. The main difference between using this method and the traditional blocklaying method is the adhesive which allows for the quick fixing time and a lack of gauging.

Cladding is the overall finish to a walled structure. This can be made from a range of materials such as stone, brick, block, timber or even plastic, which are used on the external face of a dwelling. This will be discussed later in the chapter.

The advantages of the thin joint system are:

Speed
The thin joint system allows construction times equivalent to off-site system-build solutions, without their associated **lead times**.

Quality
The improvements in build quality gained from the use of the thin joint system are:

- improved **thermal** performance

- improved stability during construction

- improved build accuracy of finished walls

- reduction of site wastage

- cleaner cavities.

Flexibility
As with traditional building methods, construction is carried out on site. This allows the builder to overcome problems which may have been overlooked or changed since the design stage and simplifies modifications to the building should it need to be extended or adapted in future.

Applications
The thin joint system can be applied to:

- cavity walls (**internal** and **external leaf**)

- solid walls

- partition walls

Timber cladding on a building

Lead time
The time between the start and completion of a process

Thermal
Having the quality of retaining heat

The thin joint system can be used in the construction of multi-storey buildings

Internal leaf
Inside skin of a building

External leaf
Outside skin of a building

- separating walls

- flanking walls

- multi-storey buildings.

PREPARATION

To build masonry cladding using brick, block and stone requires very good preparation. The position of the resources is very important, as is following the manufacturer's instructions. Working at the correct position and not having to walk to the **spot board** and brick stack is key to being efficient. Bricklayers should be able to turn in position and pick up **mortar** and a brick at the same time and lay to the line or quoin. Good positioning of the spot and brick stacks will ensure comfortable working conditions.

Health and safety considerations at the early stages of construction include ensuring good ground conditions, such as a covering of ballast or stone chippings. This provides a good firm ground on which to walk.

Mixing mortar can be done by hand or machine. The mix of different materials such as sand and cement is best when mixed mechanically. Powdered mortar is mixed using a hand held auger. Traditional mortar can be mixed as requried in a drum mixer. When mixing mortar for the thin joint system, water is the first material to be added. Water for mixing needs to be clean water that is free from dirt and other contaminates. Once the ends of the walls are established, the bricklayer can continue and infill the middle section of the walls (**infill panels**).

PLANNING

Walking onto the site and locating the plot can be determined by using the block or site plan. More information about plans can be found in Chapter 2, pages 49–50. Make sure you know which plot the cladding is being fixed to.

Spot board

A board made of durable material roughly 600mm x 600mm, on which mortar is placed

Mortar

Traditionally sand, cement and plasticiser

INDUSTRY TIP

The mortar for the thin joint system is sold in 25kg sealed bags.

Infill panel

The middle sections of a length of walling

Mortar on a spot board

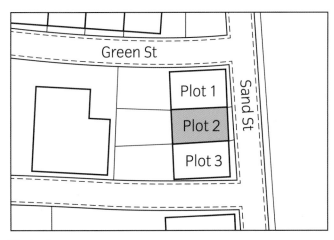

Block plan

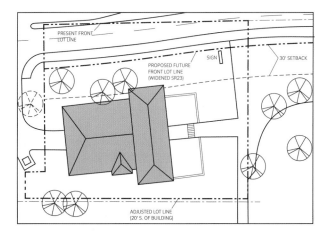

Site plan

Each stage of the construction process can be followed by the use of the assembly drawings. These drawings show a plan view of the structure both at ground and first floor level. Other areas of the project such as cross sections and foundations can also be found using the working assembly plans.

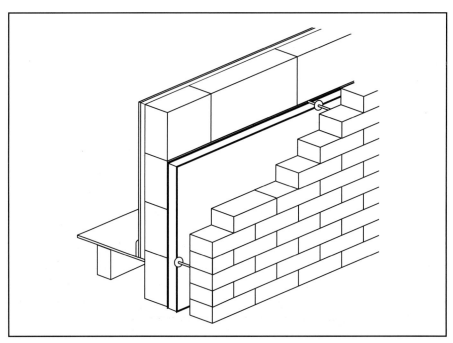

Cross sectional drawing of a cavity wall

A flat scale rule on a drawing

All working drawings are drawn to scale; the details required for the bricklayer can be shown from scale 1:10–50. The bricklayer has to learn how to measure the dimensional line to a scale using a scale rule, and calculate the full size and length of the same dimensional line. For more information on scales, see Chapter 2, page 47.

SAFETY MEASURES AND EQUIPMENT

When loading out resources such as bricks and blocks, the recommended stacking height must be adhered to. The manufacturer will always give good advice for their materials so their instructions should be followed. The general rule is that the bricks and blocks should not be stacked higher than 1.8m. This equates to two packs of blocks, both dense and lightweight. Individual stacks of bricks and blocks next to the spot board can also be stacked to a height of 1.8m. Bonded stacks are used to store blocks near to the working area, ready for the bricklayer to lay his or her block courses.

Setting out brick stacks

An operative building a block wall with stacks of blocks behind him

Working as a bricklayer involves working in areas where hazards are commonplace. The handling of materials such as heavy blocks creates hazards, such as blocks falling over onto an operative's feet. This is why safety boots are worn on site, to protect your feet from damage from heavy material. Dust from mixing and cutting materials is another common problem, so you must always use masks when cutting to avoid inhaling dust. All building sites have a glove policy, which is in place to protect the bricklayer's hands from cuts and bruising. Although bricklayers do not use many power tools, if an operative is to use one then they must be trained to use it.

PPE

Measures to protect against accidents will always be highlighted within the risk assessment of a job. Good quality PPE such as those shown in the following table are common to most activities on site. For more information on PPE, see Chapter 1, pages 20–23.

FUNCTIONAL SKILLS

4 blocks laid in thin joint **design strength** adhesive measure 4 × 440mm plus 3 joints at 2mm each = 1.766m (ie 1766mm). Calculate the length of blockwork in metres using 10 blocks.
Work on this activity can support FM2 (L2.1.1).

Answer: 10 × 440mm plus 9 joints at 2mm = 4.418m.

Design strength

The specific setting qualities of the adhesive used

Overalls

Boots

Gloves

Wet-weather clothing

Hard hat

Goggles

METHOD STATEMENTS

Using a method statement, which will include risk assessments (see Chapter 1, page 5), is key to understanding the correct and safe way to build a structure. The method of work will be detailed in a correct manner, and hazards for the bricklayer to avoid will be noted. The method statement should cover everything operatives need to construct the project in a safe way.

An example of a method of work would be for building brick and block at height: the access equipment would be planned for, detailing who would erect the scaffolding and when, so the bricklayer can have confidence in working off a platform.

TOOLS AND EQUIPMENT

A bricklayer's tools are mostly hand tools: laying and pointing trowels, spirit and pocket levels, line and pins, club hammer, comb hammer, gauge rod and tape measure. The following table explains the use of tools.

Tool	Use in thin joint masonry
Laying trowel 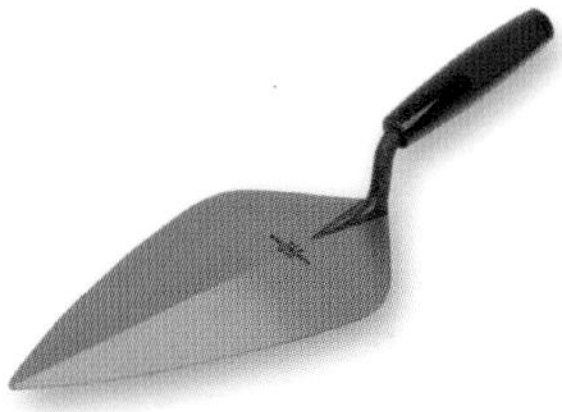	Only used on the first course of blockwork.
Pointing trowel 	Used to point areas of missing adhesive.
Pointing hawk 	Used with a pointing trowel when pointing the mortar joint.
Scoop 	A thin joint trowel used to lay the perp and bed joint adhesive. Also known as a toothed applicator.
Spirit level 	Used to maintain level between blocks.
Pocket level 	Used to make sure the blockwork is level and plumb.
Tape measure 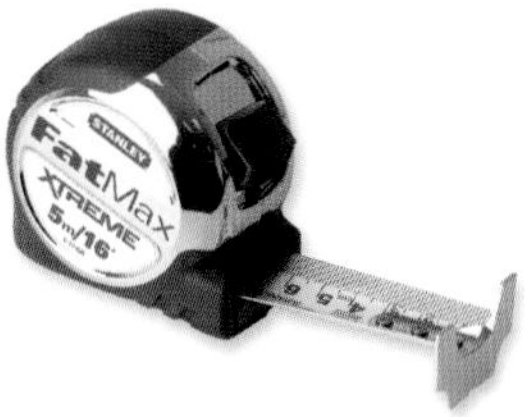	Used to measure lengths of walling and blocks.

INDUSTRY TIP

Bed and **perp joints** when applied must be full of mortar (flush) and complete at the front and rear to comply with the building regulations.

Perp joint

Vertical mortar joints which join two bricks or blocks together

Dress

To maintain a cut face

Tool	Use in thin joint masonry
Line and pins 	Used to maintain level courses between corners.
Scutch (or comb) hammer 	Used to **dress** a cut block.
Club hammer 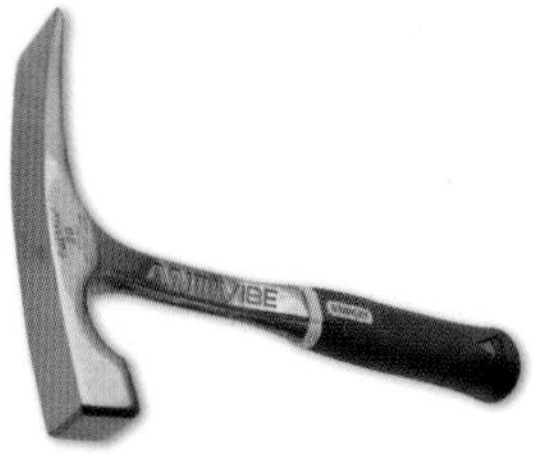	A weighted hammer used to cut blocks.
Gauge rod 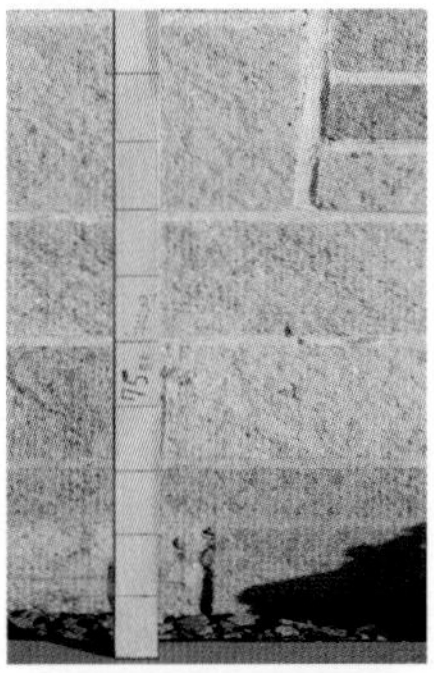	Used in gauging of block courses to maintain equal level courses.
Hammer drill 	Used to drill holes in blocks.
Drill bits 	Used to drill holes in masonry.

Tool	Use in thin joint masonry
Screwdrivers 	Used to fix screws into timber or masonry.
Masonry saw 	A hand saw with large teeth used to cut lightweight blocks.
Set square	Used to cut lightweight blocks with a masonry saw.
Grinder 	A power tool used to grind and cut materials.
Rasp 	Used to file down a block for level.
Whisk 	Used to mix adhesive in a container.
Hopper 	Applies wider and larger amounts of adhesive to thin joint blockwork.

As well as your tools, you will need equipment to build thin joint masonry. The table below shows the equipment you will need and explains their use.

Equipment	Use in thin joint masonry
Mixer	A mechanical mixer used to mix a large quantity of mortar or adhesive.
Extension leads	Electrical leads used in transferring over a long length.
Transformer	Used to transform the power output from 240V to 110V.
Shovel	Used to transport materials.
Wheelbarrow	Used to transport materials.

Equipment	Use in thin joint masonry
Spot board	A flat timber or steel board used to support the blockwork mortar at intervals along the building line.
Bucket	A container used to carry water or mortar, and waste products.

Traditional bricklaying tools have remained the same for hundreds of years. Trowel and level designs have varied from region to region. A bricklaying tool kit will contain hammers and chisels, line and pins, different sizes of trowels and jointers. Building with the thin joint system uses different tools and equipment; the traditional bricklayer will find the application of adhesive very different from laying bed and perpends in mortar.

Protecting all tools and equipment for the duration of the project is important. Check equipment and tools regularly to ensure nothing needs to be repaired. Using storage containers or lock ups to store and protect tools and equipment will ensure the item is always at hand, and regular maintenance will ensure that the item is always ready for use.

Cutting bricks and blocks can be very difficult. All bricklayers will carry the standard brick hammer and brick bolster (and occasionally a masonry saw), and these tools are suitable for most bricks, but not all. Cutting a very hard brick can create a lot of wastage, so if working with costly bricks and blocks it's better to use a mechanical piece of equipment, such as a clipper saw, Stihl saw or block splitter. This can help reduce the amount of waste produced.

ACTIVITY

Compare the two different tool kits (for normal bricklaying and for the thin joint system) and learn their application process. You could start with the laying trowels as an example.

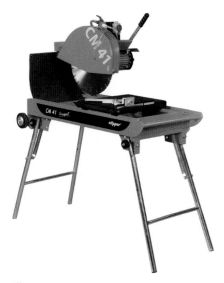

Clipper saw

Stihl saw

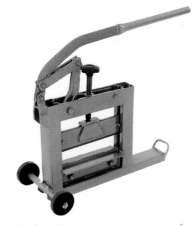

Block splitter

PROTECTING MATERIALS

Protecting your work is an important step as an operative. Making sure that the right protective measures have been taken will prevent injuries, keep your work in good condition and save time and money.

Bricklayers need to protect their work against the weather, but also against traffic and the general public. Traffic such as lorries, vans, concrete wagons and heavy machinery can cause vibration and move newly built brick or blockwork. The general public must always be kept away from the construction project, and especially from newly constructed brick or blockwork.

Other trades such as carpenters, electricians and plumbers can cause damage if they need access to the construction site or attach their work to yours. Good training and planning is required when follow-on trades are involved.

Polythene sheeting protecting bricks

CALCULATIONS

FUNCTIONAL SKILLS

If one 25kg bag of adhesive lays 60 blocks, how many blocks can be laid using five bags?
Work on this activity can support FM2 (L2.1.1).

Answer: 5 × 60 = 300 blocks.

When calculating the number of bricks required for the job, over-calculating must be avoided. Over-calculating causes too much money to be spent on materials, and can have an effect on how much the project can be sold for. A bricklayer can use the centre line method to calculate the number of bricks and blocks required for the project. This method involves accurately measuring the centre position on a plan of the internal and external corners, so as not to over-calculate at the corners.

Below is the step-by-step process for the centre line method.

1 Count the number of external corners of the building.

2 Add together the skin thickness for each of the external corners. Note that these could be different.

3 Work out the overall perimeter length by adding together all of the sides.

4 Work out the combined corner length.

5 Take away the combined corner length from the overall perimeter length.

6 Work out the true length of walling, by multiplying the perimeter length by the wall height.

7 Use the true length of walling to calculate the areas of brickwork needed. Remember that there are 60 bricks to 1m².

To properly understand this method, follow the example below.

Example

Measurements are shown in millimetres.

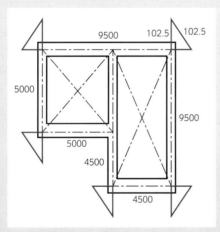

Step 1: Count the number of external corners of the building in the image above. In this example, there are five.

Step 2: Add together the skin thickness for each of the external corners. In this example, the skin thickness for one external corner is 102.5mm:
102.5 × 5 = 512.5mm

Step 3: Work out the overall perimeter length by adding together all of the sides:
9500 + 9500 + 4500 + 5000 + 4500 + 5000 = 38,000mm

INDUSTRY TIP

Using the centre line method for calculating the accurate length of a wall will allow the tradesperson to be accurate in calculating the materials and resources for the construction project. Always remember the external wall corner thickness must be taken away from the wall measurements.

Step 4: Work out the combined corner length. In this example, one corner is 102.5mm long:
102.5 × 5 = 512.5mm

Step 5: Take away the combined corner length from the overall perimeter length:
38,000 − 512.5 = 37,487.5mm, or 37.487m

Step 6: Work out the true length of walling, by multiplying the perimeter length by the wall height. In the example, the wall height is 3m, so 3000mm.
37.487 × 3 = 112.46m^2.

Step 7: Use the true length of walling to calculate the area of brickwork needed.
112.46 × 60 = 6747

The total amount of bricks needed is 6747.

WORKING METHODS

Laying bricks is hard physical work, and moving between the spot board and the wall must be kept down to a minimum. If the bricklayer has positioned the materials too far away from the face of the dwelling, more time will be spent walking between the wall and the board, instead of turning between the wall and the board and at the same time laying bricks. Being organised in this way will allow you to follow the **critical path** of the project.

Critical path
A program of stages to be followed

Organised bricklayers with their stacks of bricks close by

BONDING

Establishing the bonding at the start of the project and working below ground level can create problems when trying to work the brick or block to full components (full-sized bricks or blocks). In an ideal world, lengths of brick and blockwork would work to full brick sizes, but this is not always the case. The bricklayer can measure the length of wall using a tape measure and check to see if the length works using full bricks. Another option is to set out two courses **dry** around the complete perimeter of the dwelling to ensure the correct bond is used and cutting is kept to a minimum.

Dry

Spacing bricks or blocks without mortar to sort out potential problems with the bond

An operative showing how to set out bricks dry

Taking measurements from drawings and converting these measurements into a length of walling is an everyday task for a bricklayer. Working to full bricks and perp joints is harder, and if the wall does not work to full bricks, the bricklayer has a broken bond or reverse bond to construct (for more information on these bonds, see Chapter 4, page 151 onwards). Setting out two courses of bricks dry is more time consuming than simply measuring the length of the wall, but it is also the most accurate method. Using this method can save a great deal of time in the long term, as it reduces the amount of cutting a broken bond takes. Marking the dry bonded courses on to the foundation concrete is achieved by putting down a **thin layer** of mortar 2mm thick and using the trowel to mark the position of the perp joint into the **screed**. This operation must be undertaken all around both dry courses to establish the position of every perp on the first course.

Thin layer

2mm bed and perpend thickness

Screed

A mixture of cement, sand and water applied to the concrete foundation to give a smooth surface finish

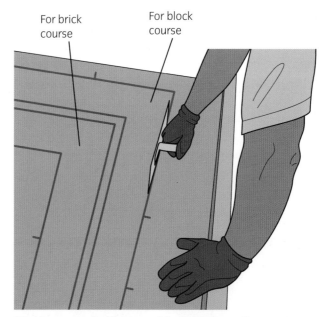

For brick course

For block course

Marking perps to the screed for a cavity wall

Reinforced blockwork known as 'clockwork reinforcement' involves fixing reinforcements into the horizontal bed joints. This reinforcement resists lateral movement of the joints and helps stop cracking. Fixing blockwork to concrete and steel frames is undertaken when large construction projects are built, such as industrial buildings. The blocks are built into the frames and anchored to the concrete or steel with ties fixed to the frame. These ties are fixed to the frame using high powered fixings such as nails driven in to the concrete and steel. The same ties are then built into the blockwork, fixing all materials together.

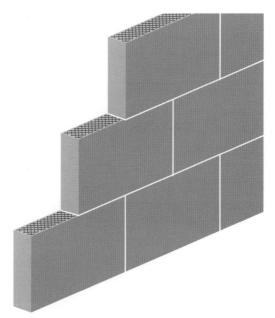

How reinforced blockwork works

When the brick and blockwork has been inserted up to **damp proof course** (DPC) level, the horizontal damp proof course (HDPC) can be laid. At this stage the bonding can be altered slightly, and the positioning of the window and door opening can be established and marked onto the face of the dwelling at DPC height. This detail will help the bricklayer to set out the openings and form the reveals.

DAMP PROOF COURSING

Ensuring damp does not enter the building in the early stages of construction is undertaken by inserting a HDPC. A DPC is inserted at a height of 150mm above finished ground level. It consists of a layer of impervious (ie watertight) membrane the same width as the wall. The DPC is sandwiched between layers of mortar to fully imbed the DPC to the horizontal course.

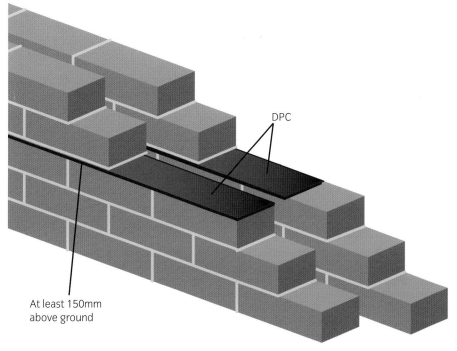

DPC

At least 150mm above ground

Horizontal DPC being laid

Damp proof course (DPC)

A layer of watertight material that prevents damp rising up through a wall. It needs to be positioned at least 150mm above ground level

INDUSTRY TIP

Always check the manufacturer's instructions. Look at the essential requirements in the document guidelines and follow them as closely as possible. The instructions will give a list of tools and equipment needed, areas where the thin joint system can be used and the correct building regulation for the system.

INDUSTRY TIP

Always lay the DPC using the roll. This will ensure the wind cannot blow the DPC as you are fixing it in place.

LAYING USING THE THIN JOINT SYSTEM

The following steps show the preparation and mixing of the adhesive, and laying using the thin joint blockwork system.

STEP 1 Using the adhesive from the bag, mix the powder in a tub or a mixer using a hand held whisk so it is ready to use.

STEP 2 When building the first course of the thin joint system use traditional sand and cement. This will provide a level base from which to use the thin joint adhesive.

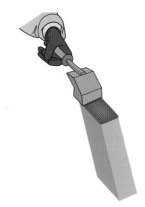

STEP 3 Using a scoop, apply the adhesive to the perp ends, making it 2mm thick.

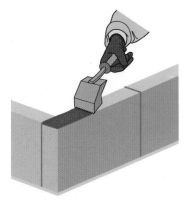

STEP 4 Again using a scoop, apply the adhesive to the bed joint, making it 2mm thick. Perping and laying the blocks using the thin joint adhesive requires greater speed due to the time the adhesive sets.

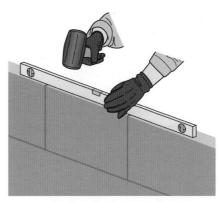

STEP 5 Check your work using a spirit level. Use a rubber hammer to gently knock the blocks into place. Remember to use the hammer on the blocks and not the level.

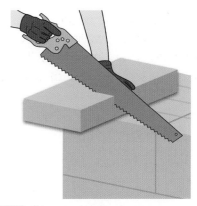

STEP 6 Use a masonry saw to cut any blocks that need to have a good cut surface. If you don't need to cut any blocks, a rasp can be used to level a block or course.

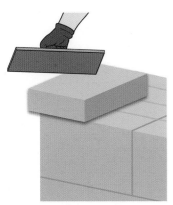

STEP 7 After cutting the block, use the rasp to level the cut face before applying the perp joint.

STEP 8 Use traditional blocklaying methods to finish the job. All joints must be full and complete and the overall appearance must be to building regulations.

OPENINGS AND ARCHES

Window openings being built on the first and second storeys of a building

Door and window openings provide access and light, as well as ventilation to a dwelling. Supporting the brick and blockwork above these openings is very important. The method of supporting the brickwork can be achieved by the use of an arch. The common forms of arches are:

■ soldier arch

■ semi-circular arch

■ segmental arch.

Solider arch

Semi-circular arch

Segmental arch

Building arches brings its own problems, such as bridging the cavity. Bridging is the term used when moisture travels across a cavity with the help of a bridge. This bridge can be made up of mortar droppings, blocks and bricks and even an ill-fitting DPC. If a material is touching both the external and internal skins then bridging can occur. Moisture will create damp patches on the inside of the dwelling especially at wet times of the year. Using different materials purely for convenience can also create a cold spot and result in damp. Inserting bricks into an insulation block wall will create a different surface temperature and condensation will be present. Always cut the bonding pieces out of the same insulating block material. The aim is to build a building with as low a **U-value** as possible.

When closing a cavity to form an opening, great care must be taken. The use of a vertical DPC (VDPC) must be used to stop any moisture travelling across the cavity (bridging). The minimum width of this VDPC is 150mm.

The step-by-step process for forming an opening is:

1   Once the brick and blockwork is complete up to DPC level, the position of the openings can be measured and marked on the top course of brickwork. This mark is usually a pencil mark, showing just where the openings will start and finish.

2   Measure the openings and take the sizes from working drawings to establish the opening. Always remember to measure from the corners in to each side of the openings.

3   Once the positions of the openings are measured and marked, the brick and blockwork needs to be set out and the correct bond established. Always remember to stop the brick and blockwork with no less than a half brick or block either side of the opening.

4   Measure the opening for height; this is important because of the door and window frame height. The lintel supports need to be inserted at the correct height ready to receive the lintel.

5   Once the blockwork and cladding are completed, fixing the door and window frames can be completed. This is done by the window and door manufacturer, and includes using fixings secured though the frames into the stopped ends of the blocks and brick cladding.

U-value

Rate at which heat escapes from a building

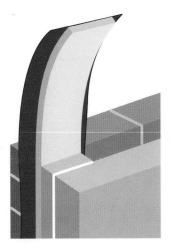

VDPC in position

LINTELS

The support used to form an opening is provided by the insertion of a lintel. Lintels come in many different forms and sizes: the two on the next page, IG and Catnic, are just two examples.

An IG lintel does not have a cavity tray built in. Catnic lintels are made in the form of a cavity tray and painted to prevent moisture penetrating through the metal. Both lintels are made from steel, but are lightweight enough that one person can lift and position the lintel over an opening. An operative should also include a flexible tray over the top of each lintel.

IG lintel

Catnic lintel

A lintel must always be backed up with the use of a cavity tray. The tray is built into the lintel and will help catch any moisture and direct it to the outside of the wall using openings called **weep holes**. This will prevent moisture from penetrating the inside of the building.

Weep holes

Gaps deliberately left in masonry perp joints to allow moisture to escape. Purpose-made plastic inserts are often used to maintain the correct size of the joint

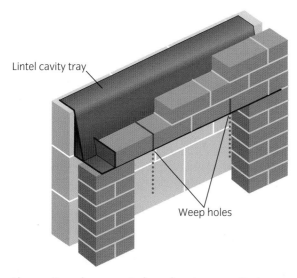

Lintel cavity tray

Weep holes

The section above a window showing a cavity tray and weep holes

OUR HOUSE

The lintel can be positioned to almost any height, due to the flexibility of the cutting of the blockwork. Look at 'Our House', especially in relation to the lintels, and compare their overall position and height. The traditional bedding of the lintels follow the height and gauge of the blockwork but the thin joint allows for the lintel to be inserted at any height in relation to the wall.

CAVITIES

Cavity closer

A PVC closer with built-in insulation that closes the cavity at openings

Closing cavities to form an opening has an effect on the insulation used. If the cavity is to be partially or totally full of insulation, the building of the cavity insulation must be accurate and have no empty joint within the insulation. The cavity is closed by inserting a PVC **cavity closer** with built-in insulation; this closer will stop heat loss at the openings and also stop water penetrating the cavity. The insulation must also be positioned as close as possible to the VDPC.

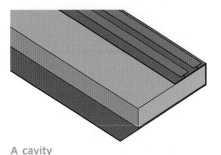

A cavity

Partial fill uses a different building method to total fill. The 30mm thick insulation is attached to the inside of the lightweight block skin. This means the blockwork has to be constructed first. The insulation is fixed to the block with the use of wall ties and plastic wheels.

Total fill cavity insulation is the most difficult to construct. The smallest amount of mortar or dust on the insulation will result in bridging, so the bricklayer has to be very careful and keep the area clean during this work.

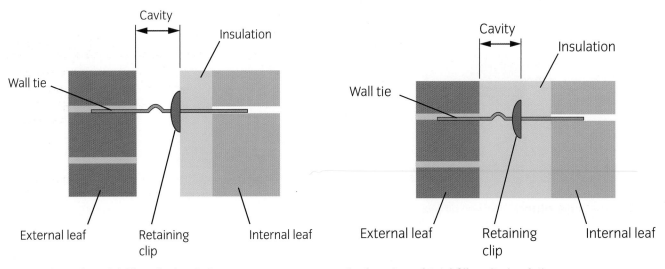

Section view of partial fill cavity insulation   Section view of total fill cavity insulation

Long lengths of cavity walling require vertical movement joints, which are vertical straight joints in the bonding arrangement constructed along the length of the wall. These joints are filled with a compressible material to allow small amounts of movement along the length of the walling.

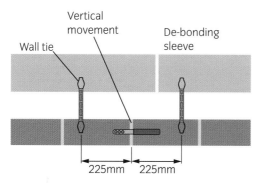

A vertical movement joint. Note the de-bonding sleeve holding the joint together

The joints also help guide any pressure to a vertical flexible compound. Cavity walling over long lengths can be constructed to withstand movement if joints are placed at regular intervals. The spacing of these joints is important and they should be positioned no further apart than 5m. For more information on vertical movement joints, see Chapter 6, page 222.

Frame tie

OUR HOUSE

The thin joint system requires the bricklayer to build blockwork to the inner leaf using a different application. Take a look in 'Our House' at the insulation and make a note of the wall tie and bonding arrangement of the insulation. These do not change just because you are using a different application. The insulation is bonded when fixed and the wall tie positions must still conform to building regulations.

ACTIVITY

Look at the area of construction you are involved with and learn the regulations relating to the type of dwelling you are building, in terms of thin joint masonry.

Working as a bricklayer, certain industrial standards apply. Bricklayers can work to a tolerance of 3mm +/– for plumbing. If high quality bricks are used then no tolerance for plumbing would be allowed, the wall has to be **plumb**.

Plumb

When brick or blockwork is completely straight, vertically

CLADDING

Internal blockwork is always required for **cladding**. Timber-framed buildings can be used and the bricklayer is only required to construct the outside cladding. As mentioned earlier in this chapter, the cladding

Cladding

When a surface has been covered in another material, eg plastic or timber

can be brick, block, or even stone. Safety requirements are different when working with buildings covered in brick cladding which have an internal timber frame. The timber frame can be erected very quickly, and secured to the over site slab or brickwork at DPC level. Bricklayers and other trades have to be mindful that timber frames are large, heavy and must not move prior to any cladding being fixed.

Working safely when fixing external brick cladding is important at each stage of the project. Timber-framed construction has many hazards, from ties protruding from the frames, to possible large sections of timber frames moving around the building site. All operations must be detailed in the method statement, and the correct control measures put into place before work begins.

A timber frame ready for the first course of bricks to be laid

A timber frame for a building

The first course of the cladding has to have a starting point. This starting point or course is established from transferring a fixed level from the site datum to the foundation concrete or house slab. This will let the bricklayer know just where to start and lay the first course of bricks.

The following step by steps explain cladding in the thin joint system.

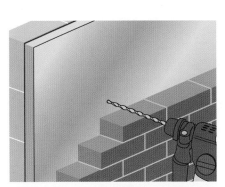

STEP 1 When the inside thin joint block-work is complete, the external brick, timber or plastic cladding can be added. Firstly, the cavity must be insulated and wall ties fixed as shown.

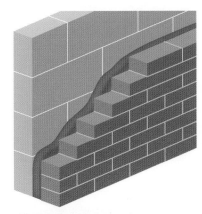

STEP 2 Follow the manufacturer's instructions when cladding the building. Brickwork will always be built as a cladding to the outside with no hint of the thin joint system used on the inside. The dwelling with the insulation can be built quickly and to building regulations.

Stacking materials on a timber-framed project has to be timed and planned accurately. To move large sections into position requires large machinery, therefore no materials for the external cladding can be stacked out until the frame is in place and secured. Cladding the external skin of a timber-framed dwelling can be done using the same methods as if the inside skin was block. The only exception is the gauging. The brick gauging must be a lot more accurate, for example the brickwork must be built up to the height of windows and door lintels. Fixing gauge strips to reveals will help the bricklayer maintain the gauge. To protect the cavities from wind, damp and spread of fire, bricklayers insert protection socks. These are long fire-retardant filler pieces inserted between cavity walls and roof timbers to stop the spread of smoke and flames.

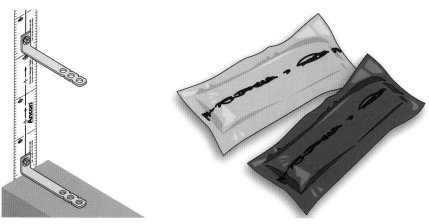

Gauge strips   Protection socks

Forming returns, reveals and stopped ends in external brick cladding can create many opportunities for bridging to occur. This is why, when bridging the cavity, a VDPC must be inserted.

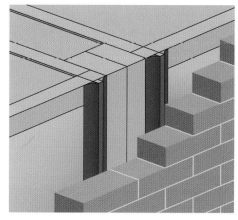

VDPC in timber framed building

Special care must be taken when building the outside skin of a timber-framed property, due to the material placed on the timber frame. The frame is covered in a vapour barrier, which is easily broken or holed. If damage occurs, this will result in water and moisture getting into the building.

Case Study: Alex

Alex runs a small to medium sized building company called Mezz Real Estate and he has recently been looking to change the method of their construction process.

For the last 10 years his company has been building with traditional brick and block. This method involves using a traditional sand and cement mix to bind both bricks and blocks together and the whole process can take a long time. The process of building houses is all about building the best possible structure in the shortest amount of time.

Alex and Mezz Real Estate have looked into a new building system called the thin joint block system. This system involves taking away the traditional sand and cement and using a 2mm-thick adhesive binding to secure bricks and blocks instead. This adhesive comes in a powder form that is mixed with a whisk and removes the need for a traditional mortar or concrete mixer. The block manufacturer has provided the company with not only the blocks and the adhesive, but also the new tools to lay the thin joint system. The company has also found storing the materials much more convenient and space-efficient than the traditional method of sand and cement.

Bricklayers working for Mezz Real Estate have found a big difference in how the blockwork construction fits together. Not only are they saving time when putting blocks together, but the whole process of building has changed using the thin joint system. Traditional blocks have to be gauged to match the brickwork. Not only does the gauge have to be correct but the level and plumb alongside has to be correct. The block manufacturer has given guidance and advice to Alex's company regarding the building process. Using the thin joint process bricklayers do not have to worry about the gauge as, along with the blocks, it can be cut and a rasp can be used to maintain the level.

Alex has saved a lot of time too – the adhesive bonding the joints initially sets within seven minutes, and sets at full strength in 20 minutes. Setting blockwork so quickly allows his company and his team of bricklayers to erect a single dwelling up to five times faster than if they were using traditional sand and cement block. Alex is thrilled with this system as his company has turned around the speed of producing domestic housing.

Work through the following questions to check your learning.

1 Which course on the thin joint blockwork requires traditional sand and cement?

a First

b Second

c Third

d Fourth

2 Which method of construction is not undertaken when using the thin joint system?

a Gauge

b Level

c Plumb

d Range

3 What size are the joints used in the thin joint blockwork system?

a 1mm

b 2mm

c 3mm

d 4mm

4 What is the correct height for stacking lightweight blocks?

a 2m

b As per the specification

c 4m

d As per manufacturer's instructions

5 The tool shown in this photo is used to maintain

a An angled cut

b A cut face

c A straight cut

d A mitred cut

6 Materials used for mortar in the thin joint system are

a Sand and cement

b Powder

c Sand and chippings

d Silicone powder

7 Powered mortar is mixed using a

a Hand held auger

b Half bag mixer

c Diesel mixer

d Dry silo mixer

8 Which type of joint finish is required on a thin joint system?

a Full on face, empty on rear

b Complete joint and flush

c Full on the rear and empty on the face

d Full and projecting

9 The full strength setting time for thin joint mortar is how many minutes?

a 5

b 10

c 15

d 20

10 Which two materials are used in the thin joint system and at the start of the blockwork?

a Sand and lime

b Sand and cement

c Sand and plaster

d Sand and chippings

11 What method of construction is undertaken to maintain level when using the thin joint system?

   a   Plumb using a plumb bob

   b   Square using a straight edge

   c   Rasping down using a rasp

   d   Measuring using a tape

12 When cutting a lightweight block, which two tools can be used?

   a   Straight edge and level

   b   Set square and masonry saw

   c   Brick hammer and goggles

   d   Line and pins

13 When loading out blocks, the correct procedure to use is

   a   Bonded stacks

   b   Un-bonded stacks

   c   Low level stacks

   d   High level stacks

14 A pocket level can be used to

   a   Plumb blocks

   b   Range blocks

   c   Check blocks are gauged

   d   Check blocks are straight

15 The mortar used for the thin joint system is sold in

   a   1 tonne bags

   b   25kg sealed bags

   c   50kg sealed bags

   d   100kg bags

16 When mixing mortar for the thin joint system, which material is added first?

   a   Powder

   b   Chippings

   c   Water

   d   Cement

17 Spreading the thin joint mortar is achieved by using a

   a   Hopper

   b   Pointing trowel

   c   Plastering trowel

   d   Gauging trowel

18 Pointing the mortar joint when using thin joint mortar can be achieved by using a

   a   Plastering hawk and trowel

   b   Pointing hawk and pointing trowel

   c   Trowel and small tool

   d   Margin trowel and hawk

19 Moving blocks using the thin joint mortar must be undertaken within how many minutes?

   a   5

   b   10

   c   15

   d   20

Chapter 4
Unit 204: Building solid walling, isolated and attached piers

In this chapter, we will look at how we build solid walling. Solid walling applies to masonry that has no cavity in the structural design and often refers to walls which are typically 215mm wide or greater. However, the term solid walling can also be applied to half-brick walling. A wall of this thickness is relatively weak on its own and is usually strengthened by adding piers. This chapter will therefore also consider how we construct piers, both those that are bonded into the wall (attached) and those that stand on their own (isolated).

By reading this chapter you will know how to:

1 Plan and select resources for practical tasks.
2 Erect solid walling to required specification.
3 Erect isolated and attached piers to required specification.

PREPARING FOR BUILDING SOLID WALLING

WHERE SOLID WALLS ARE USED

Solid walling will often be specified for use in free-standing walls such as boundary walls. Walls like this are typically built in one-brick walling bonds such as English or Flemish bond (for detailed descriptions see pages 154–155), which can resist high winds. Since a thicker wall has more weight, it's not so easy to push over.

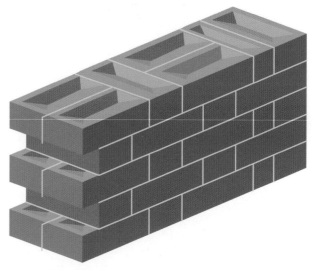

Solid walling (Flemish bond)

Retaining wall

A wall built to support or prevent the advance of a mass of earth or other material

A wall with greater weight will also be capable of resisting the force of soil behind it when it's required to function as a **retaining wall**. Retaining walls are carefully designed to perform their job and when built in brick can use variations of English and Flemish bonds to increase the thickness if required.

These days, retaining walls in brick are unlikely to exceed a thickness of 440mm (the length of two bricks). In fact, retaining walls are often designed using a combination of a skin of brick on the face of the wall, backed by concrete blocks laid flat to achieve the specified thickness.

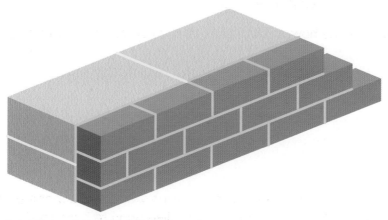

Retaining wall in brick and block

If a wall needs to be higher and thicker so as to retain more soil or other material, it is likely to be constructed using **reinforced** concrete or to use other methods which may be quicker to construct and can be more cost effective.

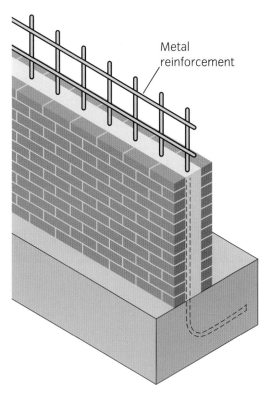

Reinforcement in a retaining wall

Reinforced

In concrete, strengthened by adding steel

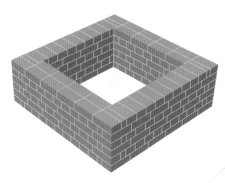

Inspection chamber in English bond

Inspection chamber

A masonry structure that allows inspection of services below ground level

INDUSTRY TIP

Inspection chambers were often referred to as 'manholes' in the past.

Stability

Resistance to movement or pressure

Inspection chambers can also be designed in solid walling to withstand the pressures of material surrounding them. They are often built in English bond since this has the greatest strength of any of the brick bonds.

Half-brick walls can also be described as solid walling when they are not built as part of a cavity wall. A wall of this thickness is obviously not as strong as the heavier walls described above and this is where the use of piers is valuable. Piers can be bonded or attached to a half-brick wall to increase its **stability**. When a pier is not attached to a wall we call it an isolated pier.

We will discuss how to build piers of both types later in this chapter.

GETTING READY TO BUILD

HEALTH AND SAFETY

Whenever we work on site or in a training workshop, our first priority has to be safety. On site we may be called upon to build solid walling in an excavation or be required to work on a scaffold at height, so we must be familiar with regulations relating to construction health and safety and the Work at Height Regulations 2005.

In the training workshop there are also many safety matters and risks we need to be aware of, including potential hazards related to the materials that we may use. Always take notice of COSHH (Control of Substances Hazardous to Health) statements and the safety guidance on products used in the workplace.

Risk assessments are important documents that help us to recognise hazards and give directions on how to make the workplace safer.

A worker consulting a risk assessment

Risk Assessment

Assessment carried out by: _____

Date assessment was carried out: _____

Date of next review: _____

Area/ activity	Hazard	Risk to (list persons)	Current precautions	Action	Action required by	Date for required action	Complete

A risk assessment form

The five main steps in writing a risk assessment are:

1 Identify actual or potential hazards.

2 Identify who might be at risk.

3 Assess how likely it is that the risk will cause an accident.

4 Design measures that will reduce the risk.

5 Monitor the risk to identify changes.

Applying risk assessments and maintaining high standards of health and safety is the responsibility of everyone working in construction. You must also make sure that you always use the correct PPE. Details about relevant safety standards and PPE that apply to building solid walling are in Chapter 1 and should be reviewed often.

ACTIVITY

Select a work task (for example, stacking out bricks) in your training workshop or place of work. Produce a table by hand or using a computer to include the five risk assessment steps and complete the table as a risk assessment for your chosen task.

INFORMATION ABOUT THE JOB

Before we can successfully build any wall, we first need to gather a range of information. One of the main methods of communicating information for any building activity is by means of drawings. A working drawing makes it possible to provide a great deal of information without having to use lots of writing.

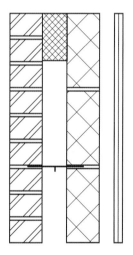

A working drawing

WORKING DRAWINGS

Architectural drawings are drawn according to a set of conventions, which include particular views (floor plan, elevations etc), sheet sizes and units of measurement. A range of symbols are used and also representations known as hatchings are used to signify a range of different materials. See Chapter 2, page 48, for examples of these.

When producing drawings, an architectural technician or a draughtsperson will draw a building to 'scale'. This means that we can represent large structures on a document that is much smaller and more manageable than the real thing. Scale is shown by using a **ratio**, such as 1 to 10. This would usually be written in the form '1:10' and means that if we wanted to draw a real wall that is 1m (or 1000mm) long, it would be shown as a drawing 100mm long. This is because 100mm is ¹⁄₁₀ of 1000mm.

If we didn't use scale we would have to draw buildings full size (called 1:1 scale). Imagine how big a full size drawing would have to be for a new football stadium. Obviously it would be impossible to produce or to use a drawing that big.

If we imagine that we are instructed to build a one-brick thick (215mm) boundary wall on a housing site, some of the following drawings will be needed. See Chapter 2, pages 49–51, for information on these and other drawings. The following table explains the use of different working drawings.

Ratio

The amount or proportion of one thing compared to another

A cross section of a cavity wall showing hatchings

Type of drawing	Description
Block plan 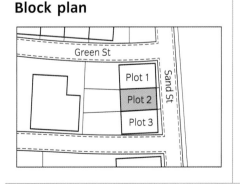	Usual scale 1:1250 or 1:2500. This will show us a bird's eye view of the whole site in relation to the area around it. It will usually show individual plots and road layouts on the site as a simple outline with few dimensions. It will show the external boundaries of the site where our boundary wall might be located.

Type of drawing	Description
Site plan 	Usual scale 1:200 or 1:500. This will give more detail of individual plots or a number of plots and will show the dimensions needed to position buildings correctly in accordance with the local authority planning requirements. It will also show the positions of drainage and other services and access roads and drives. It may show the position of trees and shrubs if they are required as part of the planning details. If the plot or plots are on the edge of the development, then a boundary wall will be included in the site plan.
General arrangement drawing 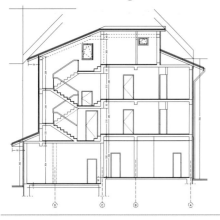	Usual scale 1:50, 1:100 or 1:200. This is sometimes used to show a single building element and what it should contain. For example, in the case of a boundary wall it could show an elevation of the wall with a decorative feature such as a course of contrasting bricks. Or the drawing could show the main elements of a structure such as the external walls, internal or partition walls, floor details, stairs and so on.
Sectional drawing 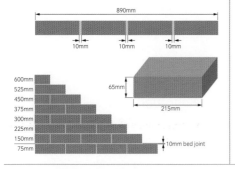	Usual scale 1:50 or 1:100. These are a slice or cut through a structure to give a clear view of details that could otherwise be hidden. For example, on a working drawing for a house, a sectional drawing could allow us to clearly see the layout of the stairs within the building. In the case of a boundary wall, a sectional drawing could show the depth of foundation required.
Assembly or detail drawings	Usual scales 1:1, 1:5 and 1:10. These are used to show all the information required to manufacture a particular component (such as a window frame or a brick to be used) or complex details in a design. They are unlikely to be used for a boundary wall, unless it has an unusual feature or detail in the design.

An important feature of the site plan is that it will often be used to show a site datum point or temporary bench mark (TBM). This is a reference point from which the correct finished floor level (FFL) and other important levels can be established. The bricklayer is responsible for building masonry to the correct height from the foundation to the FFL, so the datum should always be carefully checked. For more information on datums and benchmarks, see page 47 in Chapter 2.

Layout of drawings

When drawings are produced, they can be laid out in a number of ways. Two more common methods of presenting drawings are:

- orthographic projection
- isometric projection.

Orthographic projection is a drawing where the front elevation of a structure has the plan view directly below it. The side or end elevations are shown directly each side of the front elevation. The most commonly used type of orthographic projection is called 'first angle projection' (see Chapter 5, page 180, for an example). This method of drawing allows views of all elevations to be looked at in relation to each other to gain a good understanding of the overall layout of the structure.

A site datum

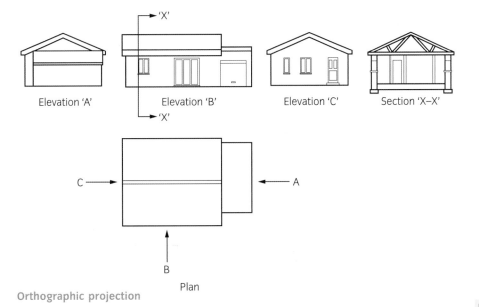

Elevation 'A'   Elevation 'B'   Elevation 'C'   Section 'X–X'

Plan

Orthographic projection

Isometric projection has the structure drawn at an angle with one corner represented as closer to the person viewing the drawing. Although it doesn't provide a true three-dimensional view (since it doesn't include **perspective**), it does provide a more 'realistic' view while maintaining accurate scaled dimensions on the drawing. In isometric projection, the vertical lines in the structure will be drawn at 90° to the horizontal baseline (or bottom edge of the page) and the

Perspective

The appearance of things as determined by their distance from the viewer

horizontal lines of the structure will be drawn at 30° to the horizontal on the page.

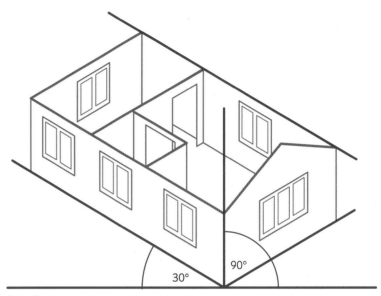

Base line

Isometric projection

OTHER INFORMATION SOURCES

As well as referring to drawings to provide us with necessary information for the job, we would also consult the specification and schedules related to the task in hand.

The specification is a contract document that gives us information about details that may not be shown on the drawing. For example the specification or 'spec' may give descriptions of materials including the type, size or quality required. It may also state the standard of work and finish required. In some cases it will state which **contractors** should be used for particular parts of the project.

A schedule is used to detail components, material types or fittings that are repeated throughout a job. For example, on a large site there may be a number of different house designs each having different door frames. A schedule would be used to show the door requirements for each type of house and would help avoid confusion.

These three documents (drawing, specification and schedule) should tie together in informing us about all the details we need to successfully complete the job. For more information on these types of documents, see Chapter 2.

Contractors

Workers or companies working to an agreement that is legally binding

Master Internal Door Schedule							
Ref:	Door size	S.O. width	S.O. height	Lintel type	FD30	Self closing	Floor level
D1	838 × 1981	900	2040	BOX	Yes	Yes	GROUND FLOOR
D2	838 × 1981	900	2040	BOX	Yes	Yes	GROUND FLOOR
D3	762 × 1981	824	2040	BOX	No	No	GROUND FLOOR
D4	838 × 1981	900	2040	N/A	Yes	No	GROUND FLOOR
D5	838 × 1981	900	2040	BOX	Yes	Yes	GROUND FLOOR
D6	762 × 1981	824	2040	BOX	Yes	Yes	FIRST FLOOR
D7	762 × 1981	824	2040	BOX	Yes	Yes	FIRST FLOOR
D8	762 × 1981	824	2040	N/A	Yes	No	FIRST FLOOR
D9	762 × 1981	824	2040	BOX	Yes	Yes	FIRST FLOOR
D10	762 × 1981	824	2040	N/A	No	No	FIRST FLOOR
D11	686 × 1981	748	2040	N/A	Yes	No	SECOND FLOOR
D12	762 × 1981	824	2040	BOX	Yes	Yes	SECOND FLOOR
D13	762 × 1981	824	2040	100 HD BOX	Yes	Yes	SECOND FLOOR
D14	686 × 1981	748	2040	N/A	No	No	SECOND FLOOR

Example of a schedule

SELECTING TOOLS

It's a good idea to make a list of the tools that will be required for the job before we start work. The tools needed to build solid walling can be split into three main groups.

- *Laying and finishing.* To build any wall we will need a trowel to lay the bricks or blocks, and for face brickwork, a pointing trowel and a jointer to provide a finish to the joints.

Trowel

Pointing trowel

Jointer

■ *Checking.* A tape measure is needed to set out and check dimensions, a spirit level to make sure the work is level and plumb, and a set of line and pins to align the bricks or blocks accurately.

Tape measure

Spirit level

Line and pins

■ *Cutting.* To cut the bricks or blocks accurately we will need a club (or lump) hammer and a brick bolster. A brick hammer and a scutch hammer (sometimes called a comb hammer) are used to trim and shape bricks or blocks.

Club hammer

Brick bolster

Ear defenders

Brick hammer

Scutch hammer

CUTTING MASONRY MATERIALS

When bricks or blocks need to be cut or shaped, we should always make sure that we use the correct PPE. Goggles or safety glasses are essential to protect our eyes from flying brick or block chips while cutting by hand or machine (such as a disc cutter). Protective gloves are also recommended. If we use mechanical means to cut masonry materials we would also use **ear defenders** and a dust mask as essential PPE.

Ear defenders

A means of personal protection from the harmful effects of noise

Never attempt to use or handle cutting machinery of any kind unless you are competent and authorised to do so. Being properly trained in using cutting machinery (in particular, how to safely change cutting discs in a disc cutter) will reduce the risk of serious injury to yourself and others working nearby.

When cutting by hand we need to take care in using and looking after the tools correctly and safely and to follow the correct work sequence.

Disc cutter

STEP 1 Make sure you are using the right PPE (safety glasses or goggles etc) and workers nearby are aware that you are cutting masonry materials.

STEP 2 Mark the position of the cut on the face, the opposite side and the bed of the brick with a pencil. For blocks, it is usually sufficient to mark the position of the cut on the face only, unless you prefer to mark it all around.

STEP 3 Placing the blade of the bolster slightly on the *waste* side of the pencil mark, strike the brick lightly but firmly with the club hammer. For blocks you will need to use several more powerful and decisive strikes across the full face of the block.

STEP 4 Now do the same on the opposite side of the brick or block. For blocks, if you've used sufficient strength in your blows the block should break as desired.

STEP 5 For bricks, turn the brick so that the face is uppermost again and strike the last blow. If the strength of the blow is adjusted correctly, this should complete the operation.

STEP 6 If the brick or block doesn't break as desired, repeat from Step 3 until a clean break is achieved.

Trauma

An event or situation that causes great distress and disruption

The aim is to produce clean, sharp arrises (edges), especially on the face side of the cut brick or block. This will ensure a satisfactory appearance in the finished wall.

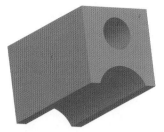

A well-cut facing brick

PRODUCTIVITY

The steps detailed above are similar to a method statement. This is a document written to clearly list the steps to successfully complete a particular job. On site there will be many method statements written as guidance for a range of work tasks which will be available for workers to consult. Using a method statement is one way to improve efficiency and safety in our work and to make sure levels of productivity are as high as possible.

Safety

When we link a method statement with a risk assessment, we make sure our work activities are as safe as possible. This also supports productivity – when a worker is injured at work, besides the **trauma** it causes for that individual, there are often delays and holdups caused while an accident is investigated and measures are put in place to make sure it doesn't happen again.

HSE inspector

Correct materials

Another way to keep levels of productivity high is by making sure we have the correct quantity and type of materials available before we start work. Calculating quantities of masonry components is easier if we remember the number of bricks and blocks in 1m² of half-brick walling. (Don't forget that you would need to double these figures for one-brick thick walling.)

- There are 60 bricks to 1m².

- There are 10 blocks to 1m².

If we remember these two figures, then all we need to do is to work out the area of the face of our wall in square metres and multiply the result by 10 or 60, depending on which material quantity we want to calculate. By now, you will know that we calculate *area* in m² by multiplying the height of a wall by its length. By including an amount for waste (say 5%) we make sure we don't run out of materials and avoid wasting time.

The specification gives details about the required materials for all construction tasks including solid walling. If the wrong type, size or colours of materials are used, the work may have to be redone (which creates unnecessary expense) and productivity will suffer.

Protecting your work

A key point to consider when thinking about productivity is the matter of protecting our materials and completed work from damage. Protecting bricks and blocks is simple but important. By covering materials (with tarpaulin or sheet polythene) when they are delivered to site and when they are set out and stacked ready for use, we prevent them from being contaminated or discoloured.

In addition, if bricks and blocks are allowed to get wet they will be difficult to lay and problems like efflorescence can develop at a later date.

Efflorescence disfigures the appearance of brickwork by leaving a white powder deposited on the surface of the wall. Although this can be removed by brushing with a stiff brush, it's better to avoid the problem by maintaining good practice in the first place.

Protecting our completed work is also important since there are many other construction operatives who will perform tasks near our work area that could damage our work. Once again, the simple matter of covering our work with a protective material like polythene may prevent damaged or contaminated work having to be rebuilt.

INDUSTRY TIP

When you cover materials, always make sure that the covering is secured strongly enough to not be blown away.

Covered materials

Efflorescence

Sustainable

Capable of being maintained without exhausting natural resources or causing severe damage to the environment

ACTIVITY

Look at brickwork in buildings as you travel around. See if you can identify some examples of efflorescence and take a picture on your mobile phone (if you have one). Discuss with your tutor or supervisor what could have been done to prevent it.

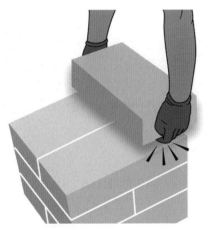

Worker trapping fingers

Components

Basic parts of something more complex

FUNCTIONAL SKILLS

Make enquiries of a local builder's merchant by phone or online and find out the approximate weight of dense concrete blocks. How much heavier is one concrete block compared to one concrete brick?

Work on this activity can support FM2: (1) and (2).

Removing waste

Finally, always keep a tidy work space and dispose of waste and rubble frequently. Moving waste from the work space to a designated site waste disposal area reduces risks of injury and increases productivity. Aim to support recycling initiatives on site so that you contribute to **sustainability**.

Segregated waste disposal area on site

PREPARING TO BUILD SOLID WALLING

STACKING MATERIALS

Remember that bricks and blocks are heavy **components** and need to be moved and handled with care. This is especially the case with dense concrete blocks. It can be very easy to trap your fingers between heavy blocks when stacking them one on top of the other.

If blocks are handled roughly they can develop cracks in them that are not easy to see. When the block is lifted at the ends it may break into two or more heavy pieces, which can fall and injure an operative's legs or feet. Careful handling is very important.

Stacks of bricks can be positioned carefully with two rows of six bricks in each layer with up to 12 layers in each stack. Stacks can be higher, but get advice from a more experienced bricklayer if you're not sure.

Brick stacks

Stacks of blocks are best arranged flat rather than **on edge**, six to eight layers high unless the base on which they are stacked is firm and level. If the base is suitable, the stacks can be higher, but it's a good idea to ask for advice from someone more experienced.

There will be occasions when materials for solid walling are stacked along the edge of an excavation trench ready to build work below ground level. Always make sure the ground supporting stacks of materials on the edge of a trench is firm and level. You may have to spend some time removing soft or loose material before starting the stacking out process.

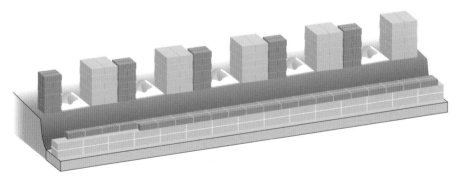

Materials correctly stacked along the edge of a trench

Pay attention to guidance provided by manufacturers and to health and safety regulations that apply to handling and positioning masonry components and materials competently and safely.

Tools for moving bricks manually, such as brick tongs or brick clamps, are designed to comfortably carry bricks in multiples of six. This helps to minimise the risk of damage to the materials and injury to the operative. Dense concrete blocks are best moved one at a

On edge
When bricks are turned so that they are resting on their face

A block stack

ACTIVITY

Check the Health and Safety Executive (HSE) website and type 'manual handling' in the search bar. Write a short report on the guidance given about how much weight a worker can safely lift.

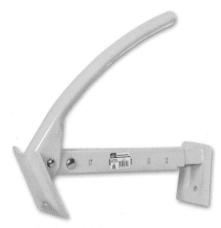

Brick tongs

time if moved by hand, and remember to use the kinetic lifting technique outlined in Chapter 1, pages 18–19. Whenever possible, arrange to move all heavy masonry components using mechanical handling methods such as a forklift or crane.

Remember that the distance that materials are placed from the wall you are going to build is also important for efficient working. Stacks of materials and spot boards for mortar should be placed around 600mm from the face line of the wall, but some bricklayers prefer to increase the working space between the materials and the wall to around 900mm.

SETTING OUT WALL POSITIONS

When setting out a solid wall, make sure that your first courses of brickwork or blockwork are level, to the correct overall dimensions and to the required line.

To set out a wall to the required line, profiles are used. These are constructed from timber at each end of a foundation trench. They allow the line of the wall to be indicated by nails or a saw cut accurately positioned on them. A string line can then be attached to the nail or positioned in the saw cut to show the face line of the wall along the length of the trench.

Batter board
Stake
AA
BB
Peg
String line also the building line
Diagonals
Nails
CC
DD

Timber profile with string line attached

Once the string line is correctly positioned and is pulled tight, use your spirit level to plumb down from the string line to the foundation and transfer the face line of the wall to the foundation concrete. The steps for setting out like this would be:

STEP 1 Spread a thin **screed** of mortar on the foundation concrete stretching from the corner, along the line of the wall, about 400mm–600mm long. (Judge the position by eye to line it up below the string line.)

STEP 2 Carefully position the spirit level alongside the string line, allowing a slight gap. (Allowing the spirit level to touch the line risks moving the line and losing accuracy.) Position the level at one end of the screed.

STEP 3 Adjust the spirit level until it is plumb. (You may need to brace the level to stop it moving about. Some bricklayers use their trowel held at an angle to steady the spirit level.)

STEP 4 Carefully make a small mark in the screed at the bottom of the level with the tip of the trowel. (Make sure the mark is the same side of the level as the string line.)

STEP 5 Now position the spirit level at the other end of the screed and repeat Steps 3 and 4.

STEP 6 Finally, lay the spirit level on the screed using it as a straight edge to join up the two marks. Make a line along the edge of the level with the tip of the trowel.

Now we have a line alongside which we can lay our first bricks or blocks, which should correspond to the string line on the profiles. Make sure you lay the bricks or blocks to the correct side of the line.

Screed

A mixture of cement, sand and water applied to the concrete foundation to give a smooth surface finish

SETTING OUT THE BOND

Setting out bricks or blocks 'dry' (without mortar) is a useful way of establishing the correct bond within the given dimensions for any type of masonry construction. Using this method will help you decide whether you need to cut bricks and blocks or **reverse** the bond in order to make things fit within the design dimensions.

Reverse bond

To change the direction of bricks or blocks so that there is a stretcher brick (or block) at one end of the wall and a header brick at the other end of the wall

Broken bond

The use of part bricks to make good a bonding pattern where full bricks will not fit in

INDUSTRY TIP

When a lot of cut bricks or blocks are needed, it's a good idea to spend some time cutting a large number at once. This can speed up the building process by allowing your bricklaying to flow without stopping for cutting as each course is laid.

FUNCTIONAL SKILLS

Produce a ruler-assisted sketch showing 'broken bond' in two courses of Stretcher bond brickwork. The first course should show a half-bat in the centre. You must determine how the cuts will be arranged in the second course.

Work on this activity can support EM 1.2.1C and FM2: (6F).

If bricks or blocks are cut in order to establish the specified bond, this is known as **broken bond**. The cuts in broken bond will be positioned so as to create an even appearance on the face of the wall. If a window or door is to be built into the structure, the cuts could be placed below them. If no openings are to be included in the elevation, then the cuts would be located as close to the centre of the wall as possible.

Broken bond

Solid walling can be constructed in a range of bonding patterns. If the wall is constructed in half-brick walling then the bond will usually be Stretcher bond (a half-bond arrangement in which the bricks overlap by half a brick length). Similar principles apply to block walling that is half-bonded.

For a wall constructed in one-brick walling, there are four main bonds that can be used. They are:

- English bond

- Flemish bond

- English Garden Wall bond

- Flemish Garden Wall bond.

These are all Quarter bond arrangements (in other words the bricks overlap by ¼ of a brick length). See pages 154–155 for more information and illustrations.

ERECTING SOLID WALLING TO THE GIVEN SPECIFICATION

Having completed your preparation and setting-out stages, it's now time to build your solid walling. Imagine you are instructed to build a length of boundary wall in one-brick thick masonry. Follow the construction process from the foundation up.

SETTING THE LEVEL

We have already discussed the method used to set out the *line* of the wall accurately onto the foundation concrete. But how do we establish the correct *level* for the wall? Previously we mentioned how some drawings provide us with a datum which is used as a reference to establish important levels in a structure. The site datum or temporary bench mark (TBM) is used by the site engineer to provide convenient additional datum points, usually in the form of timber pegs which you can refer to.

Your wall will have pegs set up at each corner or end point, the top of which will correspond to a set number of courses of brick or block from the foundation concrete. In the case of a building such as a house, the top of the peg will correspond to finished floor level (FFL) which is usually the same as damp proof course (DPC) level.

Since the peg or datum is set up near the corner or end point of our wall, it's easy for the bricklayer to place a spirit level on the top of the peg and use a tape measure or gauge rod to measure down from the spirit level to the top of the foundation concrete.

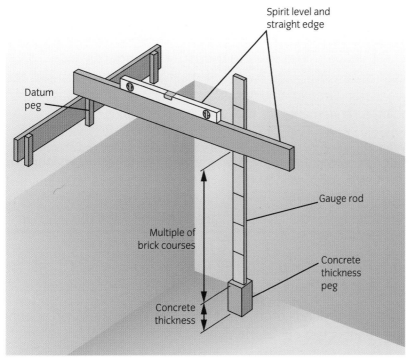

Measuring down with a gauge rod from a spirit level

INDUSTRY TIP

If the spirit level is too short to reach from the peg to the wall position in the trench, the bricklayer can place it on a straight edge to extend the range. It's a good idea to fix the level to the straight edge with some adhesive tape.

If the dimension is not correct, you can decide what needs to be done to build the masonry up to the correct level. For example, it may be decided to lay split bricks as a first course or use a thicker bed for one or two courses at the bottom of the wall.

One course of split bricks laid at the bottom of the wall

Once the level details have been established, you can build **quoins** or **racked ends** to the correct height and use a string line to build the masonry between.

CHECKING THE BOND

All construction trades work to **industrial standards** and when building solid walling the bricklayer must take care to maintain the relevant standards at all times. It's important to be familiar with the bonding arrangements for half- and Quarter bonds that are commonly used.

Half-bond is straightforward: we are required to lap each course of bricks by the dimension of the header face of a brick (102.5mm). This will result in the perps (or cross joints) in any course being lined up with the centre of the stretcher face of the bricks in the courses above and below them.

There are many different Quarter bond arrangements, but let's focus on the ones we've already mentioned in the previous section.

Study the illustrations of these bonds to see how the Quarter bond arrangement is laid out at the quoins.

- *English bond.* This is the strongest of all brick bonds arranged as **alternate** courses of stretchers and headers. Since each course of headers is laid across the width of the wall there are no straight joints in the bonding arrangement which could create weak points.

Quoins

The vertical external angles (corners) in walling

Racked ends

The ends of walls built without a corner to produce a vertical 'stopped' end

Industrial standards

A universally adopted definition of work methods

ACTIVITY

Produce a ruler-assisted sketch of an elevation of Quarter bond brickwork. Select two of the bonds to draw and sketch two elevations, six courses high, to your desired length.

Alternate

Interchanging repeatedly

English bond

- *Flemish bond.* Arranged as alternating headers and stretchers in each course. This is considered to be a more decorative bonding arrangement. In each course the centre of the header faces line up with the centre of the stretcher faces in the courses above and below.

- *English Garden Wall bond.* The arrangement consists of three, five or seven courses of stretchers to one course of headers. Although this is not as strong as English bond, it is suitable for garden walls (hence the name) and gives an acceptable standard of finish on both sides of the wall.

- *Flemish Garden Wall bond.* In this bond there is a pattern of three or five stretchers followed by one header repeated along the length of each course. The header face in a course should be centred above the middle stretcher of each group of three in the course below.

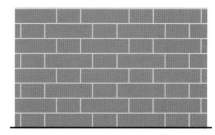
Flemish bond

English Garden Wall bond

Flemish Garden Wall bond

OUR HOUSE

Take a look in 'Our House'. What bonding arrangements for the brickwork can you see on show there?

Each of these Quarter bonds requires a **Queen Closer** to be laid next to the header at the quoin of each course. If the wall has no return corner, then the closer will be placed next to the header in alternate courses.

In maintaining standards, remember these key points:

- Avoid cutting bricks when setting out the bond.

- Keep perps to 10mm if possible – although there is an allowable **tolerance** of +/– 3mm, large perps spoil the appearance, especially in Quarter bond walling.

Queen Closer
A brick split along its length to produce a cut of 46mm

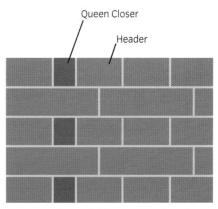
A Queen Closer laid next to a header brick

Tolerance
Allowable variation between the specified measurement and the actual measurement

Poorly bonded Quarter bond brickwork

- Remember – the width of a Queen Closer is not simply half the size of a header face. It should be cut to a width of 46mm to create the correct overlap.

- In long walls Quarter bond can be difficult to maintain if you don't take care. Perps can 'wander' so that the Quarter bond overlap is reduced.

DAMP PROOF COURSE

A damp proof course (DPC) is always installed in a structure that has a living or working area, since damp conditions are damaging to people's health and also cause long-term damage to the contents and **fabric** of a building.

A DPC is rarely specified for a boundary wall. However, the installation of a DPC might be needed if excessive moisture is present and could cause continuous saturation of the masonry. A permanently wet wall will be more likely to suffer frost damage when conditions become cold enough. Since water held in the wall will expand when it freezes, the wall can literally be pushed apart.

Let's consider the different types of damp proof course. There are two main types: rigid and flexible. There is a third type called semi-rigid which involves coating structural elements with hot **asphalt** to form a continuous membrane. This is mainly used for damp proofing underground sections of a building such as a basement, and would not usually be used in masonry.

Fabric

In this context, the structure or framework

FUNCTIONAL SKILLS

Find some online images of frost damaged masonry. Write a short description of how the appearance of the masonry is affected.

Work on this activity can support FICT2: (4A) and FE2:3 (A).

Asphalt

A thick, sticky, black mixture of petroleum tars

Section of basement walling being tanked with asphalt

THE CITY & GUILDS TEXTBOOK

RIGID DPC

Examples of materials for rigid DPC are engineering brick and slate, which were used before the introduction of flexible DPCs. Some advantages and disadvantages related to using these materials are listed below.

Material	Advantages	Disadvantages
Slate	■ Natural material. ■ Relatively easy to install.	■ Heavy to transport in bulk. ■ Will crack if there is movement in the masonry. ■ Expensive.
Engineering brick	■ Very durable and long-lasting. ■ Can be used as a decorative feature. ■ Good for garden or boundary walls.	■ Heavy to transport. ■ Needs space for storage. ■ Relatively expensive.

FLEXIBLE DPC

Examples of materials for flexible DPCs are polythene, pitch polymer and bitumen felt. Some advantages and disadvantages related to using these materials are listed in the table on the next page.

Stacks of flexible DPC materials

INDUSTRY TIP

There must be a minimum of two courses of engineering brick to form an effective DPC.

Material	Advantages	Disadvantages
Polythene	▪ Light and easy to install. ▪ Low cost. ▪ Easy to store. ▪ Suitable for stepped damp proof courses. ▪ Produced in a range of sizes.	▪ Can be punctured.
Pitch polymer	▪ Capable of withstanding high loads (for multi-storey structures). ▪ Easy to install. ▪ Produced in a range of sizes.	▪ More costly than polythene. ▪ Prone to distort if not stored properly.
Bitumen felt	▪ Relatively easy to install. ▪ Produced in a range of sizes.	▪ More costly than polythene. ▪ Prone to distort if not stored carefully. ▪ May crack if unrolled in cold weather.

When installing a flexible DPC it is always good practice to lay the material on a thin bed of mortar. This protects the DPC material from the risk of being punctured by hardened mortar, which may project from the top of the masonry in the course below.

INDUSTRY TIP

With a thin bed of mortar under the DPC and further mortar above the DPC to lay the bricks on, remember to watch your gauge. Take care not to build the joint up too much.

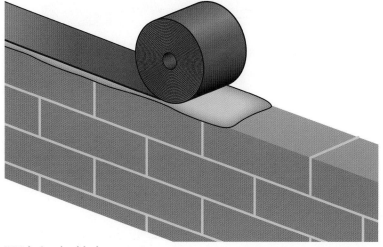

DPC being bedded on mortar

If a roll of DPC is too short to completely cover a section of wall, an additional roll should be laid to overlap the first section by a minimum of 100mm.

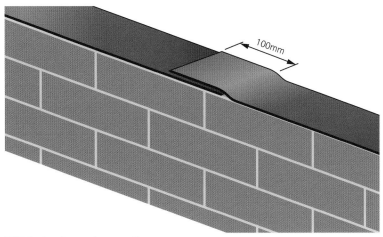

DPC being lapped correctly

An exception to this is when wider DPC is used. Then the overlap should be the same as the width of the DPC being used. So, 150mm wide DPC will have an overlap of 150mm.

DPC IN USE

So, what type of DPC would be suitable for use in a boundary wall?

If we were to use one of the flexible DPCs, we would create a weak point in the bed joint where the DPC was installed since mortar will not bond to any of the flexible materials listed. Something like a very strong wind putting sideways pressure (lateral force) on the wall could cause it to fail at this weak point and push it over.

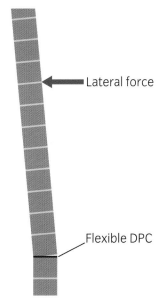

How sideways pressure could fracture the structure at the DPC

ACTIVITY

Write down what other occurrences could put sideways or lateral pressure on a boundary wall (eg accidental occurrences).

However, rigid DPC materials *will* bond to mortar and, in the case of engineering brick, the DPC will form part of the overall masonry bonding arrangement. This will serve to maintain the strength of the wall while at the same time providing a barrier to moisture.

DPC prevents rising damp caused by capillary attraction

INCREASING STRENGTH

Solid walling in brick or block is very strong in *compression* (when something is crushing the wall) but not so good in *tension* (when something is bending or pulling the wall).

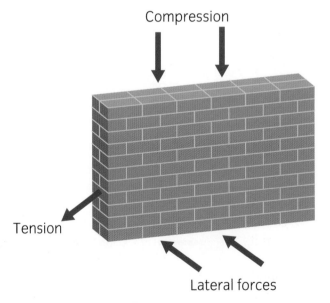

Forces in action on a wall

Reinforcement

A support that steadies or strengthens something else

If there are conditions that could place bending forces on the wall, the design may call for a means of **reinforcement** of the masonry. This means that the bricklayer will be required to build a strengthening component into the wall.

Reinforcement can be achieved in a number of ways, but the most common method is to build steel mesh into the horizontal bed joint of the walling at specified positions.

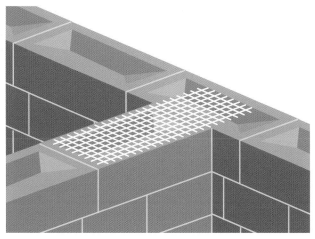

Expanded metal lathing in a bed joint of masonry

This mesh is known as expanded metal lathing (EML) and is usually treated to resist corrosion by galvanising (applying a coating of zinc during manufacture). This type of reinforcement is available in a range of widths to suit various thicknesses of solid walling.

There are occasions when reinforcement will be installed vertically in solid walling. The reason for this has already been mentioned briefly on page 137. When solid walling is specified as a retaining wall it will be required to resist sideways (or lateral) pressures. If it is expected that strong lateral pressures will be applied to a wall, then vertical reinforcement could be included into the design to enable the structure to do its job.

One way of installing vertical reinforcement in a wall is to build it using a variation of Flemish bond called Quetta bond. Study the illustration to see how this works.

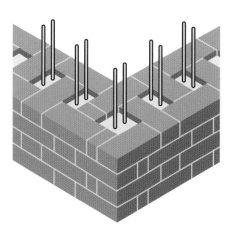

Quetta bond walling with reinforcement bars

DECORATIVE FEATURES

A boundary or garden wall consisting of large areas of plain brickwork can have its appearance improved if the design includes decorative features. Using coloured mortar is one way to add interest to the overall appearance of a stretch of solid walling. In order to keep consistency of colour throughout the job, it's better to specify ready-mixed mortar to avoid variations in colour which can occur if colouring agents are added to the mix on site.

To add even greater detail and interest, there are many different designs of brick panels and bonding arrangements that can be specified. A high standard in preparing and setting out the decorative work is needed if improvement to the appearance is to be achieved.

Coloured ready mix being delivered to site

A Soldier course

Let's discuss some common decorative features.

1 One of the most common decorative features is a Soldier course. This consists of bricks laid on end with the stretcher face showing. A contrasting brick can be used to add to the decorative appearance and the bricks can be set to project a small distance from the face line of the main wall to add more detail.

When laying a Soldier course, it's important to take care in plumbing and levelling each brick throughout the course since inaccuracies in individual bricks are easy to see and will spoil the finished job. To maintain standards of accuracy, a small spirit level such as a boat level is used.

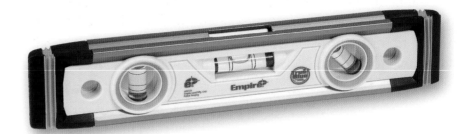

Boat level

Coping

A masonry addition that protects the top of the wall from poor weather

INDUSTRY TIP

Since the top of a wall is fully exposed to the effects of the weather, a brick on edge coping needs to be built using hard, frost-resistant bricks.

2 A free-standing boundary wall will need some protection from rain penetration at the top of the wall. This is often referred to as 'weathering' a wall and is provided by a **coping**, which can be constructed in a number of ways. One way to arrange for a coping and a decorative feature at the same time is to lay a course of brick on edge. The bricks are laid on edge with the stretcher face uppermost. This type of coping can be used on walls greater than one-brick thickness by bonding the brick on edge (using Stretcher bond) across the top of the wall.

Bonded brick on edge coping

Looking at 'Our House', can you identify any areas where decorative brick features could be included? Which ones would you choose and why?

In brick on edge coping, care is needed to make sure that the bricks are laid accurately to the line to avoid the appearance of **undulations** along the top of the wall. Some bricklayers use two lines – one at the face of the wall to maintain level and line and another at the rear of the brick on edge, just to make sure that the rear arris of the brick is accurately levelled. (Since bricks can vary slightly in length, we can't line in both front and back edges of a single brick on edge.)

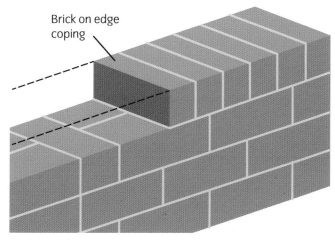

Brick on edge coping

Brick on edge coping

3 Some coping designs require the brick on edge to be laid on a **tile creasing**. This is formed by laying two courses of concrete or clay tiles, half-bonded and bedded in mortar. Since the tiles will form an overhang on either side of the wall, they allow rainwater to run off the coping away from the face of the wall. This provides both a functional and decorative feature to the wall.

Note: a specified coping may not use any bricks at all. Instead the specification may call for copings made of concrete or stone, made to suitable dimensions and shapes so that an overhang is formed either side of the wall. This is to allow water to be guided away from the face of the wall.

Set out a row of 10 bricks side by side on the training workshop floor (without mortar and positioned as headers) and line up one end of the bricks using a straight edge. Discuss with someone else how much they vary and measure the difference between the largest and the smallest.

Work on this activity can support FE2:1 (B) and (D).

Undulation

A gentle rising and falling

Brick on edge coping

A masonry addition that protects the top of the wall from poor weather, where the bricks are laid on edge with the stretcher face uppermost

Check the website of a local or national builder's merchant and look for stone and concrete copings. Make a note of the number of different sizes and designs.

Tile creasing

Two courses of concrete or clay tiles, half-bonded and bedded in mortar

A tile creasing

Band coursing

4 A Band course is formed by creating 'bands' of face brickwork (in contrasting brick colours or projecting courses) at various levels on an elevation of a structure.

The bands can be a number of courses high according to the specified design. By selecting a suitable colour of brick, the band courses can appear subtle or bold depending on the desired effect.

JOINTING

'Jointing' describes the process of producing a finish to the bed and perp joints as the work proceeds. 'Pointing' is a different process which involves raking out the mortar while it's still soft and re-filling the joints at a later date. This allows for a coloured mortar to be used or for a specialist joint to be formed which may be too time consuming to produce at the time of building.

Whatever type of solid walling we may build, if it is classified as 'face work' (or 'best brick' as older bricklayers refer to it), we will be required to produce a joint finish. There are a number of factors that will affect the choice of joint for our wall.

- The **durability** of the chosen joint.

- The time required to produce a satisfactory result.

- The appearance required as a design feature.

Let's consider how these factors apply to a number of joint finishes.

Durability

Capable of withstanding wear and tear or decay

Type of joint	Description
Half-round joint	Often referred to as 'tooled', this is probably the most commonly used joint. It is a joint finish that can be produced quite quickly and has the advantage of disguising irregularities in the arris of the brick. Since the action of ironing or tooling the joint presses the mortar against the arris of each brick, the possibility of gaps being left in the joint is reduced and the masonry has greater resistance to the effects of poor weather.
Recessed joint	Also produced as the work progresses. This type of joint is formed by using a purpose-made tool to remove the mortar from the joints to a maximum depth of 4mm. The tool can be a simple timber block cut to the right shape on site, or it can be a wheeled tool often referred to as a chariot raker. To form a satisfactory recessed joint, the bricklayer must make sure that all joints are completely full as laying proceeds. This joint should only be used with hard bricks that are frost resistant since moisture can stand in the recess on the horizontal arris of the brick.

Type of joint	Description
Weather struck joint	Formed by shaping the joint with a trowel (preferably a pointing trowel) so that it slopes to allow rain water to run off it. The top of the joint is set back from the face slightly and the bottom of the joint remains flush with the brick below. The perps are also angled with the left side of the joint sloped in slightly. As the name suggests, this joint is used where brickwork is in exposed situations and gives the masonry good protection from the effects of poor weather.
Flush joint	Often used where a more **rustic** appearance is required. It is produced by smoothing and compacting the mortar with a hardwood timber block as the work progresses. The disadvantage is that it is difficult to achieve a weather-tight finish without giving the joint the appearance of being wider than it actually is. Also referred to as a full joint.

There are many points that must be considered during construction of solid walling if we are to produce a piece of work that conforms to the relevant industrial standards. It is therefore very important that we regularly check that our work conforms to the working drawing and that it meets the specification.

A good bricklayer will have the habit of checking that the correct materials are in place before staring work. The materials should also be checked for damage before using them. Preparing for a work task properly will save time and will assist in meeting time limits set by site work programmes.

As work proceeds, there should be constant checking for accuracy in levelling, plumbing and gauging the work. The mortar joint specified should be completed to a high standard since this is the 'finish' of the job and will affect the appearance and durability of the solid wall.

If problems become obvious during construction (perhaps with mistakes in measurements on a drawing), always report the problem to your supervisor or line manager. They have the responsibility to make decisions on what to do. If alterations to the work become necessary the supervisor may think it's a good idea to put a time limit in place for completing the alterations, in order to keep to the work programme.

Carrying on and ignoring the problem could result in faults that will be expensive to put right later on and will affect your reputation and the reputation of the company you work for.

Rustic

Having a rough or textured appearance

INDUSTRY TIP

You may hear half-round joints being referred to as 'bucket handle' joints. This is because years ago, the handles of metal buckets were the right shape to use in producing a half-round joint.

Bricklayer checking work

BUILDING ISOLATED AND ATTACHED PIERS TO THE GIVEN SPECIFICATION

ISOLATED PIERS

Isolated piers are built separate from other masonry structures and are often used in situations such as gated entrances on a drive or pathway. If the pier is built in 1½ or 2 brick thickness (or more), it has the advantage of allowing reinforcement (such as steel rods or bars surrounded by concrete) to be introduced within the hollow centre. The pier can then support the weight of a heavy gate.

Isolated piers can bear the weight of a heavy gate

Purpose-made hinge support brackets for the gate can be built into the bed joints of the pier as work progresses. The bricklayer will need to take care to install the brackets perfectly plumb one above the other so that the gate will operate satisfactorily. The brackets can be spaced to suit the hinge positions on the gate, to allow for later installation.

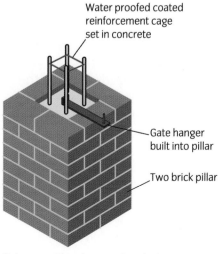

Water proofed coated reinforcement cage set in concrete

Gate hanger built into pillar

Two brick pillar

Gate mounting lugs or brackets

Isolated piers can also be used to support an arch spanning an opening. Arches will be discussed in Chapter 6.

The pier is set at the correct level using methods similar to those already described for solid walling. A datum can be provided in a position that is convenient for a bricklayer to refer to when setting out the pier. Establishing the correct position for the face line of a pier can be accomplished by the use of profiles – again using similar methods to those used for solid walling (see page 150).

The bonding arrangements already discussed can be used in building isolated piers (with the exception of the garden wall bonds). In a two-brick square pier, if we were to use Stretcher bond (half-bond), a course in the front elevation of the pier would show two stretchers side by side and the side or end elevations would show two headers with a stretcher in between.

A two brick Stretcher bond pier

Using the Quarter bond arrangements of Flemish or English bond would make it necessary to perform a great deal of cutting in each course to bond the pier correctly. Study the illustrations of two-brick square piers in Flemish bond and English bond to see how this is the case.

ACTIVITY

Try setting out the bond for some piers 'dry' in the training workshop. See if you can work out the bond for a 1½ brick square pier in English bond.

Brick pier in Flemish bond

Brick pier in English bond

ADDING DECORATIVE FEATURES

Weather-proofing used on a pier is usually referred to as a cap or capping (as opposed to a coping on a solid wall). The capping can also be used to provide a decorative feature such as a tile creasing under a plain, bonded or mitred brick on edge. Just as with solid walling, the top of a pier can be finished with materials other than brick. Capping can be specified in stone or concrete which also gives opportunities for providing additional decorative features if desired.

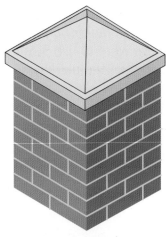

Concrete capping

Other decorative features such as a Band course can be incorporated into the elevations of a pier to enhance appearance and add interest.

Maintaining standards when building piers requires the bricklayer to pay very close attention to plumb. In a square or rectangular pier or pillar there will be eight plumbing points to control. Some bricklayers select one corner as a 'control' point which is carefully plumbed on both faces of the corner. The other corners are then set by measurement from the control corner with occasional use of the spirit level to check vertical alignment as the work progresses.

The following step by steps show how a bricklayer can use one corner of a pier to control the other corners.

STEP 1 Plumb up both sides of the corner chosen to 'control' the pier.

STEP 2 Level and measure from the 'control' corner in one direction.

STEP 3 Then level and measure in the other direction from the same point.

Whatever method is preferred, great care in plumbing, levelling and gauging is necessary to produce a job that looks good and conforms to the specification. Just as with solid walling, a good bricklayer makes regular checks for quality so as to avoid expensive and time consuming adjustments or the need to rebuild the job.

ATTACHED PIERS

Unlike isolated piers, attached piers are not free-standing and are used in a structure or wall to add strength or reinforcement. The term 'attached' means that the pier is bonded into the main section of masonry following the specified bonding arrangement.

Some typical situations where attached piers could be used are:

- A garage wall built in half-brick walling. The attached piers would be incorporated into the wall at intervals of no more than 3m and will usually be included at the end of the wall to provide a solid fixing point for a door. (The dimensions of a pier at this location may be increased to take the weight of a door.)

- Low level boundary walls which are built in thinner masonry. By adding attached piers it can make them more **economical** to build.

- A boundary wall which needs reinforcement because of its height. Even walls built in one-brick thick walling may need additional support in the form of attached piers, if built above 1.8m in height.

When bonding attached piers into face brickwork, the bonding arrangement must be set out so as to maintain the specified bonded appearance of the face of the wall. Study the examples of bonding arrangements to see how this works.

An attached pier

Economical

Using the minimum of resources necessary for effectiveness

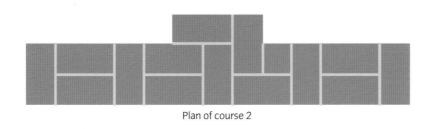

Plan of course 2

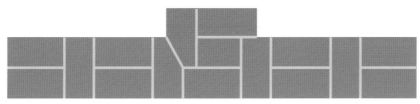

Plan of course 1

Different bonding arrangements

Case Study: Dave

Dave's uncle has asked him to build a new garden wall to replace a crumbling frost-damaged one. Dave goes to look at the job to work out a price for materials. He decides to reduce the labour costs since it is a job for family.

Dave explains to his uncle that the wall could be built in half-brick walling but then he would have to include attached piers to strengthen it and it wouldn't look as good from the neighbour's side. He decides it would be best to build the wall in Flemish Garden Wall bond. It's strong enough and will look good viewed from either side.

After working out the quantities of materials needed, Dave gives the list to his uncle to place an order.

When the materials have arrived, Dave starts the job on his weekend off. At lunch time things have gone well, but it looks like there won't be enough bricks to complete the job. Dave wishes he had been on hand to check the quantities of materials when they were delivered.

When he counts the number of bricks on site, he's surprised to find that the amount he told his uncle to order *has* been delivered.

Dave realises his mistake. When he had worked out the quantity of bricks, he'd calculated 60 bricks per 1m², when in actual fact a one-brick thick wall has 120 bricks per 1m².

Dave tells his uncle that it looks like he'll be back next weekend to finish the job.

Work through the following questions to check your learning.

1 How many blocks are there in 1m²?

   a 8

   b 10

   c 12

   d 15

2 The point from which wall levels are transferred is a

   a Starting point

   b Datum

   c Temporary fixed point

   d Solid location

3 The strongest brick bond is

   a Flemish

   b English Garden Wall

   c Flemish Garden Wall

   d English

4 A building line would be found on which **one** of the following drawings?

   a Block plan

   b Detail drawing

   c Site plan

   d Assembly drawing

5 A sectional drawing shows

   a The site split into sections

   b A slice or cut through a structure

   c A drawing produced by a section or department of a construction company

   d A drawing showing only elevations of a structure

6 The most commonly used type of orthographic projection is

   a Right angle

   b First angle

   c Correct angle

   d Third angle

7 A schedule is used to list

   a Rest breaks on site

   b The type of drawings required for the job

   c Components, material types or fittings repeated throughout a job

   d A bricklayer's hours of work

8 What does the abbreviation FFL mean?

   a First floor level

   b Fast finish liquid

   c Front feature leaf

   d Finished floor level

9 When setting out the face line of a solid wall, the string line is attached to the

   a Edgings

   b Profiles

   c Boards

   d Frames

10 To establish the best bonding arrangement in a solid wall it is helpful to set out the bricks or blocks

   a Slowly

   b By eye

   c Dry

   d By yourself

11 Broken bond in solid walling should be located

   a   At the ends of the wall

   b   In the centre of the wall or under doors or windows

   c   In the quoins or corners of solid walling

   d   Only in Stretcher bond walling

12 To reverse the bond means that a

   a   Stretcher brick is required at both ends of the wall

   b   Header brick is required at one end and a stretcher brick at the other end of the wall

   c   Header brick is required at both ends of the wall

   d   Half brick is required at one end of the wall

13 The site datum is also known as the

   a   Standard bench mark

   b   Main reference point

   c   Temporary bench mark

   d   Site level

14 What is the dimension of the header face of a brick?

   a   100.5mm

   b   102.5mm

   c   105.2mm

   d   150.0mm

15 What width dimension should a Queen Closer be cut to?

   a   35mm

   b   46mm

   c   50mm

   d   52mm

16 The best material for a damp proof course in a garden or boundary wall is

   a   Bitumen felt

   b   Pitch polymer

   c   Engineering brick

   d   Polythene sheet

17 If steel is galvanised, this means that it has been coated with

   a   Lead

   b   Resin

   c   Zinc

   d   Paint

18 What type of level is it good practice to use when laying a Soldier course?

   a   Cigar

   b   Boat

   c   Laser

   d   Feature

19 What is the minimum number of courses of engineering brick needed to form an effective DPC?

   a   1

   b   2

   c   4

   d   5

20 Modern lintels are made from

   a   Steel

   b   Plastic

   c   Timber

   d   Brick

Chapter 5
Unit 205: Interpreting working drawings to set out masonry structures

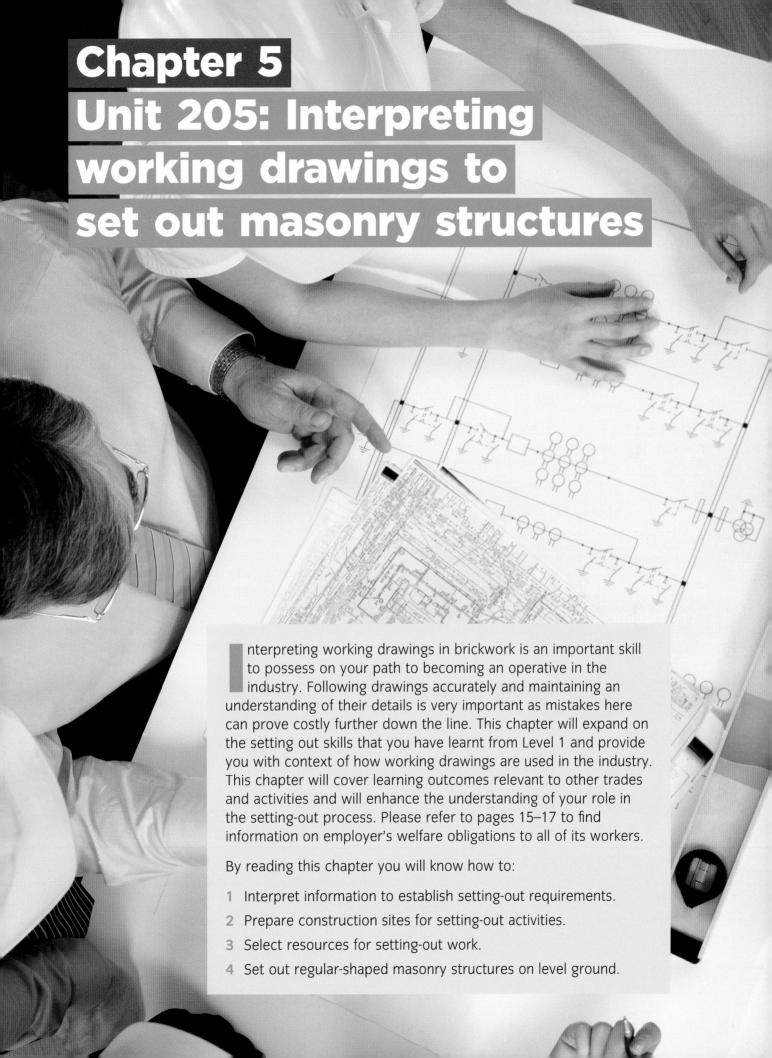

Interpreting working drawings in brickwork is an important skill to possess on your path to becoming an operative in the industry. Following drawings accurately and maintaining an understanding of their details is very important as mistakes here can prove costly further down the line. This chapter will expand on the setting out skills that you have learnt from Level 1 and provide you with context of how working drawings are used in the industry. This chapter will cover learning outcomes relevant to other trades and activities and will enhance the understanding of your role in the setting-out process. Please refer to pages 15–17 to find information on employer's welfare obligations to all of its workers.

By reading this chapter you will know how to:

1 Interpret information to establish setting-out requirements.
2 Prepare construction sites for setting-out activities.
3 Select resources for setting-out work.
4 Set out regular-shaped masonry structures on level ground.

HOW TO INTERPRET INFORMATION FOR SETTING OUT MASONRY STRUCTURES

A working bricklayer will be required to interpret construction drawings. The drawings are drawn by an architect or an architectural technician. A bricklayer will receive copies of the plans on paper and electronically.

Before setting out, make sure that you are have checked the working drawings thoroughly. Information on the symbols, hatchings and abbreviations commonly found in working drawings can be found in Chapter 2.

Setting out a structure from the beginning of a construction project can raise many health and safety issues. Risks to operatives' health and safety can arise in areas such as services present in the site, eg gas, water and electricity, to the condition of the **subsoil**.

Prior to starting a project, a risk assessment with be undertaken and all hazards identified on the risk assessment paperwork. The assessments will be included in the **method statement** produced by the health and safety team (see Chapter 1, page 6). Remember that this should be up to date with the latest legislation and meet the requirements of your local authority. The method statement will refer to the work schedule on how to find and identify the services.

SERVICES

Locating the **services** on site has to be completed from an early stage of the construction project. Local authorities will have drawings in place which will identify boundaries, pavements and roads, and in some cases the runs of gas and water installation. Not all drawings are kept with the local authority; service providers now have their own drawing base from which locations can be determined. The tradesperson will conduct a search, including a general walk over the site to locate any sign of the services. The tradesperson can use a detector to locate pipework such as for electricity and drainage. Once the services are located, permits will be required to mark the position of the said services, and in all cases the right to expose the services must be requested from the relevant service provider.

CONTROL MEASURES

The method statement, produced by the contractor, will give all the detail on how the project will be constructed. This will explain step-by-step procedure on the **assembly** of a project. The risks involved can only be identified if each task is identified: for example, bricks and blocks carry a risk of dust and particles getting into the eyes. The risk assessment will detail the **control measures** necessary, such as the use of PPE (in this case goggles).

Subsoil

Earth covering the site, that has low compression strength

Method statement

Document detailing the work schedule and risk assessment

Services

Those provided by the utility companies, eg gas, electricity and water

Cable detector

Assembly

Putting together the brick or block walls

Control measures

Specific instructions to work to and control work practices

When setting out a structure, hazards such as machinery and traffic must be identified and control measures put into place. Setting out may require pegs or metal rods driven into the ground as markers. Control measures must be identified in case buried underground services are found – these measures would include good site investigation prior to any work commencing. The surrounding area must be taken into consideration when spotting hazards. Trees and hedges which cannot be cut down, and other structures on the site, can cause accidents and must be included in any method statement. Additionally, each employee must undergo training and induction to the site.

Working to a method statement which includes a risk assessment is the responsibility of all staff, and line managers should regularly check that staff are working in line with the method statement.

ACTIVITY

Chose a location and imagine you are setting out to build a boundary wall. Assess the position of the building; the surrounding area may contain hazards, and these must be identified. Record the hazards on a risk assessment or a method statement and report these to your line manager.

METHOD STATEMENT

Revision Date:	Revision Description:		Approved By:
Work Method Description	Risk Assessment	Risk Levels	Recommended Actions* (Clause No.)
1.			
2.			
3.			
4.			

RISK LEVELS:　　Class 1 (high)　　Class 2 (medium)　　Class 3 (low)　　Class 4 (very low risk)

Engineering Details/Certificates/Work Cover Approvals:		Codes of Practice, Legislation:	
Plant/Equipment:		Maintenance Checks:	

Sign-off

Print Name:	Print Name:	Print Name:	Print Name:
Signature:	Signature:	Signature:	Signature:
Print Name:	Print Name:	Print Name:	Print Name:
Signature:	Signature:	Signature:	Signature:

Example of a method statement

DRAWINGS USED IN SETTING OUT

When a contractor arrives on site, the information required for the early stages of construction is detailed within either block plans or site plans. General location plans can also show drainage and setting out measurements too. Working as a bricklayer will at some point require the use of different working drawings:

- A block plan will help with the location of the plot in relation to the surrounding streets.

- A site plan will help with locating the plot between many building plots.

- A general location plan will detail the area of work.

- An assembly plan will show the detailed project up close and locate further detailed points.

- An elevation plan generally shows the front and back of a building revealing the window and door configurations and the shape of the roof.

- Section and sectional drawings show the inside of a building and use hatching symbols to show what type of resource is being used.

We will now look at the different areas on the drawings.

BLOCK PLANS

A block plan

The above block plan shows how a bricklayer would read the location of the site, adjoining roads and **boundary** lines. It's common practice to highlight the working area in a different colour to make it clearer.

An advantage of this bird's eye view of the site is the boundaries. The clear dividing line between properties can be determined. Good, clear drawings and photographs can also help when individuals have a problem about the ownership of land and buildings. These drawings can help to resolve disputes.

FLOOR PLANS

This bird's eye view of the planned construction is often the most informative one for a bricklayer. The general layout of the building, shown floor by floor, is easily definable. A good drawing will always show the dimensions of the rooms and the structure.

Measurements and dimensions are always written in metric form (see Chapter 2). The plan view allows bricklayers to take the sizes of the structure and relate these measurements to the site.

INDUSTRY TIP

Not all drawing dimensions work to scale. Always check the full-scale requirements on site and confirm the measurements with the line manager, architect or client.

ACTIVITY

Use your scale rule to measure and check the length and width of the garage in the plan view drawing. Use the 1:50 scale on your rule.

Dining / Lounge

External Walls:
100mm   Brickwork
50mm   Cavity
9mm   Plywood with vapour barrier
140mm   Framing (140mm × 47mm studs @600 ctrs
        with 150mm Glass fibre Insulation to achieve
        min U-valve: 0.35w/m K
12.5mm Foil backed Plasterboard and skinn

Stair construction:
Total 13 Risers
Riser: 204mm
Going: 225mm
Hand rail height: 850mm
Landing Gaurding height: 900mm

W.C.

Kitchen

Entrance Doors
to have a minium clear
opening width of 775mm

2 layers 12.5mm
plasterboard
fire protection

Garage

All new timber walls
to have sound resistance of min. 40dB. formed from 15mm plasterboard (to achieve 9.8kg/m2) both sides on 89×39 sw studs at 400
ctrs, with sole plate, head and cross noggings. Sound insulation quilt
(min. density 10kg/m3) filled between studs.

A clear plan of a ground floor showing brickwork sizes in millimetres

ELEVATIONS

Front elevation

A front elevation

This elevation generally shows the:

- entrance

- window and door configuration

- shape of the roof.

This view can be very informative for bricklayers and operatives.

Details about access to the front door of a **property** can be found on the block plan.

The elevation may also show substructure brick and blockwork and superstructure brick and blockwork, such as the brickwork for the chimney construction.

Property

A building and the land belonging to it

Side elevation

A side elevation

Like the front elevation, this elevation also generally shows the:

- entrance

- window and door configuration

- shape of the roof.

Details about rear access will be shown with this type of elevation.

Information about the garden area and any patio surface will be found on drawings relating to floor plans.

SECTION VIEWS

The **section drawings** are always informative and give bricklayers a view of the inside of the structure being built.

Drawings showing a cross-section use **hatchings** to indicate what type of resource is to be used. An example of a hatching symbol is two diagonal lines close together at an angle of 45° used for brickwork. See Chapter 2, page 48 for more examples of these symbols.

Look at 'Our House' and imagine it as a drawing. What hatching symbols would be used on the plan to show the different materials in the house?

Section drawings

Repeated views of different structures

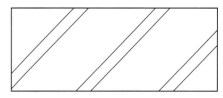

Hatching symbol for brickwork

Hatching

Patterns used on a drawing to identify different materials to meet the standard BS1192

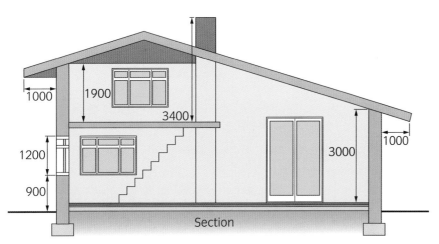

A diagram of a cross-section of a house. Measurements are in mm

Many section drawings continue underground and give bricklayers information about the foundation type and size. The illustration above shows a traditional strip foundation, where both bricks and blocks are built below ground level, up to damp proof course (DPC) level. A strip of concrete built to building regulations is placed at the bottom of the trench.

Sectional drawings can help when looking to see how the structure is built; these drawings can detail a cross-section of a wall or structure. If the tradesperson wants to look at multiple elevations at any one time, the **orthographic** and **isometric projection** drawings can help. Examples of these are shown on the next page. In bricklaying, isometric always refers to 30°/60° angles and these drawings show at least two sides of a structure. Orthographic drawings are used to show as many sides of a building as possible.

Sectional drawing

Drawing detail cut through an object

Orthographic projection

Drawing showing elevational and plan views

Isometric projection

Drawing showing a three dimensional (3D) view

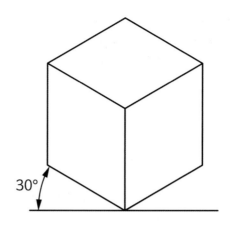

Isometric projection

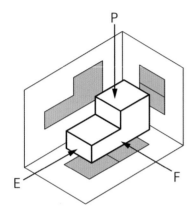

Orthographic projection

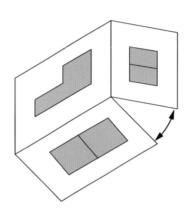

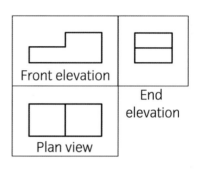

Front elevation

End elevation

Plan view

SITE PLANS

A site plan is one of many drawings and working plans the tradesperson has when working on a building site. The site plan will

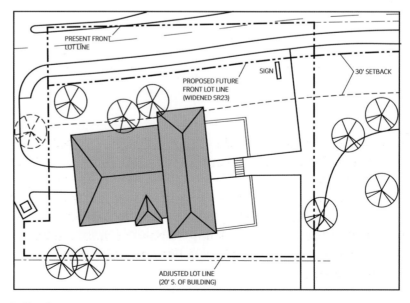

A site plan

show a plan (bird's eye view) of the plot in more detail, with drain runs, road layouts and the size and position of the existing building (and any extensions proposed) in relation to the property boundary.

GENERAL LOCATION PLANS

The most useful part of a location plan to the tradesperson is that it shows the location of services. The location plan shows a bird's eye view of the building and the surrounding area, the type of detail on a location plan will include such items as trees, fencing, and boundaries. Location plans are very useful for showing the positions of material compounds during the construction process.

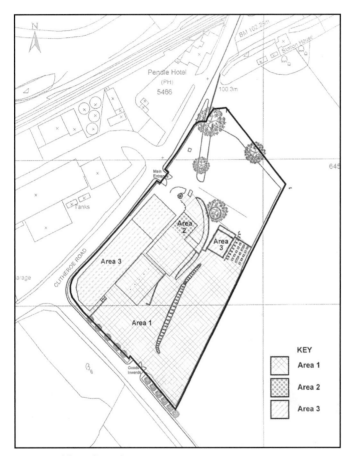

A general location plan

ASSEMBLY PLANS

The assembly plan is usually a bird's eye view and front elevation of a wall or construction project. The scale used for this plan will allow the operative to look in detail up close to the wall or project being built. For the bricklayer this will show dimensions and brick bond and the sizes of the wall (see the example on the next page). Setting out a wall will need to have clear instruction on how the wall is to be assembled; this is useful if the wall has a design feature built into it such as a decorative panel.

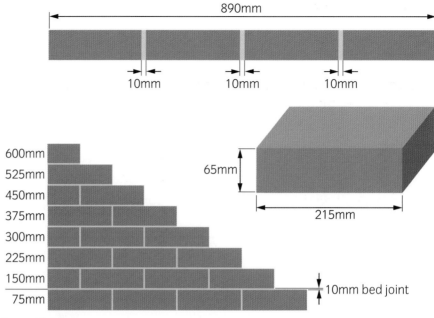

Assembly plan

For more information on these types of drawings, refer back to Chapter 4, page 140.

WORKING PLANS

The block plan will detail the surrounding area for ease of use and the site plan will detail the position of the building or structure and surroundings. The main assembly drawings showing the structural details are supplied separately to block and site plans.

The purpose of this range of drawings is to provide a detailed format to enable site personnel to locate the site, set out a given structure, and assemble the required resources. Working drawings use scales: the smaller the scale, the more detail given on the drawing. For example a 1:2500 scale will show details of the plot and surrounding areas, while a 1:10 scale will detail the brick and blockwork assembly.

When taking measurements from the working drawing, using a scale rule, refer to the architect's stated scale. It's up to the operative to translate the measurements into full scale and transpose them to the working area. Using a scale rule against the drawing is key to determining the correct length of a structure. Understanding how to use a scale rule and calculating the scaled down or scaled up measurement is the only way to determine the project's size. Always use the written measurement stated by the architect in the first instance, as this written dimension can be checked for accuracy during the build. Various scales will be used for taking different measurements from drawings. The operative will need to use a specific scale for each different type of information, for example:

- Scales of 1:2500 will detail a block plan.

- Scales of 1:100, 1:50 and 1:20 can give an overview of the project, such as a full-length wall, its foundation type and its finish.

- Scales of 1:10, 1:5 and 1:2 will detail the assembly, and areas such as **BOE** sill details.

Taking a measurement from a drawing will inform the bricklayer of the length, thickness and location of walls. Using a scale rule is a simple task if the user can match the drawing scale to the scaled measurement on the rule.

BOE

An abbreviation for 'brick on edge'

INDUSTRY TIP

Use a scale rule and locate the architect's given scale. The rule when applied to the drawing will enable the tradesperson to convert the drawing to full size measurement. For more information on scales, see Chapter 2, page 47.

FUNCTIONAL SKILLS

At a scale of 1:10, 1m is equal to 10mm (1cm). How would a measurement of 14.5m represent at a scale of 1:10?

Work on this activity can support FM2 (C2.3).

Answer: 1,450cm

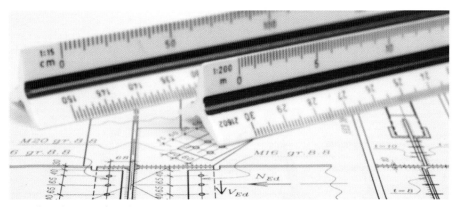

A scale rule on a drawing

Working drawings can sometimes be inaccurate: the measurement and the known length of brickwork does not always work to full bricks or blocks, and in this case your line manager or site agent must be informed. Looking at an object and knowing just how it's assembled and put together can be enhanced with the use of orthographic drawings. As we have seen, these drawings can show many elevations at the same time, ready for interpretation by the operative.

USING DATUM POINTS

When looking for a fixed level point, a site datum will be established. This datum, which can be made up of a concrete plinth or a peg surrounded by a protecting wooden frame, will detail the FFL (finished floor level). This datum enables all other vertical measurements to be calculated. For more information on datum points, see Chapter 2, page 47.

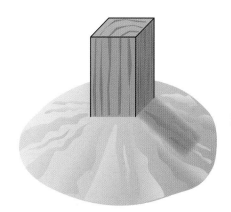

A site datum

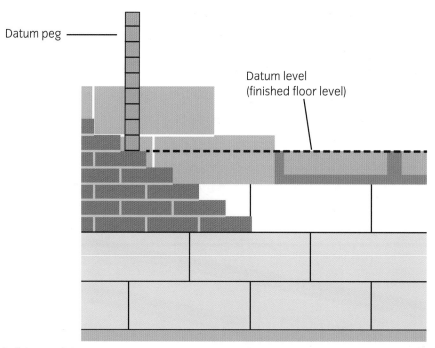

Datum peg

Datum level
(finished floor level)

A datum point

ESTABLISHING SETTING-OUT REQUIREMENTS

When drawing the site plan the architect will detail known starting points for measuring. These structures can include a tree, a boundary wall or a building – these are called 'fixed given structures'. The measurements from these given structures can be recorded and supplied to the builder or operative to help establish the corner of a new structure or building, or even the face line of new brickwork.

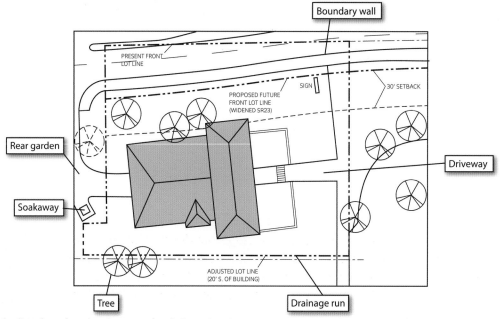

Boundary wall

PRESENT FRONT LOT LINE

SIGN

30' SETBACK

PROPOSED FUTURE FRONT LOT LINE (WIDENED SR23)

Rear garden

Driveway

Soakaway

ADJUSTED LOT LINE (20' S. OF BUILDING)

Tree

Drainage run

A site plan showing trees and existing structures

If any information is incorrect, don't be afraid to contact the architect to discuss this, eg if a measurement is not working when referenced from a given structure. Always contact the site manager and record these mistakes, usually in the site diary or log.

Using the **specification** to identify a given material, such as a type of brick on a given structure, will help when setting out; the architect will record in the specification a description of existing resources when recording setting-out positions.

Specification

A contract document that gives information about the quality of materials and standards of workmanship required

TECHNICAL SPECIFICATION

Brick Type	HANDMADE	TRADITIONAL WIRECUT	RECLAIM
Appearance	Lightly creased genuine handmade	Extruded wirecut smooth, rustic, plain or sandfaced	Prematurely 'aged' during the production process
Specification	Bricks are manufactured to BS EN 771-1 (BS 3921:1985	now withdrawn)	Specials are manufactured to the proposed BS 4729:2005
Sizes	Metric: 215mm x 102.5mm x 50mm, 65mm, 73mm, 80mm	Imperial: 9" x 4 $^5/_{16}$" x 2", 2 $^1/_4$", 2 $^3/_8$", 2 $^1/_2$", 2 $^5/_8$", 2 $^7/_8$", 3", 3 $^1/_8$"	Non Standard: Most sizes can be accommodated in our production process
Specials	A full range of standard BS and	purpose made Specials is available	
Compressive Strength	24.5 N/mm²	71.6 N/mm²	71.6 N/mm²
Durability	F2	F2	F2
Tolerances	T1	T2	T1
Liability to Effloresce	Nil to slight	Nil to slight	Nil to slight
Soluble Salt Content	S2	S2	S2
Water Absorption	14 - 16 %	8 - 10 %	8 - 10 %
Average Bulk Density	1650 kg/M³	1650 kg/M³	1650 kg/M³
Packaging	Shrinkwrapped and wire banded with holes for forklift use	Shrinkwrapped and wire banded with holes for forklift use	Shrinkwrapped and wire banded with holes for forklift use
Pack Sizes & Weights	Size Qty/pack Weight (t) 50mm 650 1.229 65mm 500 1.223 73mm 500 1.280 80mm 400 1.213	Size Qty/pack Weight (t) 50mm 650 1.070 65mm 500 1.072 73mm 500 1.195 80mm 400 1.100	Size Qty/pack Weight (t) 50mm 650 0.927 65mm 435 0.929 73mm 400 1.009 80mm 400 1.051
Workmanship	The recommendations of good practice made in the relevant British or European Standards regarding design	and workmanship must be fully observed. Always mix from four packs, working vertically down the blades, not	horizontally across the tops of packs. Bricks & brickwork should be covered to prevent saturation.
Performance	Guidance on the use of these bricks in specific situations is readily available from us. Liability cannot be accepted	for the performance of the product if used outside our recommendations in areas of high exposure/saturation	the use of Sulphate Resisting Cement is recommended.
Samples	Available on 48-hour despatch		
Important Advice	Colours and textures reproduced here are as accurate as the printing process allows	and final choices should not be made from this brochure in isolation. For the latest updates	on technical information, please visit our website on **www.northcotbrick.co.uk**

An example of a specification commonly found on a working drawing

PREPARING FOR SETTING OUT

Working with method statements requires the operative to wear the correct PPE when carrying out setting-out procedures. The working site can contain many toxic substances (poisonous and dangerous to health) in the early stages of setting out, especially on a green or brown site (see next page). Refer back to Chapter 1 pages 20–23 for more information on using PPE.

Waterproofs for setting out in certain weather conditions

INDUSTRY TIP

Safety boots are not always sufficiently waterproof for work on waterlogged sites. A good pair of wellington boots with steel toe cap are far more suitable in this situation.

Groundwater table

The natural level of water found on site

PPE is always necessary on site, and different sites require different PPE. Once the **groundwater table** is known, appropriate wet weather equipment such as waterproof footwear will be required.

TYPES OF LAND

Greenfield land

This type of land is almost always rural or land being worked as farmland or used for some sort of countryside activity. Greenfield development has increased over the last 50 years due to demand for housing in this country. Greenfield land is highly sought after because of its rural location and outlook, meaning that when a plot becomes available for sale it can achieve high prices. There are many groups that have protested against greenfield development for environmental reasons, and because they are unhappy that the countryside is being eroded.

Brownfield land

This land is the most common form of land that builders build on. Brownfield is classified as being occupied either by humans or industry. Brownfield can include industrial buildings such as warehousing and industrial occupation; which in turn can be converted to housing or apartments for sale or rent. In general brownfield sites need further development before any building takes place. This may be because chemicals from a previous use have affected the site. Many brownfield sites are cleaned and developed for housing.

Site investigation

Looking at areas underground, such as the water table and ground conditions

Dumpling

A mound of top soil which can be saved and used for gardens and landscapes

SITE INVESTIGATION

At the start of the project the clearance of the site, which includes all vegetable matter and top soil, is important because of the low load-bearing capacity of the material. The top soil, if clean, can be stored and reused for making good to the landscaped area, for example using the **dumpling** method.

Dumpling method of storing top soil

The dumpling method is a stock pile of good top soil, placed out of the way on the building site to be used later on to make good to the gardens of the site.

The services must be located at this stage: the gas, electric, water and possible existing drainage present on the site have to be found and recorded. The depth and size of the services plus their direction must all be located and recorded for further investigation. Re-diverting services may be an issue later on during the project. If no services are present, these will need to be established as the work proceeds. Safety at the early stages of construction is important, as any one of the services can cause harm and delay the project. This in turn will affect the overall budget.

All service pipes and cables should be located before starting work on a project

The type of matter removed from the site may be recycled. For instance if hardcore, brick, stone or chippings are found, these materials can be reclaimed and sold on. Not all of the found resources should be removed; if possible the trees and shrubs on site, which are not affected by the construction, should be left to enhance the site upon completion.

All construction projects require some form of demolition such as removing fence posts or existing structures; these obstacles are removed ready to prepare the working area. The surface strip involves removing all vegetable matter such as turf, top soil and plants, because these have a low load-bearing factor. Construction projects need to have a strong sub base and the previous matter will not provide this.

Top soil being removed

If at all possible sloping sites may be levelled to enhance the outside areas.

The quantity and type of tools and equipment required for setting out a building will vary upon the size of the contract. To set out a large structure the following equipment may be required.

TOOLS AND EQUIPMENT USED FOR SETTING OUT

The tools and equipment used for setting out will always require some form of maintenance; this will range from cleaning on a regular basis to replacing parts that are not repairable, such as an optical level and squares. Even something like a stretched measuring tape can affect the setting out – whenever possible use metal tape measures. The table on the next pages explains the use of different tools and equipment in setting out.

Tool/equipment	Use in setting out
Setting out chain 	Measuring linear distances over a long length.
Ranging poles 	Red and white rod fixed to indicate set distance points.
Tape measure 	Measuring tool, comes in a range of sizes: 3m, 5m, 10m, 30m.
Optical level 	Fixed level on a tripod, using the eye, with the help of a telescope.
Optical square 	Fixed level on a tripod, using the eye, with the help of a pair of telescopes, fixed at right angles.
Pegs and profiles 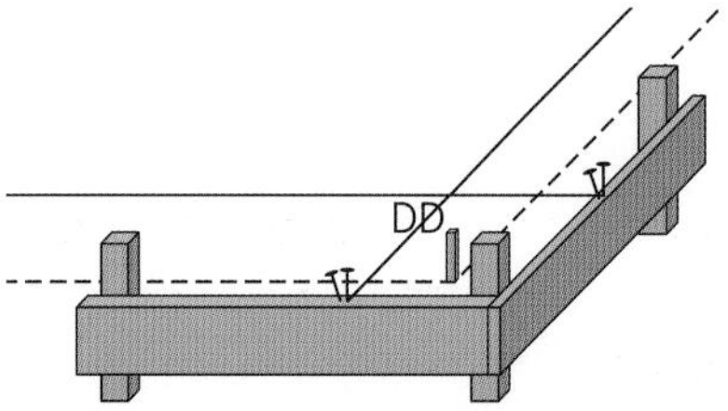	Square wooden pegs fixed to horizontal rails to form a **profile**.

ACTIVITY

Selecting equipment when setting out is always important – using the correct equipment can save time and money. Compare two different tape measures and try to measure over a large distance. A typical 5m tape is good for normal brick and block lengths in a dwelling but when setting out a large building greater lengths are required. Compare a 30m fabric tape to a 5m steel tape.

Profiles

Boards fixed horizontally to ground pegs at the ends of a wall before construction commences in order that lines may be stretched across to mark the position of the foundations and wall

Tool/equipment	Use in setting out
Line and pins	A string held with metal pins used to guide the blocks or bricks to make them straight.
Straight edge	A straight piece of metal or timber. Tool used in conjunction with a spirit level to help transfer a level.
Spirit level	Straight metal level with fixed vials (bubbles) for horizontal levelling and vertical plumbing.
Ranging line	Nylon line used to take the place of the level when laying bricks or blocks.
Builder's square	A tool used to mark corners as square when building quoins.
Spray paint	Paint used to mark the ground underneath the profile ranging lines.
Cable detector	Battery-powered detector used to locate electrical power cables.

INDUSTRY TIP

Proper storage of the setting out equipment is vital. Keep it clean and treat it with respect; this will ensure the equipment is in good working condition when required.

SETTING OUT

Prior to setting out, a method statement will be produced and followed. This statement will detail each stage of the operation and will highlight the risks involved, and the control methods that need to be followed.

MORTAR

In the early stages of construction, mortar will be required for marking out ranging lines, setting up datums and general use around the site, such as fixing **hoardings** and posts. To mix mortar, the site will require an electricity supply from the beginning of the contract. If this isn't possible, petrol or diesel mixers can be used during the time of no power supply.

Hoarding

Barrier surrounding the site to protect against theft and unauthorised entry

Electric mixer

Mixing by hand, and using small amounts of mortar for setting out, can be undertaken in a wheelbarrow or on a level concrete or boarded surface. Mixing small amounts of mortar or concrete can be done by hand:

1 Place the correct ratio of sand and cement, or aggregates, on a solid, level surface, and mix in a dry state.

2 Mix completely using a shovel, prior to adding any water.

3 When adding the water, hollow out the centre of the dry mix and pour it in, taking care not to let the water run out of the mix.

4 Use the shovel to take the dry mix from the edges and, working to a clockwise motion, mix in the dry materials while adding water to the desirable thickness.

INDUSTRY TIP

The ratio for mortar or concrete is governed by the job in hand and decided on by the architect.

An operative loading premixed cement into a mixer

An operative mixing by hand

PROTECTING THE SITE

Protecting the working site on a day to day basis can be achieved with the use of hoardings. These barriers can stop individuals from entering the site. Protecting the work area from traffic is also important; the **trench barrier** system should be used to stop work personnel and vehicles falling into excavated foundations. Always be mindful of the weather conditions, as bad weather can cause damage to existing and newly completed work. Always cover up and support the completed work at the end of the day.

Trench barrier

Barrier erected to stop traffic and personnel falling into a trench

Sheeting over a construction site

Hoarding around a construction site

Once setting out has begun, the site foundations must be protected and boundaries must have a hoarding. All areas must be kept clean, and ground material such as **ballast** or chippings added to reduce the amount of mud and water being walked over the site. At this stage sustainable resources can be determined and stored for later use.

Ballast

Aggregate mixture of sand and chippings up to 50mm deep

Sustainable resources are the materials that have been reused and made into blocks, bricks concrete etc. The materials are then purchased and stored on site in a material compound.

Ballast on a construction site

Top soil is the top 150mm of soil containing vegetable matter

FUNCTIONAL SKILLS

Calculation formula for area = length × width. Calculation formula for volume = length × width × thickness.
A plot measures 10m × 25m, and the soil is 0.2m thick.

1 Calculate the area of the plot.
2 Calculate the volume of soil to be removed.

Work on this activity can support FM2 (C2.32 and C2.7).

Answers: 1) Area = 250m², 2) Volume of soil = 50m³

CALCULATIONS

At the planning and surveying stage calculations can be made regarding the area of the plot and the volume of top soil to be removed. These calculations are vital to the work involved at the early stage of the project. Knowing just how many cubic metres of soil is to be removed will enable the contractor to calculate the type of plant and length of time that will be required.

When the calculations for the areas and volumes are complete, the contractor can calculate the number of truckloads needed to transport the soil and in turn calculate the cost of removal. This is done by finding out from the transport contractor how many cubic metres each truck will carry and the length of time it will take to load and empty each truck. Calculating the total area of a plot and working out the thickness of top soil to be removed can be achieved by using a simple formula. This formula for a basic rectangular plot is:

$$\text{width} \times \text{length} \times \text{depth}$$

If the area of the plot is known (the width multiplied by the length), multiplying this by the thickness of soil to be removed (the depth) will generate the total volume.

When calculating during the setting-out process, certain formulas are to be used. Calculating areas, volumes and perimeters are all important. For example, adding up all the sides of a plot to find the total length of a perimeter will help when calculating such items as fencing or hoardings. Refer back to Chapter 2 pages 60–72 for more information.

BULKING

When calculating the removed soil, the **bulking** effect must be taken into account. When the soil is removed from the ground, air will be introduced to the soil, and this will affect the volume of the excavated soil. Bulking must be allowed for when calculating the number of truckloads needed to remove the soil.

Bulking

An increase in volume of soil or earth, caused by introducing air

Example 1

One truck carries 10m³ and a total excavated amount for a site equals 250m³. A bulking allowance of 30% must be added to this.

Step 1
To find 30% of 250, you multiply them together and divide by 100:

$$250 \times 30 = 7500$$
$$7500 \div 100 = 75m^3$$

Step 2
To find the total amount excavated plus 30%, add them together:

$$250 + 75 = 325m^3$$

The true volume of soil to be removed by truck is **325m³**.

A total of 33 trucks, or trips by trucks, would be needed to remove all the soil from the site.

As well as knowing the volume of top soil to be removed, it will be useful to know how to work out how much time it would take a contractor to remove the soil, and how much they would charge to do this.

FUNCTIONAL SKILLS

Calculation formula for area = length × width. Calculation formula for volume = length × width × thickness.

A plot measures 10m × 25m, and the soil is 0.2m thick.

1 Calculate the area of the plot.
2 Calculate the volume of soil to be removed.

Work on this activity can support FM2 (C2.32 and C2.7).

Answers: 1) Area = 250m²
2) Volume of soil = 50m³

Example 2

A contractor requires 400m³ of soil to be removed from a site, and the contractor charges £500.00 per working hour. They also charge an additional flat fee of £500.00 for machinery and personnel hire. How long will it take to remove the soil, if 1m³ of soil can be removed in 15 minutes?

Step 1
First, you need to work out how much soil can be removed in 1 hour, because the cost is charged per hour. You need to multiply the amount removed in 15 minutes by 4, because 60 minutes (1 hour) divided by 15 is 4.

$$1m^3 \times 4 = 4m^3$$

Example 2 cntd.

Step 2
To find out how many hours this will take, you need to divide the total amount to be removed by the amount that can be removed in 1 hour:

$$400m \div 4m^3 = 100$$

So it will take 100 hours to remove 400m³ of soil.

Step 3
To work out how much it will cost to remove all the soil, you need to multiply the amount of hours by the hourly price.

$$500 \times 100 = £50,000.00$$

Step 4
You then need to add the cost of machinery and personnel hire.

$$50,000.00 + 500 = £50,500.00$$

So it will take a total of 100 hours to remove 400m³, and will cost £50,500.00.

OUR HOUSE

Look at 'Our House' and turn the structure upside down (you can do this by clicking the blue directional arrow and moving your finger up or down until you are looking at the underneath of the building). The outline of the foundations will be visible. You can now compare the wall positions in relation to the overall width of the concrete foundations. This is key when setting out a structure.

ASSISTING WITH SETTING OUT

BUILDING AND FRONTAGE LINES

Setting out requires certain known fixed points, such as the building line. The building line represents the front of the new structure, and can be found on the site and location drawings. This line must be adhered to, and no building can be developed in front of this line, between the front of the building and the frontage line. The frontage line is the front boundary of the plot. No construction can take place between the frontage line and the pavement.

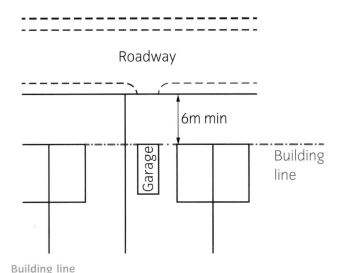

Building line

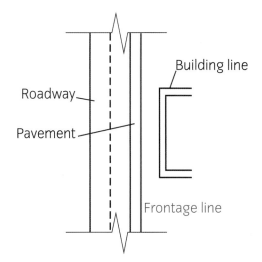

Frontage line

Building in the wrong position can result in heavy fines or even the demolition of the structure. It is the responsibility of the architect to establish the building and frontage lines at the start of the contract. The contractor must, at the start of the project, establish the first corner of the structure, and then start setting out the other corners, both internal and external. All corners must be square. The contractor and trades personnel will not only use a builders' square but also a site optical square. They also need to set out right angles.

Checking for square

When setting out an L-shaped building it's always wise to measure all the diagonals to check for square. Set out a simple small scale L-shaped building and follow the diagonals shown here – this will not only enable you to check individual rooms for square but the overall shape too. The dimensional arrows must be the same length if the building is to be square.

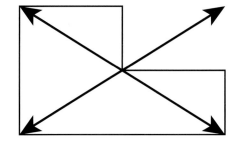

How to set out a right angle

On site, bricklayers use a range of methods and tools to set out a right angle. The most common method is the 3:4:5 ratio. This is a calculation formula used to set out a right angle at 90°. The bricklayer can use metres and the ratios, eg 3m:4m:5m, will form a right angle when setting out.

For example, to set out a right angle using a tape and spirit level use this process:

1 Establish a base line.

2 Measure 400mm along the base line. Call your starting point 'A', and end point B.

3 From 'A', measure 300mm up. This is point C.

4 Join points B and C. This line will be 500mm long.

5 You have formed a right angle at point A.

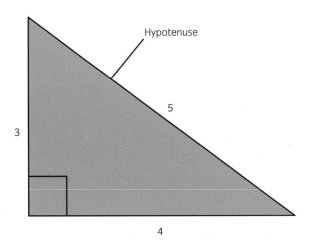

Calculating the length of the hypotenuse (the longest size of a right angle) is critical in determining the length of the diagonals of a structure. The 3:4:5 method often requries two people to set out.

Establishing a 90° angled corner can be achieved by using a range of tools and equipment; the most common tool is the builders square. The square is made from steel or timber and fixed to an angle of 90°. When using a builder's square the checking factor is important: always check for accuracy. An optical square uses telescopes to view by eye. These telescopes are set at right angles to each other and will help establish the positions of up to three corners if the level is positioned over the first corner. Laser levels come in many different forms, the most common being a fixed level using a beam of light to transfer over a distance.

Optical square

Builder's square

SETTING OUT USING INSTRUMENTS AND TAPE MEASURES

Setting out using instruments and tape measures carries a risk of inaccuracies, so the industry allows a **tolerance** in all cases of measurement. Measuring linear measurements +/– 5mm over a

Tolerance

Excess measurement allowed

distance of 30m is allowed, but operatives should always try and be as accurate as possible. Transferring levels across the working site can be achieved by using a straight edge and spirit level or an optical and laser level.

Transferring levels

Using different levels will always involve a checking process, ie checking in the first place if the level is accurate. The calibration of all laser and optical levels are defined by making sure that the stand or tripod is positioned using a fixed vial or bubble fixed to the tripod or stand. Most modern laser or optical levels once damaged cannot be repaired until sent to the manufacturer. Inspecting a laser or optical level will involve checking the fine adjustment screws and quality of the eyepieces. Any damage will result in poor levelling operations.

Transferring a level over a distance can only be achieved by using a laser or optical level. All levels are taken from a fixed datum level established near to the site office for safety. This height can then be transferred using a levelling instrument across the site to establish areas such as DPC height, corners of buildings, and even depth of foundations. By measuring from a known fixed datum height and calculating vertical measurements, the height or depth of work below ground level and heights above ground level can be established.

Using a laser or optical level requires the operative to stage the level at different places over the working area. Always remember to remove the level and store correctly prior to lifting the stand or tripod. Setting up the levelling instrument requires good positioning; the view from the level needs to be accurate and to the point. It pays to cover a large area from one position, because this will help keep the mistakes to a minimum.

A correctly stored optical level

Storage of all expensive equipment needs to be well planned and reviewed on a regular basis: this equipment is expensive and a target for theft. Leaving such equipment in vans overnight is not recommended. These items need to be stored in a secure building under lock and key.

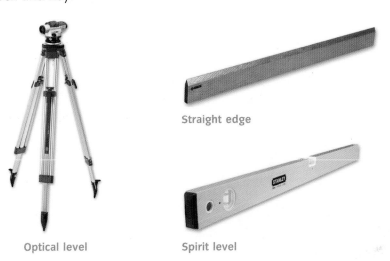

Straight edge

Optical level   Spirit level

PROFILES

Marking out the findings of square and face lines requires the contractor to establish the profiles. The use of a straight or corner profile will be determined by the resources available, space on site, and the ease of use for establishing more than one direction on a temporary profile.

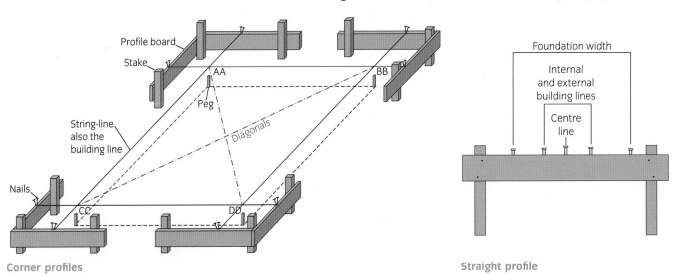

Corner profiles   Straight profile

The profile markings are determined by the working drawings (site drawing and location drawing). The architect will enter the foundation and wall widths on the drawing and the specification. These measurements will then be established on to the top rail of the profiles by the tradesperson.

This type of information is very important to the contractor, and the profiles must stay in position for the duration of the build, or at least until the brick and blockwork are well underway. The position of the temporary profiles on site is very important. They need to be not too far away from the location of the structure, but not so close that machinery will damage or destroy the profiles. Contractors will establish these profiles at least 5m away from the building. The two types of profile you will be setting out are straight profiles and corner profiles.

The top rail of a profile will carry the saw cuts or nails enabling the contractor to mark out the overall width of the foundation, and the cavity or solid wall. Once the ranging lines are fixed to the profiles, the contractor will be able to transfer down from the ranging lines to the foundation concrete and mark the wall and trench positions.

Marking trench positions on site

OUR HOUSE

This chapter requires you to set out a building and adjoining structures, square with each other. Look at the side extension on 'Our House' and check the foundation level. This will show just how square the extension is compared to the main house.

SETTING OUT BRICK AND BLOCKWORK

Bricklayers need their materials to be at arm's length. This helps with the production targets and speed of laying. The bricks and blocks need to be 600mm from the face line of the wall being built.

Preparation of the materials on site and in the workshop must always be carried out with health and safety in mind. Materials

Pallets
A storage base used to carry and store materials

should not be stacked too high. Where possible, **pallets** should be used and stacked to a maximum height of two pallets. General tidiness when working with trowel trade materials will lend itself to a better overall finish to the walls.

Brick stacks set out

BUILDING STRAIGHT AND CORNERED WALLING

While working as a bricklayer, the correct procedure for the construction of a wall must be followed. The bricklayer will set out the structure to ensure the building works will bond. The quoin is built and the infill brickwork is completed using corner blocks or line and pins.

Straight walling

Cornered walling

JOINTING

Jointing
To make a finish to the mortar faces as work proceeds

Jointing brickwork must be completed while the construction is in progress. The bricklayer can form a range of joint finishes. The most common form is the half-round (bucket handle) joint. At Level 2 the bricklayer will use the half-round, flush and **weather struck** joint finishes.

An operative jointing a solid wall

The jointing procedure should always be adhered to. The bricklayer must:

- ensure the bricks are laid with full and complete joints
- work with good timing
- complete the perp joints
- joint from the ends of the wall into the middle.

If the **bed** and perp joints are not full and complete, the bricklayer must infill the joints with a pointing trowel prior to using the **jointer**.

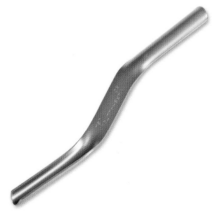

Jointer

Pointing trowel

Weather struck

An angled joint, which means one side of the joint is pressed further into the joint than the other

Bed joint

Continuous, horizontal mortar joint supporting the bricks

Jointer

A tool used for making a jointed finish

INDUSTRY TIP

Perp joints are finished first when applying weather struck.

Case Study: Beth and Wayne

Wayne has run a local building business for five years and has a good reputation as a builder. He is a qualified bricklayer, and has had many opportunities to complete different types of house construction.

The start of the project is always important and the setting out is vital to all accurate construction. The setting out of the project requires skills in measuring and using different optical levels to obtain building lines, and on the whole requires more than one person to undertake these operations. Wayne has decided to employ Beth, a local surveyor, to help with the initial stages of the house, such as setting out the plot and establishing the frontage and building lines of the property. Beth has worked in the same local area as Wayne for the last 15 years, working as a self-employed surveyor. The general type of work Beth will take on includes new build and local authority housing.

Day one on the plot requires Beth to determine the frontage and building line of the front elevation of the new house; this information is taken from the drawings produced by Wayne's architect. Wayne positions setting-out pegs as Beth confirms the setting-out positions using tape measures and optical levels.

It's not long before Beth gives Wayne the first position of the first corner peg. This in turn allows Wayne to set out all profiles for the house set well back from the construction and ranging line attached. Beth and her surveying instruments such as optical and laser levels and builder's square are now coming into their own.

Once Wayne has ranging lines established, corners set out square, and profiles fixed into position, Beth's work is done. Wayne can remove the ranging lines after marking the ground with spray paint and excavation of the trenches can take place.

Working together with a qualified surveyor in the early stages of construction will save Wayne time and money in the long term, and being accurate in the early stages helps maintain good quality work as the project expands and nears completion.

Work through the following questions to check your learning.

1   Which document provides detailed stage working content for the bricklayer to follow?

   a   Method statement

   b   Risk assessment

   c   Specification

   d   Accident book

2   What information is included is a risk assessment?

   a   Measurement

   b   Written instructions

   c   Control measures

   d   Photographs

3   A block plan can

   a   Locate the position of the plot

   b   Locate the position of the services

   c   Locate the position of car parks

   d   Locate the position of the site office

4   A site plan can

   a   Locate the position of the services

   b   Locate site buildings

   c   Locate the position of car parks

   d   Locate the position of the site office

5   Which plan will give details of the driveway and entrance to the property?

   a   Service plan

   b   Assembly plan

   c   Block plan

   d   Elevation plan

6   Which drawing will allow the reader to look inside a cavity wall?

   a   Service plan

   b   Assembly plan

   c   Block plan

   d   Sectional drawing

7   What is the correct gauged height of eight courses of bricks?

   a   375mm

   b   600mm

   c   525mm

   d   900mm

8   Setting out the alignment of the face work at a corner can be achieved by using a

   a   Line and pins

   b   Builder's square

   c   Spirit level

   d   Profile

9   On a working drawing, which detail should be drawn to a scale of 1:10?

   a   Overall size of a house

   b   Brick on edge detail

   c   Garden fencing

   d   Rain water details

10 On a working drawing, where does the fixed levelling point come from?

   a   Datum point

   b   Detailed point

   c   Drainage point

   d   Drawing point

11 The frontage line represents the

   a   Fencing line

   b   Boundary line

   c   Building line

   d   Setting-out line

12 The building line represents the

   a   Fencing line

   b   Boundary line

   c   Face line of the building

   d   Setting-out line

13 Which document provides the details on the quality of materials?

a   Programme

b   Assembly plan

c   Specification

d   Sectional plan

14 To stop operatives falling in a trench it is best to use

a   Ropes

b   A barrier

c   Fencing

d   A line of vans

15 Ballast is made up of different size aggregates, up to

a   50mm

b   25mm

c   100mm

d   12mm

16 Which item of equipment is best used to transfer a level over a distance?

a   Straight edge

b   Optical level

c   Site square

d   Spirit level

17 When reading working drawings, which item of information takes priority?

a   Size of the drawing

b   Written measurements

c   Specification

d   Scales used

18 Using a 3:4:5 method for setting out requires

a   Two people to set out

b   Three people to set out

c   Four people to set out

d   One person to set out

19 Why would you use spray paint in setting out?

a   To mark the ground underneath the profile ranging lines

b   To transfer levels

c   To take the place of the level when laying bricks

d   To check corners

20 Which **one** of these would a front elevation drawing not show you?

a   Entrance

b   Shape of the roof

c   Window and door configuration

d   Furniture

Chapter 6
Unit 206: Construct cavity walling forming masonry structures

This chapter discusses the skills and knowledge required to build cavity walling as an important element of a masonry structure. Building cavity walls is a more complex process than building solid walling. This is because additional components are included in the design in order for the cavity wall to fulfil its purpose and function. High standards of work are essential in building cavity walling so that the finished product will last a long time and work effectively as a major part of a structure.

By reading this chapter you will know how to:

1 Plan and select resources for practical tasks.
2 Erect cavity walling to required specification.
3 Form openings in cavity walling.

A client and a bricklayer checking a working drawing

Facing brick

Kiln

A type of large oven

Brick kiln

PREPARING FOR BUILDING CAVITY WALLING AND FORMING MASONRY STRUCTURES

SELECTING RESOURCES

A cavity wall consists of two individual skins or leaves of masonry separated by a cavity of specific dimensions. When preparing to build cavity walling, the bricklayer will need to carefully refer to working drawings and the specification to find out the exact details and design of the work to be constructed. The materials specified will have particular characteristics that make them suitable for use in cavity walling and it's important that the bricklayer selects the correct materials before work starts.

Many of the principles already covered regarding information sources used in selecting resources for solid walling can be applied to the building of cavity walling.

For example, review the points in Chapter 4 on pages 139–142 concerning:

- The different types of drawings and conventions commonly used (block plans, site plans, different types of projections etc).

- Ways of interpreting information from drawings (scales, symbols, hatchings etc).

- The information provided by specifications and schedules.

After you have reviewed these points in relation to solid walling, consider how they also apply to selecting resources for cavity walling. Understanding plans, drawings and specifications is vital in making sure that the right materials are used for the job.

CHARACTERISTICS OF MATERIALS

The range of masonry materials that could be specified for cavity walling includes:

CLAY BRICKS

- *Facing brick.* These are the bricks that can form the 'face' of the building. They are available in a vast range of colours and textures from many different manufacturers. The clay they are manufactured from is easily moulded and consists mainly of quartz and clay minerals. The moulded clay is converted into durable bricks by a heating process known as firing, which heats the bricks in a **kiln** to temperatures between 900°C and 1250°C. This process may produce bricks with considerable variations in size since the heating process causes the materials to change their form, which can result in shrinkage and distortion.

A lot of thought and care can go into choosing the right brick to achieve the desired finish to a building.

Facing bricks on a new house

- *Engineering brick.* These are bricks that have a high compressive strength. This means that they can resist squeezing forces such as those that might be present in a high-rise structure like a block of flats or in a load-bearing arch.

  Also, engineering bricks don't absorb water, which makes them suitable for cavity walling below ground level (or for use as a damp proof course).

A railway bridge built with engineering bricks

- *Common brick.* A lower quality brick that is usually used in locations where the finished work will not be on show. For example, they could be used in constructing internal partition walls that adjoin a cavity wall.

Common brick

Aggregate

The coarse mineral material, such as sharp sand and graded, crushed stone (gravel), used in making mortar and concrete

Hydrated

Caused to heat and crumble by treatment with water

Cure

To set hard, often using heat or pressure

OTHER BRICK TYPES

- *Sand/lime brick.* A brick which is relatively easy to cut and shape. These bricks are sometimes referred to as 'calcium silicate bricks' since they are composed of a fine **aggregate** which is bonded together by **hydrated** calcium silicate. Pigment can be added to produce bricks in a range of colours.

The mix is moulded under high pressure in hydraulic presses to produce the shape and then subjected to high-pressure steam in an apparatus called an autoclave, for up to 12 hours to **cure** the bricks. This process produces bricks that have very little variation in overall dimensions and so they are often used for decorative work.

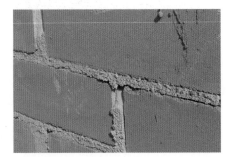

A sand/lime brick wall

Brick autoclave

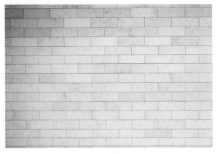

A concrete brick wall

■ *Concrete brick.* Like sand/lime bricks, concrete bricks are not fired in a kiln and therefore also have more accurate dimensions than clay bricks. They are manufactured from a mix of aggregate, cement and water. They can be coloured during manufacture and given a range of textures if desired. Since they are usually made in solid form without a **frog** and are therefore heavier than clay bricks, concrete bricks are effective in reducing noise transmission and give good fire protection.

BLOCKS

■ *Lightweight insulation block.* In cavity walling these blocks are usually specified above a damp proof course (DPC) for the internal skin. Certain types of lightweight blocks can be used below a DPC, but these are expensive. They reduce heat transmission through the walls of a structure and therefore improve energy efficiency. Because they are lightweight these blocks are easy to work with and can be readily cut and shaped. However, especially when they're dry, they generate a lot of fine dust when being cut to shape or moved from storage. Suitable PPE should always be used to protect against dust contamination, such as a dust mask.

■ *Dense concrete block.* These can be specified in cavity walls where the outer skin is not built in brick. To provide a suitable finish, a sand/cement render or other coating would need to be used. They are also used extensively in work below ground such as in the **footings** of a cavity wall. They are made from a coarser aggregate than concrete bricks.

Have a look at the cavity walls in 'Our House' and think about the sort of blocks used for that kind of building.

MORTAR

Bricks and blocks are, of course, bonded together using mortar to produce the bed and cross (or perp) joints. Preparing mortar for cavity wall construction requires care in the mixing process to produce a material that is easy to use and durable when set. A specification for cavity walling may give precise details about the colour of the mortar, the proportions of the different materials in the mortar mix, and any additives that are required.

After reading the descriptions of the different brick types, discuss with another student which type of brick would be suitable for use in the basement of a three-storey house. Write down the description of your chosen brick in your own words and two reasons for your choice.

Work on this activity can support FE2:3 (A) and (B).

Frog
The indentation in a brick

To reduce the dust generated by cutting or moving lightweight insulation blocks, they can be lightly sprayed with water. Be careful not to saturate them.

Dense concrete blocks in storage

Footings
The section of masonry from the foundation to the start of the superstructure

Dense concrete block

Jointing mortar

ACTIVITY

Check a builder's merchants' website (for example www.jewson.co.uk) and type 'mortar additives' in the search box. Write down the names of at least two additives and describe what they do.

Sharp

In this context, sand that has pointed or angular grains

Mortar for cavity walling must meet a number of important requirements throughout the entire life of the structure. It must possess:

- adequate compressive strength

- durability – resistance to chemical attack and frost damage

- strong bonding with masonry components

- a sealed surface to protect against wind-driven rain.

To fulfil these demands, the materials mortar is produced from need to have certain qualities. Let's look at the materials for mortar one at a time.

Sand

Sand for brick- or blocklaying comes from two main sources.

It can be sand dug from pit deposits, which is appropriately known as 'pit sand'. This type of sand produces a mortar that is easy to work with and the finished product has a pleasing colour.

Alternatively, as sand deposits decline and planning permission for removing sand from pit locations becomes more difficult to obtain, sand is increasingly being extracted (referred to as dredged) from the sea. This type of sand has to be thoroughly washed to remove salts before it can be used, to avoid affecting the quality of the mortar. Dredged sand is usually more **sharp** than pit sand and may require an additive to make it easier to work with.

Dredged sand processing plant

All sand used for masonry must be well graded. This means that it must contain a uniform mix of fine, medium and coarse particles. Mortar made from poorly graded sand will be weaker since there will be more tiny spaces that need to be filled. These tiny spaces or voids can cause shrinkage as the mortar hardens, which can result in cracks forming. Rain can then penetrate the cavity walling which will cause deterioration over time.

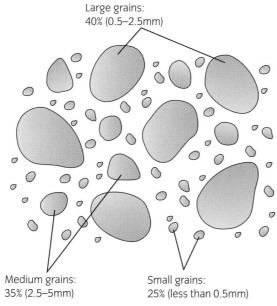

Large grains:
40% (0.5–2.5mm)

Medium grains:
35% (2.5–5mm)

Small grains:
25% (less than 0.5mm)

Grading grains of sand

ACTIVITY

Enter 'Educational Guide to Aggregates' (on the CEMEX website) into an online search engine. Check out the different sources of sand and how they are graded.

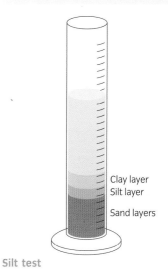

Clay layer
Silt layer

Sand layers

Silt test

Sand used for mortar must be free of mud and silt. A mortar mix containing excessive mud or silt will be weakened over time and could lead to structural failure. A specification may require a 'silt test'. In this test, the clean sand sinks to the bottom of the test vessel (tube) so that the amount of silt and mud or clay can be clearly seen.

Cement

Cement powder is produced from limestone and is used in mortar as a 'binder'. It effectively fills the voids between the sand and makes sure that the finished mortar is hard and durable enough for the job. A chemical reaction occurs between the cement powder and water added to the mix. This is called 'hydration' and this reaction makes the mortar set hard.

The proportions of sand and cement are stated as a **ratio,** which will be designed to make sure that the finished mortar has sufficient compressive strength (resistance to squeezing) while not being overly brittle. As a general rule of thumb, the mortar should be slightly weaker than the bricks or blocks being laid. This allows for any slight movement in the masonry caused by thermal expansion or by shrinkage occurring during hardening. A ratio of 1:3 (1 part cement and 3 parts sand) would be described as a strong mix whereas a ratio of 1:8 would be weaker (or leaner). There are a number of different types of cement that can be specified according to the requirements of the job:

- *Ordinary Portland Cement* (OPC). This is the most commonly used cement. It is suitable for general masonry work and if used correctly will produce a mortar of high quality and strength.

- *Masonry Cement.* This is similar to OPC but contains 25% inert filler (meaning the filler is not chemically active), so a mortar using this

Cement manufacturing plant

Ratio

The amount or proportion of one thing compared to another

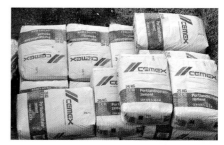

Ordinary Portland Cement (OPC)

Masonry Cement

Sulphate

A salt of sulphuric acid

A tap with clean flowing water

Plasticiser

An additive that is used to make the mortar pliable and easier to work with

type of cement requires a higher proportion of cement powder to provide adequate bonding characteristics.

- *Rapid Hardening Portland Cement* (RHPC). This can be used where a shorter setting time is required. Whereas the setting and hardening of OPC takes place in seven days or more, RHPC will set and harden to working strength in about four days.

- *Sulphate Resisting Portland Cement* (SRPC). This cement is better than OPC at resisting **sulphate** attack in damp conditions.

Water

Water is an essential constituent and without it mortar would not harden or set. The water used in producing mortar should be *potable*, which means that it is suitable to drink. Using water of drinkable quality means that no chemicals will be present that could interfere with hydration (the hardening process) or affect the mortar in undesirable ways. For example, if we were to use water from a stream or pond near a building site, it could contain substances that could affect the hardening process or discolour the mortar.

Plasticiser

If we were to simply mix sand, cement and water together to produce a mortar for brick or blocklaying, we would find it difficult to use. To make it more 'workable', a **plasticiser** must be added.

Modern plasticisers are chemical additives that are included in the mixing process as a liquid or a powder. They should be used carefully in accordance with the manufacturer's instructions. Chemical plasticisers work by introducing tiny air bubbles, which allow the particles of sand to move over each other more freely. This is called 'air entrainment'.

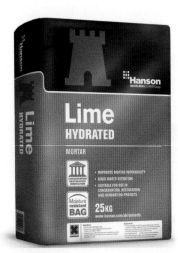

Hydrated lime

Plasticiser

Powdered plasticiser

In the past, it was common practice to use hydrated lime as a plasticiser. This increases the powder content of the mix, which forms a paste that lubricates the particles of sand. Hydrated lime is still specified on occasions but it has more health and safety considerations (and can be more hazardous to health) than chemical plasticisers, which are easier to work with.

MIXING MORTAR

Mortar for cavity walling can be produced in a number of ways:

- Mixed by hand on site

- Mixed by machine on site

- Mixed by machine off site and delivered to site ready to use.

BY HAND

Mixing mortar by hand is hard work, but if we follow a simple sequence and work on a clean solid base, it can be made a little easier. The common rule when mixing by hand is 'three times dry – three times wet'. This means that we move the dry materials from their placed position to the side and then back again three times in order to mix the sand and cement (and lime if specified) thoroughly before adding water.

INDUSTRY TIP

When mixing by hand, don't use a shovel that's too big for you to handle. It's more efficient and much easier if you use a smaller 'taper nose' shovel.

Taper nose shovel

Once the dry materials are well mixed and positioned in a tidy mound, a large circular dip is formed in the centre and water is added carefully. The water is gradually mixed in, until it is **uniformly** spread through the materials. It can then be turned three times 'wet' in a similar manner to the dry mixing and more water slowly added as required. If a plasticiser is used, this should be added to the water and not to the dry materials.

Uniformly

Evenly and consistently

The following step by steps show the correct method for mixing.

STEP 1 Add the cement to the sand in accordance with the specified ratio.

STEP 2 Mix the sand and cement three times 'dry'.

STEP 3 Add water to the dry mix (taking care not to add too much).

STEP 4 Mix the sand and cement three times 'wet'. Add water as needed to improve the mortar consistency.

BY MACHINE ON SITE

Mixing on site is usually done using a drum mixer. This can be powered by electricity, a diesel engine or a petrol engine. A drum mixer of any size is a powerful piece of machinery and must be treated with respect.

Never put your hand or a shovel into the revolving drum when the mixer is running. Wearing loose clothing can also be dangerous. It could get caught in the moving parts and drag an operative into the machinery causing potentially severe injury.

When mixing mortar with a drum mixer, always add an amount of water first, the cement second and the sand third. When the cement is added to the water, it forms a paste to which the sand is then added. If the cement is added after the sand, it can form into small balls, which prevent thorough mixing and have an effect on the final strength of the mortar. It takes time and experience to produce a mortar mix that matches all the specified requirements.

Whichever method of mixing is used, measuring the correct proportions of materials is vitally important. Measuring materials 'by

Drum mixer

FUNCTIONAL SKILLS

Enter 'cement mixer hire' into an online search engine. Browse your search results and develop a short presentation about the different types of mixers that are available besides drum mixers.

Work on this activity can support FE2:1 (B).

the shovelful' will not produce a consistently reliable mix. A shovelful of dry powdery cement will have much less volume than a shovelful of damp sand.

A shovelful of dry cement

A shovelful of damp sand

Providing accurate amounts of materials for mortar is known as 'gauging'. A gauge box is a bottomless steel or timber square or rectangle which is placed on a clean flat surface and filled with either sand or cement flush with the open top of the box. If a ratio of 1:4 is required, four boxes of sand will be mixed with one box of cement. (A suitably sized strong bucket could also be used.) To mix larger amounts, multiples of the gauged amounts will be used.

The carefully measured separate piles of sand and cement can then either be mixed by hand or loaded into a drum mixer as previously described.

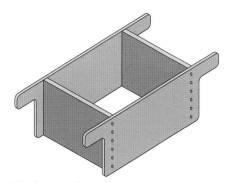

Steel gauge box

BY MACHINE OFF SITE

Mortar mixed off site will usually be mixed by weight batching and not by volume. This is a very accurate method of making sure that the correct proportions are used. The mixed mortar delivered to site may include a 'retarder', which is a chemical additive to slow down the hydration of the cement. Adding this keeps the mortar workable for up to 48 hours, sometimes longer.

Premixed mortar being delivered to a site

Mortar batching plant

SELECTING TOOLS

As has been frequently mentioned, to aid efficiency and productivity it is important to make a list of tools needed before we start work. The tools needed to build cavity walling are broadly the same as the tools required to build solid walling and are detailed in Chapter 4 (see pages 143–144). Tools for constructing masonry are grouped under three headings:

- *Laying and finishing.* Trowel, pointing trowel and jointer.

- *Checking.* Tape measure, spirit level, and line and pins.

- *Cutting.* Club (or lump) hammer, brick bolster, brick hammer and scutch hammer.

There are some additional tools which will be needed for cutting materials used in cavity wall construction. A masonry saw is useful for cutting lightweight insulation blocks and a jack saw and craft knife are useful for cutting cavity wall insulation materials. (Insulation materials are discussed in more detail later in this chapter.)

Craft knife

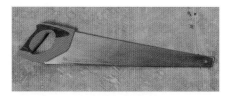

Jack saw

INDUSTRY TIP

Keep an eye out for carpenters who are disposing of worn jack saws on site. Even if the teeth are not sharp enough for cutting timber, they will be fine for cutting insulation materials (and even insulation blocks).

An operative using a masonry saw

SAFETY AND EFFICIENCY

A detailed description of safe and efficient methods used to cut masonry materials by hand can be found in Chapter 4. Cutting masonry materials by machine, such as a disc cutter, should only be undertaken after proper training has been completed.

Disc cutter training in progress

As with all construction activities, when selecting resources and materials for cavity walling, health and safety considerations have to be of the utmost importance. Important things to think about come under three main headings:

- Health and safety regulations and guidance (the Work at Height Regulations 2005, product safety guidance etc)

- PPE requirements (including goggles, gloves etc)

- Interpreting and using risk assessments.

Chapter 1 and Chapter 4 expand on these headings comprehensively. Review these two chapters to refresh your knowledge of the important health and safety points related to selecting resources and preparation for building cavity walling.

Chapter 1 also contains information about the importance of calculating the quantities of materials needed for the job, to support efficiency (see page 57 onwards). Calculating quantities for cavity walling uses the same principles as working out what's needed for solid walling. We need to first calculate the area of the face of our wall in m² by multiplying the length by the height. Then we simply multiply the number of square metres by 60 for bricks and 10 for blocks, adding 5% for wastage.

Finally, cavity walling should be protected when completed and this is something that must be planned for during the preparation stage. Before you start building, make sure that suitable materials and resources, such as polythene or hessian sheeting, are in place to protect your finished work from poor weather and other construction activities.

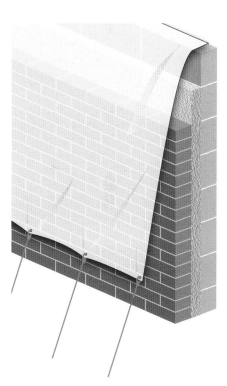

A cavity wall protected with polythene sheeting

ACTIVITY

Go to the Brick Development Association (BDA) website and enter 'frost protection' in the search box. Write down any information you can find about the effects of frost damage and how to prevent it.

ERECTING CAVITY WALLING TO THE GIVEN SPECIFICATION

GOOD PRACTICE

You should already be familiar with methods used to set out and build masonry corners, junctions and straight lengths in solid walling. (Also check Chapter 4 for details on transferring wall positions onto foundations and using datum points.) The principles for building cavity walling are similar in terms of setting out the bond and keeping plumb, level and gauge to maintain industrial standards. The following step by steps illustrate the main points to keep in mind when constructing cavity walling:

STEP 1 Set out the first course carefully and accurately.

STEP 2 Check the specified dimension for the width of cavity required.

STEP 3 Make sure that the work is set out to the correct overall dimensions and to the required level.

STEP 4 Carefully refer to and observe provided datum points.

Accurately setting out the first course will help to make sure that the rest of the construction process is completed to a high standard. Taking care to work to high standards at all times means that work will not have to be re-done, which can be costly and time consuming.

BONDING

The most commonly used brick bond in the outer skin (or leaf) of cavity walling is Stretcher bond. Take some time to establish the brick bond for the face of the cavity wall. Consider the possibility of using **reverse bond** to avoid introducing cut bricks into the face. If **broken bond** *has* to be used, plan where it will be placed (if possible under a door or window opening) and set out the bonding arrangement below ground level.

Reverse bond

In the same course, starting with a stretcher and ending with a header

Broken bond

The use of part bricks to make good a bonding pattern where full bricks will not fit in

Reverse bond

Broken bond

Carefully setting out the bond below ground level will make sure that the appearance of the cavity wall throughout the rest of the structure will be the best you can achieve. Face brickwork (where specified for the outer skin of a cavity wall) is the 'finish' of the building and will potentially be on view for a very long time.

Never build too high at any one time. Each individual skin or leaf of masonry should not be raised too high without support from the other skin. The British Standards official guidance states that a single wall in a cavity wall design should not be built higher than six courses of block or 18 courses of brick in one operation (BS EN 1996-3:2006).

FUNCTIONAL SKILLS

Go to the Brick Development Association (BDA) website and find their image gallery. Look through ten of the examples and write down the name of the project and the brick that is used in the example you like most.

Work on this activity can support FICT2 (4A).

Building too high in one operation can be dangerous. A single skin of unsupported masonry is relatively fragile and can easily be blown over by strong winds even when the mortar has hardened.

A single leaf of blockwork seven courses high, unsupported by the brickwork

Make sure all bed and especially perp (or cross) joints are full. To speed up the job, some bricklayers have the bad habit of 'tipping and tailing' their perp joints. This means that instead of completely filling the joint, a small amount of mortar is placed on the front and back edges of the header face, which leaves a **void** in the finished joint.

Void

An open space or gap

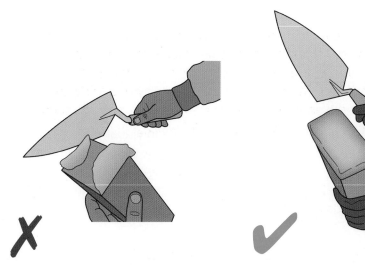

Bricklayer incorrectly 'tipping' the perp joint

Bricklayer correctly making a full perp joint

The use of cavity walling was adopted in preference to solid walling because it gives greater protection against moisture penetration.

This protection can only be fully provided if all joints are full. It may be quicker to 'tip and tail' in the short term while building, but in the long term, expensive problems can be caused by careless or shoddy workmanship.

KEY FEATURES

A cavity wall is more complex to build than solid walling. There are a number of additional components included in a cavity wall design such as wall ties, insulation and a DPC.

INDUSTRY TIP

Some solid walls may have a DPC specified in their design but this is relatively unusual and is unlikely to be a flexible damp proof course. See Chapter 4 for more details.

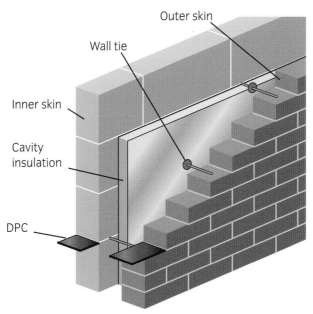

Outer skin

Wall tie

Inner skin

Cavity insulation

DPC

Components of a cavity wall

In addition, since a cavity wall is usually wider at the base than a solid wall (unless the solid wall is built to one and a half brick thickness or more), it places lighter loads on the foundation. This means that the design of the foundation for cavity walling can be simplified or reduced in thickness since it doesn't need to support the greater concentrated weight of solid walling.

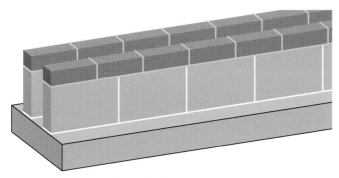

Cavity walling is wider at the base

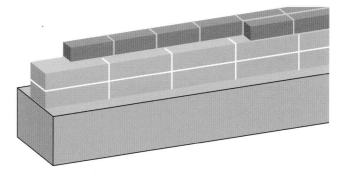

Narrower solid walling concentrates loading on the strip foundation

ACTIVITY

Do you think a foundation could be affected by trees nearby? Do some research and write down your conclusions.

Thermal movement

Changes in dimension of masonry or concrete as a result of changes in temperature over time

ACTIVITY

When you're travelling around the area you live in, look for examples of movement joints in brickwork. If you have a mobile phone with a camera, take a picture and discuss with your tutor why the movement joint has been used in that location.

Lateral movement

Movement or pressure from the side

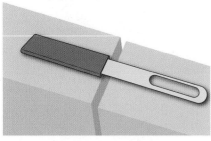

Wall tie with de-bonding sleeve

The usual design of foundation for cavity walling is a *concrete strip* foundation. This can have measurements that are wide and shallow or narrow and deep depending on ground conditions and other design considerations such as cost and timescale requirements.

Experience has shown that since a cavity wall creates lighter loads than a solid wall, it must be designed with provision to prevent cracking caused by **thermal movement** and continuous wetting and drying.

To allow for movement, cavity walling may be designed with *vertical movement joints* constructed at intervals along the length of the wall. These are constructed as a vertical 'straight joint' in the bonding arrangement, and are filled with a compressible material to allow small amounts of expansion and contraction along the length of the masonry.

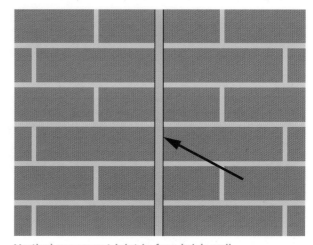

Vertical movement joint in face brick wall

The length of masonry panels between movement joints varies according to the type of brick used. In clay brickwork the distance between movement joints may be 10m or more, whereas brickwork in calcium silicate bricks may have movement joints as close as 6m apart. This detail will be clearly stated in the specification and on working drawings.

A bricklayer is often required to use specially designed ties in the bed joints at vertical movement joints. This assists the masonry to resist **lateral movement** at the joint location while still allowing horizontal movement. This is achieved by one end of the tie being firmly bedded in mortar and the other end of the tie having a moveable sleeve, called a de-bonding sleeve, bedded in the horizontal mortar joint to allow the tie to move inside it.

DAMP PROOF COURSE

A damp proof course (DPC) is an essential part of a cavity wall design and will be positioned in a number of locations in a structure. Without a correctly positioned DPC, the ability of the cavity wall to prevent the entry of moisture into the living or working area of a structure will be severely **compromised**.

Moisture, or 'damp' as it's more commonly referred to, enters a cavity wall in two main ways.

- *Penetrating damp.* This describes moisture that travels through a wall above finished floor level (FFL) when the masonry material becomes saturated. The cavity separating the inner and outer skins of masonry has the job of breaking the path of the moisture through the wall. (Preventing moisture penetrating at openings will be discussed in the next section.)

- *Rising damp.* This refers to moisture that is drawn upwards from ground level and below by a process known as *capillary attraction*. A horizontal damp proof course installed at a minimum of 150mm above finished ground level is designed to halt the progress of rising damp. The position of a horizontal DPC usually corresponds to FFL.

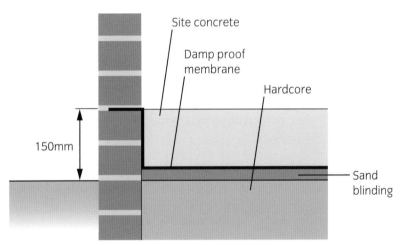

Horizontal DPC 150mm above ground

A third, less frequent, point of entry for moisture is where a cavity wall projects above a roof line in the form of a **parapet**. Moisture can penetrate from above and this requires special DPC arrangements to protect the structure from damage. This chapter will concentrate on horizontal DPC and provision of DPC around openings.

A damp proof course is described as *flexible* or *rigid* according to the material used. See Chapter 4 pages 157–158 for a detailed description of a number of materials that can be specified for each type of DPC along with an analysis of the advantages and disadvantages of each.

The bricklayer is responsible for the correct installation of a DPC into cavity walling and must give careful attention to the following points of good practice:

Compromise
To reduce the quality or value of something

Penetrating damp

ACTIVITY

Refer back to Chapter 4, page 158 and check the advantages and disadvantages of different types of flexible DPC. Which type would you select for the horizontal DPC in a four-storey block of flats? State the reasons for your choice.

INDUSTRY TIP

A parapet cavity wall is usually in an exposed position and may include a purpose made coping to close the cavity and 'weather' the top of the wall. The coping will usually be manufactured from pre-cast concrete or impermeable stone.

Parapet
A low wall along the edge of a roof or balcony

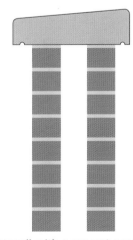

Parapet wall with a precast concrete coping on top

Flexible DPC materials in stacks

■ Store rolls of DPC correctly. Stack rolls on end, no more than three rolls high. Rolls of DPC that are stored flat are prone to distortion which can make them difficult to lay. If possible store in an even temperature.

■ Make sure the specified material is used. Once the DPC is built into a cavity wall, it's a major task to change it if it isn't the correct type.

■ Lay flexible DPC on a thin bed of mortar to protect it from possible puncture by hardened mortar projections in the previously laid work.

■ If rolls of flexible DPC have to be overlapped, make sure the lap is a minimum of 100mm. If a DPC wider than 100mm is specified, then the lap should be the same as the width of DPC used.

■ Never allow the DPC to project into the cavity. If necessary, cut it off with a craft knife. If mortar builds up on a projecting DPC, it can allow moisture to 'bridge' the cavity and enter the living or working area of the building.

WALL TIES

A cavity wall consists of two leaves or skins of masonry that in isolation are relatively weak. When properly tied together with suitable wall ties, the stiffness and load-bearing capacity of the combined skins can be almost equal to a similar solid wall. Providing an adequate number of correctly positioned and installed wall ties is the bricklayer's responsibility.

The image below shows the correct spacing of wall ties in accordance with regulations and codes of practice.

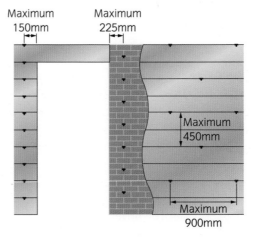
Wall tie spacing

There are a number of different types of wall tie currently in use which are available in a range of sizes to suit various cavity widths. The specification will state the type of wall tie to be used for a particular job. Ties were previously manufactured from **galvanised** steel which suffered from long-term failure due to corrosion and rust. Modern ties are commonly made from stainless steel which is much

Galvanise

To cover iron or steel with a protective zinc coating

more durable. More rarely, wall ties have been manufactured using polypropylene (a type of plastic).

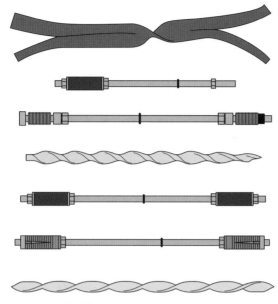

A variety of wall ties

A safety consideration that must be kept in mind in relation to the installation of wall ties is their potential for causing injury. When they are built into the first skin of masonry that's constructed, they project from the wall and can cause injury to the bricklayer as the second skin or leaf is constructed. Always be aware of this, especially with regard to wall ties at eye level.

Wall ties are designed with a feature known as a 'drip', which is usually in the form of a twist or a bend along the length of the tie. This serves to shed any moisture that may track across them from the outer skin, preventing it from reaching the inner skin or leaf.

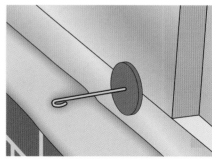

Wall tie correctly bedded in a bed joint

The competent and careful bricklayer should always keep the following points in mind when installing wall ties:

■ Bed the ends of ties at least 50mm into the bed joint of each masonry skin.

■ Make sure that the 'drip' is positioned centrally in the cavity.

■ Never just push the ties into the bed joint – they will not be effective in tying the two skins or leaves together.

■ To achieve maximum strength, press the ties down into the mortar – do not lay the mortar over the ties.

■ Make sure the ties are level between the two skins, or inclined towards the outer skin. If ties are inclined towards the inner skin, they can conduct moisture across the cavity.

■ Keep all ties clean – remove mortar droppings to avoid creating a bridge for moisture.

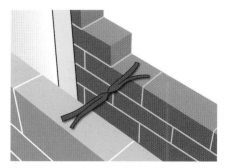

Wall tie with drip positioned in a cavity wall

INSULATION

The requirement to improve energy efficiency (see Chapter 2) and reduce carbon emissions in new buildings has led to the introduction of increasing levels of insulation. Cavity walls provide a convenient and efficient way to control heat transfer, and the opportunity to locate insulation materials in a major element of a structure.

There are three main methods of installing insulation in a cavity wall.

Method name	Description
Full fill 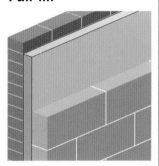	Sometimes called total fill. As the name suggests, this method fully fills the cavity with insulation material so that no air gaps remain. The material used is usually manufactured in the form of flexible slabs or 'batts'. This form of insulation can also be effective in preventing the spread of fire.
Partial fill 	This method allows an air gap of a minimum of 50mm to be maintained. The insulation material is in the form of rigid sheets of material and is fixed to the inner skin or leaf by special clips attached to the wall ties.
Injection 	The method of pumping insulation into the cavity after the building is complete. In new-build work the insulation material is injected through holes drilled in the inside skin of the structure. If an older building is insulated by injection, the holes are drilled in the outer skin or leaf of masonry, usually through the mortar joints rather than through face bricks.

The range of materials suitable for use as insulation includes:

Material	Description	Use
Mineral fibre	Flexible sheets or batts made from glass or rock.	Suitable for full fill.
Expanded poly-styrene (EPS) and polyisocyanurate foam (PIR)	Rigid sheets or boards.	Suitable for partial fill.
Expanded poly-styrene	Beads and chopped strands of mineral fibre.	Suitable for injection.

A newer form of insulation that is effective but expensive is sheep's wool, which is currently not widely used.

DECORATIVE FEATURES

If the outer skin or leaf of a cavity wall is built in face brick, there are opportunities to introduce decorative features to enhance the appearance of the building. Chapter 4 details a number of features that can also be used in cavity walling. These include **Soldier courses**, which are commonly used when spanning openings, and

Soldier course above a window

Soldier course

Bricks laid on end with the stretcher face showing

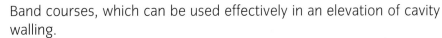

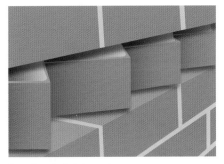

Dog-tooth brickwork

Castellated

Having or resembling repeated square indentations

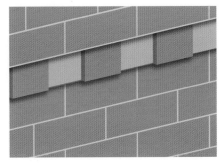

Dentil brickwork

Band courses, which can be used effectively in an elevation of cavity walling.

A feature not already mentioned which is commonly used in the face of cavity walling is a String course. A String course can include face bricks laid in a pattern known as Dog-tooth. This involves laying bricks diagonally in relation to the face line of the wall to give the String course a serrated effect (meaning it has a jagged edge, like a knife).

Another bonding arrangement that can be used in a String course is known as a Dentil course. This involves stepping alternate half bricks (showing the header face) back from the face line accurately along the course to produce a type of **castellated** effect. Look at the illustrations to see the bonding arrangements for these two types of String course.

JOINTING

Jointing refers to the method of providing a finished joint as the work proceeds. This method differs from *pointing*, which involves raking out the mortar joints at the time of building and refilling (or pointing) them at a later stage, perhaps with a coloured mortar.

This would also be done, for example, if the specified joint was too time consuming to allow completion at the time of building (such as a weather cut and struck joint which takes a high level of skill and a great deal of time to produce correctly).

The following step by steps show racking out of joints followed by pointing to refill the joints.

STEP 1 Use a chariot raker to rake out the mortar joints ready for pointing (12–15mm deep).

STEP 2 Point the new mortar into the raked out joints. Always provide a finish to the perps first, followed by the beds.

STEP 3 Use a pointing trowel to give a weather struck finish to the bed joints.

In Chapter 4 you will find a detailed discussion of joint finishes that can also be used in cavity walling, including:

- half-round

- recessed

- flush

- weather struck.

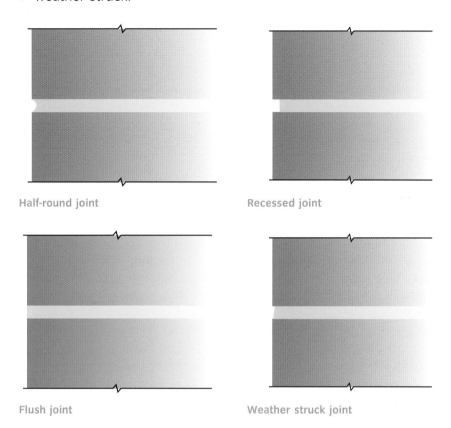

Half-round joint

Recessed joint

Flush joint

Weather struck joint

Whichever joint finish is specified, the effort put forth and the level of skill employed by the bricklayer will determine the quality of the finished job.

To produce work that looks good and conforms fully to the industrial standards requires commitment. It is important that the bricklayer develops good habits during preparation, checking that the correct undamaged materials are in place while preparing for the work.

Regularly checking for accuracy in levelling, plumbing and gauging as the cavity walling proceeds will contribute to the production of work that is durable and fit for purpose. If problems become obvious during construction, always report the issue to your supervisor or line manager.

It's not appropriate to try to tackle difficult problems without direction from authorised personnel. The decision made regarding any necessary **remedial work** may have consequences for other operatives who follow on from your work, so always get direction before proceeding. In addition your supervisor or line manager will want remedial work to fit in with the programme of work, so a timescale for the work may be set out.

Remedial work

Necessary alterations or adjustments to work due to errors, damage or poor work practices

Finally, remember to take account of risk assessments and method statements to be safe and efficient in your work. Chapter 4, pages 137–138 detail the steps involved in producing risk assessments and method statements.

FORMING OPENINGS IN CAVITY WALLING

DIFFERENT METHODS

Openings in cavity walls are constructed by the bricklayer to allow for the installation of doors and windows. The methods used to set out and create an opening vary according to the type of door or window frames specified. Openings are also formed to allow for services like water and electricity below ground, but in this section we'll concentrate on forming openings for doors and windows.

For example, if softwood timber frames are specified, they can be 'built-in' to the masonry as work proceeds. The frame is set up and temporarily braced in the correct position on the masonry at the door or window sill level and the brickwork or blockwork is carefully formed around it. A range of different types of frame fixings to secure the frame can be built into the bed joints of the masonry at the required spacing as the work around the frame is built up. The fixings are simply screwed into the side of the frame.

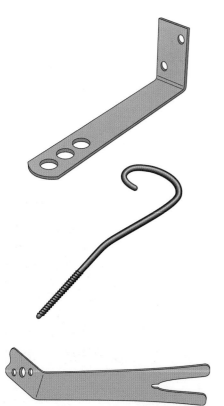

Different types of frame fixings

A timber window frame set up on a cavity wall and braced with temporary support to keep it plumb

If **PVC** frames are to be used, they will need to be installed after the masonry work is completed since they can easily be damaged during construction activities like bricklaying. The openings are formed using 'dummy' frames: these form a temporary profile around which the masonry can be built. They are later removed to leave an opening ready for the PVC frames to be inserted into. This method might also be used when expensive hardwood frames are specified which could suffer damage during the building phase.

PVC

Polyvinyl chloride, a type of strong plastic

Dummy frame in use

The dimensions of the dummy frame are usually increased by 10mm or so, to create an opening slightly larger than the finished frame – this allows ease of fitting later.

CUTTING AROUND THE OPENING

When constructing openings in masonry, a considerable number of cut bricks and blocks will be required. Some bricklayers prefer to spend time preparing the required cuts before building commences, to improve the flow of work.

If the inner skin is constructed in insulation block and is returned into the outer skin to close the cavity at the **reveals**, care is needed to make sure that the cutting operation produces accurately sized components. This is because a vertical DPC may be specified at this location, and this will need to be held firmly in place without the risk of it being punctured.

The outer skin will have cut bricks (or batts) laid to maintain the bond either side of the opening. If the cuts are half-bats, the cut end should be placed in the perp or cross joint to make sure that a

An operative cutting bricks

Reveals

The masonry forming the side of a window or door opening

smooth rear face is presented against the vertical DPC, again to make sure there is minimal risk of puncturing the DPC. This also ensures that the position of the DPC follows the correct vertical line.

MORE ON DPC

There are modern flexible vertical DPCs that have an insulation material attached to them to reduce what is known as the 'cold bridge' effect around a door or window frame. This material can be easily damaged and must be handled with care. The rolls of insulated DPC can also be bulky, so you must plan where you will store them.

Insulated vertical DPC in position at the reveal of a window

Proprietary

An item manufactured and distributed under a trade name

Jamb

A vertical inside face of an opening in a wall

More frequently, no vertical DPC is specified, but instead a **proprietary** PVC cavity closer may be used. This has the advantage of simplifying the cuts required since no masonry closes the cavity at the **jamb** area. The rigid PVC profile closes the cavity, acts as a DPC and can also be designed to include insulation material. In addition, fixings for the door or window frame can be included in the design to make a simple-to-use multi-purpose component.

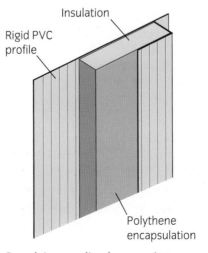

Insulation

Rigid PVC profile

Polythene encapsulation

Proprietary cavity closer system

WALL TIES AT OPENINGS

Creating an opening in a cavity wall will inevitably cause an area of weakness in the **structural integrity** at that location. To improve the strength at the opening, a greater number of wall ties are built into the jamb area either side of the opening.

You will remember from your Level 1 studies that the vertical spacing of wall ties in a cavity wall is set at 450mm. This spacing is reduced to 225mm at the reveals so that the strengthening effect provided by the wall ties is significantly increased. See the image on page 224 for a labelled diagram of wall tie spacings.

In the rare instance that both skins of a cavity wall are built in brick, the vertical spacing at the reveals is then set at 300mm, or at every four courses of brick.

BRIDGING OPENINGS

When forming openings in cavity walling, a means of supporting the masonry built above the opening must be provided. Steel or concrete **lintels** are used for this purpose and are manufactured in a large range of designs and dimensions.

CONCRETE LINTELS

Concrete lintels have to be reinforced with steel to enable them to withstand the forces (tension) placed on them by masonry bearing on them from above. Concrete performs well under compression when a load is squeezing it, but is not good where it is required to withstand tension in situations where it is stretched or subject to bending.

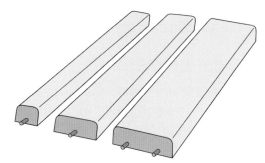

Concrete lintels showing steel reinforcement

The reinforcement is placed at the bottom of the lintel when it is cast since this is where the greatest stretching forces will be. The bricklayer must therefore be sure that a concrete lintel is installed the right way up. It is usual for manufacturers to label the top of the lintel with the letter 'T'.

Structural integrity

A structure's ability to safely resist the loads placed on it

Lintel

A horizontal member for spanning an opening, such as a door, to support the structure above

Concrete lintel showing 'T' marking on the top

Concrete lintels are mostly used where appearance is not important, such as in bridging openings in partition walls within a structure or for providing openings for service entry points underground.

STEEL LINTELS

Steel lintels are more commonly used in cavity walls which have the outer skin constructed in face brickwork and the inner skin or leaf constructed in lightweight insulation block. This is because a steel lintel is lighter than a concrete lintel of the same span and unlike a concrete lintel very little of the steel lintel can be seen when viewed from the outside of the structure. In addition, steel lintels are manufactured to incorporate insulation materials as part of their design.

Steel combination lintels

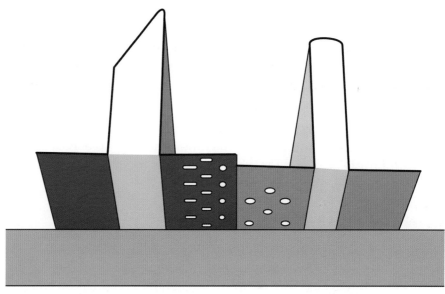
Different steel lintels with insulation

Whichever type of lintel is used, it is the bricklayer's responsibility to make sure that the correct lintel is properly installed and that the **bearing** is as per the specification (a minimum of 150mm).

POSITIONING OF LINTELS

The position at which lintels are installed is termed the 'head' of the door or window opening. This position is vulnerable to moisture penetration and must be protected by a damp proof course tray, which is installed above the lintel. Study the illustration of a DPC tray and note how any moisture travelling down the inside of the outer skin will be directed out of the structure (through openings called **weep holes**) and will be prevented from penetrating the living or working area of the building.

Bearing

The portion of the lintel that sits on the wall and transmits structural weight

Weep holes

Gaps deliberately left in masonry perp joints to allow moisture to escape. Purpose made plastic inserts are often used to maintain the correct size of the joint

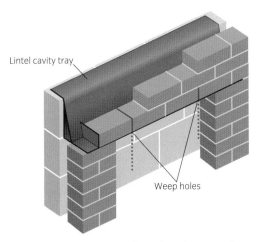

Lintel cavity tray

Weep holes

The section above a window showing a cavity tray and weep holes

APPEARANCE

To give character to the appearance of a building, the architect may specify the use of arches to bridge openings. Since an arch requires more technical expertise and care to construct than installing a lintel, there will need to be greater time allowance in the programme of work. This adds to the expense of a project.

Brickwork arches

To save time and cost and to make construction easier, brick manufacturers can produce special brick components to construct **axed** segmental and semi-circular arches. This removes the need for bricklayers on site to set out and cut bricks to shape.

The process of setting up the temporary supports (arch centre or turning piece) is detailed on page 237 onwards. The principles discussed in relation to setting out and building arches for solid walling are the same for cavity walling.

Axed

Bricks cut into a 'v' shape to fit around the radius of an arch

CILLS

Cills (sometimes spelled 'sills') under door and window frames can be formed from a variety of materials. They can be manufactured in different types of stone, slate or tile, or precast in concrete. Cills may be constructed as a decorative feature in brickwork to enhance the architectural design of a building.

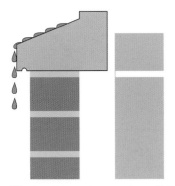

Cill showing water moving off the top surface and being thrown clear of the cavity wall

Fall

A downward slope or decline

A brick window cill

Whatever material or decorative design is specified, the cill has the important function of directing rainwater away from the face of the wall. This can be achieved in brick by laying a brick on edge set at an angle or '**fall**'. Clay or concrete tiles can also be laid with a distinct fall away from the base of the frame. Precast concrete cills can be formed with a slope or fall to conduct water away from the frame and wall.

JOINTING

Types of jointing and their advantages and disadvantages are discussed in the previous section and in Chapter 4. When performing jointing around openings in cavity walling, the following additional points are important to remember.

Not only does jointing provide a finish to a cavity wall at openings, but it also serves a vital function in the weather proofing of the jamb area of an opening. At the point where the face of the wall returns into the frame, the bed joints must be fully filled and compressed during the jointing process.

Poorly jointed work at the corners of a brick quoin

Carelessness in completing the work properly can result in gaps and voids being left which will make the cavity wall vulnerable to the effects of poor weather. When moisture enters the poorly finished bed joint, it may stay there for some time and may freeze during cold weather.

Since water expands as it freezes, it can potentially destroy the bed joint at that point and will make it likely that further deterioration will take place over time.

ARCHES

For many centuries, arches have been used to **span** openings. Many houses and other structures built in the past 200 years used arches spanning doors and windows and are still in use today. In fact some arches are still standing after well over 1000 years, in structures built by the Romans.

The curved shape of an arch spreads the load carried above it evenly to the walls (or abutments) either side of it. This means an arch can deal with large forces compressing it from above.

Span

The space or distance between two points

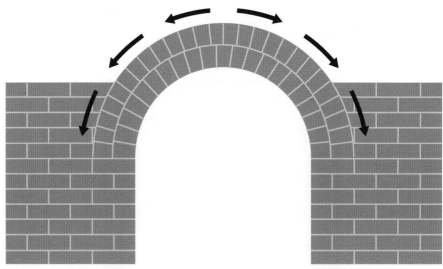

How an arch distributes the load

Find out what other arch designs are used besides semi-circular and segmental. You could check the Brick Development Association website for ideas.

Segment

A part of a curve between two points on the circumference of a circle

Although the modern method is to span openings by using lintels manufactured from steel (see page 234), there are still occasions when arches are specified in modern buildings to add character to the design.

Arches can be designed in many shapes, but the most commonly used types are semi-circular and segmental arches.

If we were to draw a complete circle, a semi-circular arch would be formed by half of the circle and a segmental arch would be formed by a **segment** of the circle.

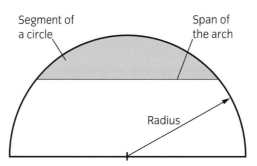

A circle split into a semi-circle and a segment

If speed of construction is a consideration or if the arch is not required to have the best quality of appearance, then the bricklayer would build what is known as a rough ring arch. In this type of arch construction, the bricks forming the arch are not cut to fit around the radius. Instead, the joints between the arch bricks are laid in a wedge shape so that the arch brickwork follows the curve across the span.

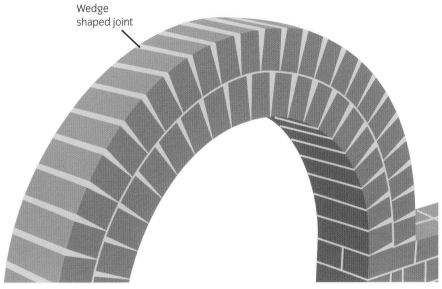

Wedge shaped joints around the arch radius

SETTING OUT

To set out and build an arch successfully, we have to be familiar with the **terminology** that is specific to arch construction. Study the labelled illustration showing the names of the various parts of an arch.

Terminology

The special terms that apply to an item or object

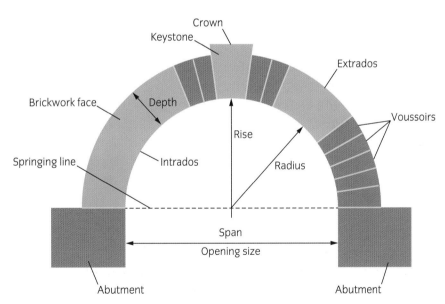

The parts of an arch

To span an opening, we obviously need a way to support the arch bricks until the radius is complete from one side of the opening to the other. This is provided by a temporary timber support called a turning piece when constructing a segmental arch, or an arch centre when constructing a semi-circular arch. Since the weight of bricks carried by these temporary supports can be considerable, they need to be well-made, sturdy carpentry items.

INDUSTRY TIP

An arch centre is usually used for a semi-circular arch and a turning piece is usually used for a segmental arch with a rise that does not exceed 150mm.

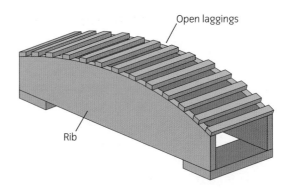

Open laggings

Rib

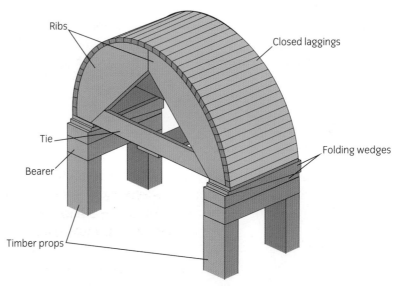

Ribs

Closed laggings

Tie

Folding wedges

Bearer

Timber props

A turning piece (top) and an arch centre (bottom)

In order to allow the arch centre or turning piece to be easily removed on completion of the arch, it should be supported on folding wedges placed on props or struts carefully wedged against the walls or abutments either side of the opening. The term 'folding wedges' refers to a pair of wedges that are placed on top of each other, with their shallow taper in opposite directions. These allow for fine height adjustment.

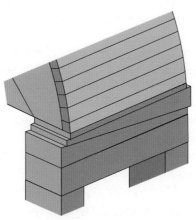

Folding wedges

By using folding wedges, the temporary support can be slightly lowered or 'eased' prior to its removal so that the arch brickwork settles and tightens on itself and bonds securely together.

Once the arch centre or turning piece has been set up correctly, the bricklayer marks the centre point of the opening on the timber support and then marks a plumb vertical line to the top or crown of the radius. This will indicate the position of the centre of the key brick. Pencil markings can then be made around the radius of the arch centre or turning piece that will indicate the evenly spaced position of the arch bricks from the springing line (refer back to the illustration on page 239) to the key brick.

The spacing of the pencil marks may have to be adjusted by trial and error to make sure the appearance is even across the radius, with the joint size slightly reduced from the standard 10mm at the bottom of the joint so as to avoid too large a dimension at the top of the joint.

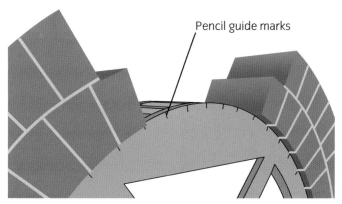

Pencil guide marks

Markings around an arch centre to build to

GOOD TECHNIQUE

Once the preparation work is complete, we can start laying the header bricks (on edge) around the radius. Always start from the springing points, laying two or three bricks on each side in turn so that the weight of the bricks is shared evenly over the arch centre or turning piece as the work progresses. Important points to remember are:

- Never allow mortar to accumulate between the bricks and the arch centre or turning piece. This will stain the **soffit** of the arch which will be visible once the timber support has been removed. It will also make it difficult to create an arch with a uniform radius.

- Remember that the face-plane of the arch must be maintained in relation to the walls either side of it. This can be achieved by building accurately plumbed 'dead men' either side of the arch to which a string line can be attached. Timber or metal profiles could be used instead.

Soffit

The underside of a part of a building (such as an arch)

The 'dead man' method

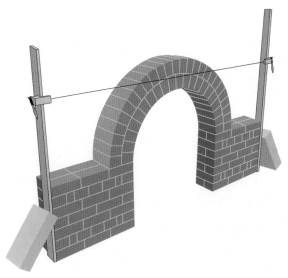

Timber profiles can be used to build an arch

- Make sure all perp joints are full but pay special attention to forming full joints when laying the key brick.

Good technique also extends to the attention we give to jointing and finishing our work. Always check the accuracy of any work you produce to make sure that it fully meets the specification and never be afraid to consult with your supervisor or a more experienced bricklayer to sort out any problems that may arise.

INDUSTRY TIP

Try to form the joints in a wedge shape so that the joints are full and you don't have to tap the bricks too much to form the radius.

CHECK YOUR WORK

The specification contains important details including, among other things, what materials should be used, the standards of workmanship required and the methods of work that should be employed. The finished job will only meet the design requirements if the bricklayer continually checks that his or her work fully complies with the given specification.

Case Study: Lee and Scott

Lee and his bricklaying partner Scott are working on a housing construction site for a major developer. The unit they're working on is a five bedroom detached house with masonry cavity walls.

As they work on the end elevation of the house Scott mentions to Lee that they are running low on wall ties. They'll need to get a supply from the stores in the site compound in the morning. Lee says, 'Not to worry – we'll just space the ties out a bit more to make them last.'

Scott is not sure that's a good idea but says nothing . . . Lee has been working on this site longer than Scott so maybe that's what he's done before.

As they drive home at the end of the day, they pass through a large estate of social housing which was built in the 1960s. A lot of contractor's vehicles are parked in the streets. Lee says, 'I wonder what contract is going on here?'

Scott says that he remembers that there was a report in the local paper that the council were going to spend a lot of money on installing replacement wall ties that had rusted away. A surveyor had caused real worries for the residents when he said that the houses could fall down if the ties weren't replaced.

Lee thinks for a moment about his suggestion to space the wall ties out more on their job. He turns to Scott and says quietly, 'I think we'd better make sure we pick up some ties from the stores in the morning.'

Work through the following questions to check your learning.

1 Engineering bricks have high
   a Passive strength
   b Compressive strength
   c Torsional strength
   d Lateral strength

2 Moulded clay facing bricks are produced in a kiln by
   a Hydrating
   b Soaking
   c Firing
   d Purging

3 The term used for accurately measuring proportions of materials for mortar is
   a Setting
   b Gauging
   c Sorting
   d Placing

4 If sand for masonry is described as 'sharp', to make a workable mix we will need to add a
   a Smoother
   b Retarder
   c Plasticiser
   d Accelerator

5 Sulphate Resisting Portland Cement (SRPC) is best for use in conditions that are
   a Dry
   b Hot
   c Sealed
   d Damp

6 Chemical plasticisers make mortar workable by causing air
   a Entrapment
   b Entrainment
   c Elongation
   d Elevation

7 A retarder added to mortar keeps it workable for longer by slowing down the
   a Hydrolysis
   b Batching
   c Hydration
   d Gauging

8 Cement powder is produced from
   a Glass fibre
   b Granite
   c Pit sand
   d Limestone

9 Moisture moving across a cavity wall above finished floor level (FFL) is referred to as
   a Travelling damp
   b Rising damp
   c Penetrating damp
   d Connecting damp

10 If cut bricks have to be introduced into a bonding arrangement it is called
   a Best bond
   b Cut bond
   c Broken bond
   d Secondary bond

11 To prevent moisture from travelling across wall ties, the ties have a feature called a

   a   Drop

   b   Drip

   c   Strip

   d   Cut

12 The minimum distance that wall ties should be bedded into a bed joint is

   a   25mm

   b   50mm

   c   75mm

   d   100mm

13 The method of providing a joint finish as the work proceeds is called

   a   Pointing

   b   Flashing

   c   Jointing

   d   Sealing

14 If a String course has a 'castellated' pattern, it will be laid as a

   a   Diagonal course

   b   Dentil course

   c   Detail course

   d   Dovetail course

15 A course of face bricks laid on end with the stretcher face showing is a

   a   Long course

   b   Special course

   c   Dog-tooth course

   d   Soldier course

16 To allow for thermal expansion, a cavity wall may be designed to include a

   a   Horizontal movement joint

   b   Lateral movement joint

   c   Vertical movement joint

   d   Intermediate movement joint

17 The building regulations state that vertical spacing of wall ties at the jamb area should be at intervals of

   a   150mm

   b   200mm

   c   225mm

   d   300mm

18 Steel reinforcement in concrete lintels is placed

   a   In the ends

   b   Through the middle

   c   At the bottom

   d   At the top

19 In order for a cill to direct water away from the face of a cavity wall, the top surface of the sill is designed to have a

   a   Fall

   b   Tumble

   c   Funnel

   d   Spill

20 The section of a lintel at each end that transmits the weight of masonry from above an opening to the walls either side is called the

   a   Loading

   b   Bearing

   c   Padding

   d   Stiffening

TEST YOUR KNOWLEDGE ANSWERS

Chapter 1: Unit 201

1   c   Risk assessment
2   d   Blue circle
3   b   Oxygen
4   a CO_2
5   b   Control of Substances Hazardous to Health (COSHH) Regulations 2002
6   c   75°
7   c   Glasses, hearing protection and dust mask
8   d   Respirator
9   a   410V
10 b   80 dB(A)

Chapter 2: Unit 202

1   a   Specification
2   a   1:5
3   a   Door
4   b   Insulation
5   a   A point of a known height used for setting out
6   c   Trench
7   b   Raft
8   c   Coarse aggregate
9   a   Insulation
10 b   English

Chapter 3: Unit 203

1   a   First
2   a   Gauge
3   b   2mm
4   d   As per manufacturer's instructions
5   b   A cut face
6   b   Powder
7   a   Hand held auger

8   b   Complete joint and flush
9   d   20
10 b   Sand and cement
11 c   Rasping down using a rasp
12 b   Set square and masonry saw
13 a   Bonded stacks
14 a   Plumb blocks
15 b   25kg sealed bags
16 c   Water
17 a   Hopper
18 b   Pointing hawk and pointing trowel
19 d   20

Chapter 4: Unit 204

1   b   10
2   b   Datum
3   d   English
4   c   Site plan
5   b   A slice or cut through a structure
6   b   First angle
7   c   Components, material types or fittings repeated throughout a job
8   d   Finished floor level
9   b   Profiles
10 c   Dry
11 b   In the centre of the wall or under doors or windows
12 b   Header brick is required at one end and a stretcher brick at the other end of the wall
13 c   Temporary bench mark
14 b   102.5mm
15 b   46mm
16 c   Engineering brick

17 c Zinc

18 b Boat

19 b 2

20 a Steel

Chapter 5: Unit 205

1 a Method statement

2 c Control measures

3 a Locate the position of the plot

4 b Locate site buildings

5 c Block plan

6 d Sectional drawing

7 b 600mm

8 b Builder's square

9 b Brick on edge detail

10 a Datum point

11 b Boundary line

12 c Face line of the building

13 c Specification

14 b A barrier

15 a 50mm

16 b Optical level

17 b Written measurements

18 a Two people to set out

19 a To mark the ground underneath the profile
ranging lines

20 d Furniture

Chapter 6: Unit 206

1 b Compressive strength

2 c Firing

3 b Gauging

4 c Plasticiser

5 d Damp

6 b Entrainment

7 c Hydration

8 d Limestone

9 c Penetrating damp

10 c Broken bond

11 b Drip

12 b 50mm

13 c Jointing

14 b Dentil course

15 d Soldier course

16 c Vertical movement joint

17 c 225mm

18 c At the bottom

19 a Fall

20 b Bearing

INDEX

greenfield land 186
grinder 115
ground floors 85–86
groundwater table 186

H

half-round joint 164, 229
hammer drill 114
hammers 144
hand arm vibration syndrome
    (HAVS) 23, 31
hand washing 34
hard hat 22
hardcore 85
hatching symbols 48, 179
HAVS *see* hand arm vibration
    syndrome
hazardous gases 23
hazardous substances 9–11
hazards 5–6, 32–33, 111, 175
health and safety
    construction site 111
    control measures 174–175
    hazards 5–6, 32–33, 111, 175
    hoardings 190–191
    legislation 3–42
    and productivity 146
    risk assessment 138
    sources of information 8
    stacking materials 148–150
Health and Safety Executive (HSE)
    8–9
Health and Safety at Work Act
    (HASAWA) 1974 4–9
height, working at 24–30
high visibility (hi-viz) jacket 22
hipped roof 92
hoardings 190–191
hollow floors *see* suspended
    floors
hopper 115
hygiene, personal 34
hypotenuse 196

I

I-beam 85
imposed load 79
improvement notice 8

inductions 6
infill panels 109
injuries
    reporting 12–13
    statistics 2–3
insulation 85, 99–101
    blocks 108
    cavity 128–129, 226–227
    types of 100–101
internal leaf 108
internal walling 91
invoices 74
isolated piers 137, 166–169
isometric projection 141–142,
    179–180

J

job sheet 72
jointer 143
jointing 164–165, 200–201,
    220–222, 228–230, 236–247
joints
    flush 165, 229
    half-round 164, 229
    recessed 164, 229
    weather struck 165, 201,
    229
joists 85

K

kinetic lifting 18–19

L

ladders 25–27
land, types of 186
lateral movement 222
laying trowel 113
lead time 108
lean-to roof 92
leptospirosis 12
levels *see* spirit level
lifting 18–19
    equipment 30
    kinetic 18–19
Lifting Operations and Lifting
    Equipment Regulations
    (LOLER) 1998 30

lightweight insulation blocks
    209
lime 88
line and pins 114, 144
linear length 61–63
lintels 87, 126–127, 233–235
location drawing 140
location plan 49, 110, 181

M

mandatory signs 41
Manual Handling Operations
    Regulations 17–19
masonry cement 211–212
masonry saw 115
materials
    calculating quantities
    57–72, 118–120, 147,
    192–194
    delivery note 75
    protecting 118, 147
    recycling 186–187
    stacking 148–150
    sustainability of 97–99
measurement, units of 59
measures 113
method statement 6, 112,
    174–175
mixer 116
mortar 88, 109, 190–191
    materials for 209–213
    mixing 213–215

N

noise levels 19–20

O

openings 125–127
    arches 125, 235, 237–242
    in cavity walling 128–129,
    230–236
    cills 236
optical level 188
optical square 188, 195
Ordnance bench mark (OBM) 47
Ordinary Portland Cement (OPC)
    211

orthographic projection 141, 179–180

PICTURE CREDITS